Legal Notice

ISBN-13: 978-1481019330
ISBN-10: 1481019333

This book is dedicated to all my students over the past 15 years, I have learned just as much from all of you as you have learned from me.

BOOKS BY DR. STEVE WARNER FOR COLLEGE BOUND STUDENTS

28 SAT Math Lessons to Improve Your Score in One Month
- Beginner Course
- Intermediate Course
- Advanced Course

320 SAT Math Problems Arranged by Topic and Difficulty Level

320 SAT Math Subject Test Problems Arranged by Topic and Difficulty Level
- Level 1 Test
- Level 2 Test

SAT Prep Book of Advanced Math Problems

The 32 Most Effective SAT Math Strategies

SAT Prep Official Study Guide Math Companion

ACT Prep Red Book – 320 ACT Math Problems with Solutions

CONNECT WITH DR. STEVE WARNER

www.facebook.com/SATPrepGet800

www.youtube.com/TheSATMathPrep

www.twitter.com/SATPrepGet800

www.linkedin.com/in/DrSteveWarner

www.pinterest.com/SATPrepGet800

plus.google.com/+SteveWarnerPhD

28 SAT Math Lessons to Improve Your Score in One Month

Score in One Month
Lessons to Improve Your

Advanced Course

For Students Currently Scoring Above 600 in SAT Math and Want to Score 800

Steve Warner, Ph.D.

Table of Contents

Actions to Complete Before You Read This Book

1. Purchase a TI-84 or equivalent calculator

It is recommended that you use a TI-84 or comparable calculator for the SAT. Answer explanations in this book will always assume you are using such a calculator.

2. Take a practice SAT from the Official Guide to get your preliminary SAT math score

Your score should be at least a 600. If it is lower, you should begin with the beginner or intermediate book in this series.

3. Claim your FREE book

Simply visit the following webpage and enter your email address to receive an electronic copy of the *SAT Prep Official Study Guide Math Companion* for FREE. You will also receive solutions to all the supplemental problems in this book.

www.thesatmathprep.com/28Les800.html

4. 'Like' my Facebook page

This page is updated regularly with SAT prep advice, tips, tricks, strategies, and practice problems. Visit the following webpage and click the 'like' button.

www.facebook.com/SATPrepGet800

INTRODUCTION
STUDYING FOR SUCCESS

This book was written specifically for the student currently scoring over a 600 in SAT math. Results will vary, but if you are such a student and you work through the lessons in this book, then you will see a substantial improvement in your score.

Each strategy in this book is numbered in accordance with the same strategy that is given in "The 32 Most Effective SAT Math Strategies." Note that not every strategy from that book is covered here – the focus of this book is on advanced techniques and concepts. If you discover that you have weaknesses in applying more basic techniques (such as the ones reviewed in the first lesson from this book), you may want to go through the intermediate course before completing this one.

The book you are now reading is self-contained. Each lesson was carefully created to ensure that you are making the most effective use of your time while preparing for the SAT. It should be noted that a score of 700 can usually be attained without ever attempting a Level 5 problem. Readers currently scoring below a 700 on practice tests should not feel obligated to work on Level 5 problems the first time they go through this book.

The optional material in this book contains what I refer to as "Level 6" questions and "Challenge" questions. Level 6 questions are slightly more difficult than anything that I have seen on an actual SAT, but they are just like SAT problems in every other way. Challenge questions are theoretical in nature and are much more difficult than anything that will ever appear on an SAT. These two types of questions are for those students that really want an SAT math score of 800.

1. Using this book effectively

- Begin studying at least three months before the SAT
- Practice SAT math problems twenty minutes each day
- Choose a consistent study time and location

You will retain much more of what you study if you study in short bursts rather than if you try to tackle everything at once. So try to choose about a twenty minute block of time that you will dedicate to SAT math each day. Make it a habit. The results are well worth this small time commitment. Some students will be able to complete each lesson within this twenty minute block of time. If it takes you longer than twenty minutes to complete a lesson, you can stop when twenty minutes are up and then complete the lesson the following day. At the very least, take a nice long break, and then finish the lesson later that same day.

- Every time you get a question wrong, **mark it off, no matter what your mistake**.
- Begin each lesson by first redoing the problems from previous lessons on the same topic that you have marked off.
- If you get a problem wrong again, **keep it marked off**.

As an example, before you begin the third number theory lesson (Lesson 9), you should redo all the problems you have marked off from the first two number theory lessons (Lessons 1 and 5). Any question that you get right you can "unmark" while leaving questions that you get wrong marked off for the next time. If this takes you the full twenty minutes, that is okay. Just begin the new lesson the next day.

Note that this book often emphasizes solving each problem in more than one way. Please listen to this advice. The same question is never repeated on any SAT (with the exception of questions from the experimental sections) so the important thing is learning as many techniques as possible. Being able to solve any specific problem is of minimal importance. The more ways you have to solve a single problem the more prepared you will be to tackle a problem you have never seen before, and the quicker you will be able to solve that problem. Also, if you have multiple methods for solving a single problem, then on the actual SAT when you "check over" your work you will be able to redo each problem in a different way. This will eliminate all "careless" errors on the actual exam. Note that in this book the quickest solution to any problem will always be marked with an asterisk (*).

2. Calculator use.

- Use a TI-84 or comparable calculator if possible when practicing and during the SAT.
- Make sure that your calculator has fresh batteries on test day.

Below are the most important things you should practice on your graphing calculator.

- Practice entering complicated computations in a single step.
- Know when to insert parentheses:
  - Around numerators of fractions
  - Around denominators of fractions
  - Around exponents
  - Whenever you actually see parentheses in the expression

Examples:

We will substitute a 5 in for *x* in each of the following examples.

Expression	Calculator computation
$\frac{7x+3}{2x-11}$	(7*5 + 3)/(2*5 – 11)
$(3x-8)^{2x-9}$	(3*5 – 8)^(2*5 – 9)

- Clear the screen before using it in a new problem. The big screen allows you to check over your computations easily.
- Press the **ANS** button (**2nd (-)**) to use your last answer in the next computation.
- Press **2nd ENTER** to bring up your last computation for editing. This is especially useful when you are plugging in answer choices, or guessing and checking.
- You can press **2nd ENTER** over and over again to cycle backwards through all the computations you have ever done.
- Know where the $\sqrt{\ }$, π, and **^** buttons are so you can reach them quickly.
- Change a decimal to a fraction by pressing **MATH ENTER ENTER**.
- Press the **MATH** button - in the first menu that appears you can take cube roots and nth roots for any n. Scroll right to **NUM** and you have **lcm(** and **gcd(**. Scroll right to **PRB** and you have **nPr**, **nCr**, and **!** to compute permutations, combinations and factorials very quickly.

The following graphing tools can also be useful.

- Press the **Y=** button to enter a function, and then hit **ZOOM 6** to graph it in a standard window.
- Practice using the **WINDOW** button to adjust the viewing window of your graph.
- Practice using the **TRACE** button to move along the graph and look at some of the points plotted.
- Pressing **2nd TRACE** (which is really **CALC**) will bring up a menu of useful items. For example selecting **ZERO** will tell you where the graph hits the *x*-axis, or equivalently where the function is zero. Selecting **MINIMUM** or **MAXIMUM** can find the vertex of a parabola. Selecting **INTERSECT** will find the point of intersection of 2 graphs.

3. Tips for taking the SAT

Each of the following tips should be used whenever you take a practice SAT as well as on the actual exam.

Check your answers properly: When you go back to check your earlier answers for careless errors *do not* simply look over your work to try to catch a mistake. This is usually a waste of time.

- When "checking over" problems you have already done, **always redo the problem from the beginning** without looking at your earlier work.
- If possible use a different method than you used the first time.

For example, if you solved the problem by picking numbers the first time, try to solve it algebraically the second time, or at the very least pick different numbers. If you do not know, or are not comfortable with a different method, then use the same method, but do the problem from the beginning and do not look at your original solution. If your two answers do not match up, then you know that this is a problem you need to spend a little more time on to figure out where your error is.

This may seem time consuming, but that is okay. It is better to spend more time checking over a few problems, then to rush through a lot of problems and repeat the same mistakes.

Guess when appropriate: Answering a multiple-choice question wrong will result in a $\frac{1}{4}$ point penalty. This is to discourage random guessing. If you have no idea how to do a problem, no intuition as to what the correct answer might be, and you cannot even eliminate a single answer choice, then *DO NOT* just take a guess. Omit the question and move on.

- Take a guess on a multiple-choice question if you can eliminate one or more answer choices.
- Always guess on grid-in questions that you do not know.

You are *not* penalized for getting a grid-in question wrong. Therefore you should always guess on grid-in questions that you do not know. Never leave any of these blank. If you have an idea of how large of a number the answer should be, then take a reasonable guess. If not, then just guess anything—do not think too hard—just put in a number.

Pace yourself: After you have been working on a question for about 30 seconds you need to make a decision. If you understand the question and think that you can get the answer in another 30 seconds or so, continue to work on the problem. If you still do not know how to do the problem or you are using a technique that is going to take a long time, mark it off and come back to it later if you have time.

If you have eliminated at least one answer choice, or it is a grid-in, feel free to take a guess. But you still want to leave open the possibility of coming back to it later. Remember that every problem is worth the same amount. Do not sacrifice problems that you may be able to do by getting hung up on a problem that is too hard for you.

Now, after going through the test once, you can then go through each of the questions you have marked off and solve as many of them as you can. You should be able to spend 5 to 7 minutes on this, and still have 7 minutes left to check your answers. If there are one or two problems that you just cannot seem to get, let them go for a while. You can come back to them intermittently as you are checking over other answers.

Grid your answers correctly: The computer only grades what you have marked in the bubbles. The space above the bubbles is just for your convenience, and to help you do your bubbling correctly.

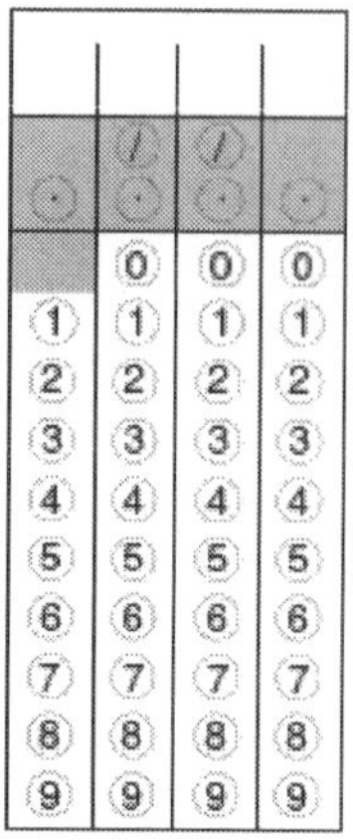

Never mark more than one circle in a column or the problem will automatically be marked wrong. You do not need to use all four columns. If you do not use a column just leave it blank.

The symbols that you can grid in are the digits 0 through 9, a decimal point, and a division symbol for fractions. Note that there is no negative symbol. So answers to grid-ins *cannot* be negative. Also, there are only four slots, so you cannot get an answer such as 52,326.

Sometimes there is more than one correct answer to a grid-in question. Simply choose one of them to grid-in. *Never* try to fit more than one answer into the grid.

If your answer is a whole number such as 2451 or a decimal that only requires four or less slots such as 2.36, then simply enter the number starting at any column. The two examples just written must be started in the first column, but the number 16 can be entered starting in column 1, 2 or 3.

Note that there is no zero in column 1, so if your answer is 0 it must be gridded into column 2, 3 or 4.

Fractions can be gridded in any form as long as there are enough slots. The fraction 2/100 must be reduced to 1/50 simply because the first representation will not fit in the grid.

Fractions can also be converted to decimals before being gridded in. If a decimal cannot fit in the grid, then you can simply *truncate* it to fit. But you must use every slot in this case. For example, the decimal .167777777... can be gridded as .167, but .16 or .17 would both be marked wrong.

Instead of truncating decimals you can also *round* them. For example, the decimal above could be gridded as .168. Truncating is preferred because there is no thinking involved and you are less likely to make a careless error.

Here are three ways to grid in the number $\frac{8}{9}$.

	8	/	9

.	8	8	8

.	8	8	9

Never grid-in mixed numerals. If your answer is $2\frac{1}{4}$, and you grid in the mixed numeral $2\frac{1}{4}$, then this will be read as $\frac{21}{4}$ and will be marked wrong. You must either grid in the decimal 2.25 or the improper fraction $\frac{9}{4}$.

Here are two ways to grid in the mixed numeral $1\frac{1}{2}$ correctly.

	1	.	5

	3	/	2

Lesson 1
Number Theory

In this lesson we will be reviewing four very basic strategies that can be used to solve a wide range of SAT math problems in all topics and all difficulty levels. Throughout this book you should practice using these four strategies whenever it is possible to do so. You should also try to solve each problem in a more straightforward way.

<u>Strategy 1</u> – Start with Choice (C)

In many SAT math problems you can get the answer simply by trying each of the answer choices until you find the one that works. Unless you have some intuition as to what the correct answer might be, then you should always start with choice (C) as your first guess (an exception will be detailed in Strategy 2 below). The reason for this is simple. Answers are usually given in increasing or decreasing order. So very often if choice (C) fails you can eliminate two of the other choices as well.

Try to answer the following question using this strategy. **Do not** check the solution until you have attempted this question yourself.

Level 2: Number Theory

1. Seven consecutive integers are listed in increasing order. If their sum is 350, what is the third integer in the list?

    (A) 45
    (B) 46
    (C) 47
    (D) 48
    (E) 49

Solution

Begin by looking at choice (C). If the third integer is 47, then the seven integers are 45, 46, 47, 48, 49, 50, and 51. Add these up in your calculator to get 336. This is too small. So we can eliminate choices (A), (B) and (C).

Since 336 is pretty far from 350 let's try choice (E) next. If the third integer is 49, then the seven integers are 47, 48, 49, 50, 51, 52, and 53. Add these up in your calculator to get 350. Therefore the answer is choice (E).

Before we go on, try to solve this problem in two other ways.

(1) Algebraically (the way you would do it in school).
(2) With a quick computation.

Hint for (2): In a set of consecutive integers, the average (arithmetic mean) and median are equal (see the optional material at the end of Lesson 20 for a proof of this).

Solutions

(1) An algebraic solution: If we name the least integer x, then the seven integers are x, $x + 1$, $x + 2$, $x + 3$, $x + 4$, $x + 5$, and $x + 6$. So we have

$$x + (x + 1) + (x + 2) + (x + 3) + (x + 4) + (x + 5) + (x + 6) = 350$$
$$7x + 21 = 350$$
$$7x = 329$$
$$x = 47$$

The third integer is $x + 2 = 49$, choice (E).

Important: Always remember to check what the question is asking for before choosing your answer. Many students would accidently choose choice (C) here as soon as they discovered that $x = 47$.

It is not a bad idea to underline the word *"third"* as you read the question. This may help you to avoid this kind of error.

*** (2) A quick, clever solution:** Divide 350 by 7 to get that the fourth integer is 50. Thus, the third integer is 49, choice (E).

Justification for the last solution: Recall from the algebraic solution above that $7x + 21 = 350$. Thus, $7(x + 3) = 350$, and so $x + 3 = \frac{350}{7} = 50$. Finally, we have $x + 2 = 50 - 1 = 49$.

Note that $x + 3$ is the median of the seven integers (the fourth integer in the list), $\frac{350}{7}$ is the average of the seven integers, and these two quantities are equal. See Lesson 20 for more details.

Strategy 2 – When not to start with Choice (C)

If the word **least** appears in the problem, then start with the smallest number as your first guess. Similarly, if the word **greatest** appears in the problem, then start with the largest number as your first guess.

Try to answer the following question using this strategy. **Do not** check the solution until you have attempted this question yourself.

LEVEL 3: NUMBER THEORY

2. What is the largest positive integer value of k for which 7^k divides 147^{15} ?

   (A) 3
   (B) 7
   (C) 15
   (D) 28
   (E) 30

Solution

*Pull out your calculator. Since the question has the word **"largest"** in it, we will start with the largest answer choice which is choice (E), and we divide 147^{15} by 7^{30}. We type 147^15 / 7^30 into our calculator and the output is 14,348,907. Since this is an integer, the answer is choice (E).

Note that all five answer choices give an integer, but 30 is the largest positive integer that works.

Before we go on, try to solve this problem directly (without using the answer choices).

Solution

The prime factorization of 147 is $147 = 3 \cdot 7^2$. Therefore

$$147^{15} = (3 \cdot 7^2)^{15} = 3^{15}(7^2)^{15} = 3^{15}7^{30}.$$

So 7^{30} divides 147^{15}, but 7^{31} does not. Thus, the answer is choice (E).

Note: Prime factorizations will be reviewed in Lesson 5.

Strategy 3 – Take a guess

Sometimes the answer choices themselves cannot be substituted in for the unknown or unknowns in the problem. But that does not mean that you cannot guess your own numbers. Try to make as reasonable a guess as possible, but do not over think it. Keep trying until you zero in on the correct value.

Try to answer the following question using this strategy. **Do not** check the solution until you have attempted this question yourself.

Level 3: Number Theory

3. Dana has pennies, nickels and dimes in her pocket. The number of dimes she has is three times the number of nickels, and the number of nickels she has is 2 more than the number of pennies. Which of the following could be the total number of coins in Dana's pocket?

    (A) 14
    (B) 15
    (C) 16
    (D) 17
    (E) 18

Solution

* Let's take a guess and say that Dana has 3 pennies. It follows that she has $3 + 2 = 5$ nickels, and $(3)(5) = 15$ dimes. So the total number of coins is $3 + 5 + 15 = 23$. This is too many. So let's guess that Dana has 2 pennies. Then she has $2 + 2 = 4$ nickels, and $(3)(4) = 12$ dimes for a total of $2 + 4 + 12 = 18$ coins. Thus, the answer is choice (E).

Before we go on, try to solve this problem the way you might do it in school.

Solution

If we let x represent the number of pennies, then the number of nickels is $x + 2$, and the number of dimes is $3(x + 2)$. Thus, the total number of coins is

$$x + (x + 2) + 3(x + 2) = x + x + 2 + 3x + 6 = 5x + 8.$$

So some possible totals are 13, 18, 23,... which we get by substituting 1, 2, 3,... for x. Substituting 2 in for x gives 18 which is answer choice (E).

Warning: Many students incorrectly interpret "three times the number of nickels" as $3x + 2$. This is not right. The number of nickels is $x + 2$, and so "three times the number of nickels" is $3(x + 2) = 3x + 6$.

Strategy 4 – Pick a number

A problem may become much easier to understand and to solve by substituting a specific number in for a variable. Just make sure that you choose a number that satisfies the given conditions.

Here are some guidelines when picking numbers.

(1) Pick a number that is simple but not too simple. In general you might want to avoid picking 0 or 1 (but 2 is usually a good choice).
(2) Try to avoid picking numbers that appear in the problem.
(3) When picking two or more numbers try to make them all different.
(4) Most of the time picking numbers only allows you to eliminate answer choices. So do not just choose the first answer choice that comes out to the correct answer. If multiple answers come out correct you need to pick a new number and start again. But you only have to check the answer choices that have not yet been eliminated.
(5) If there are fractions in the question a good choice might be the least common denominator (lcd) or a multiple of the lcd.
(6) In percent problems choose the number 100.

(7) Do not pick a negative number as a possible answer to a grid-in question. This is a waste of time since you cannot grid a negative number.

(8) If your first attempt does not eliminate 4 of the 5 choices, try to choose a number that's of a different "type." Here are some examples of types:

  (a) A positive integer greater than 1.
  (b) A positive fraction (or decimal) between 0 and 1.
  (c) A negative integer less than -1.
  (d) A negative fraction (or decimal) between -1 and 0.

(9) If you are picking pairs of numbers try different combinations from (8). For example you can try two positive integers greater than 1, two negative integers less than -1, or one positive and one negative integer, etc.

Remember that these are just guidelines and there may be rare occasions where you might break these rules. For example sometimes it is so quick and easy to plug in 0 and/or 1 that you might do this even though only some of the answer choices get eliminated.

Try to answer the following question using this strategy. **Do not** check the solution until you have attempted this question yourself.

LEVEL 4: NUMBER THEORY

4. n is a two-digit number whose units digit is 3 times its tens digit, which of the following statements must be true?

   (A) n is less than 15
   (B) n is greater than 30
   (C) n is a multiple of 3
   (D) n is a multiple of 10
   (E) n is a multiple of 13

Solution

Let's choose a value for *n*, say *n* = 13. Notice that we chose a number whose units digit is 3 times its tens digit.

Now let's check if each answer choice is true or false.

(A) True
(B) False
(C) False
(D) False
(E) True

Since (B), (C), and (D) are each false we can eliminate them. Let's choose a new value for *n*, say *n* = 26. Let's check if each of choices (A) and (E) is true or false with this new value for *n*.

(A) False
(E) True

Choice (A) does not give the correct answer this time so we can eliminate it. Thus, the answer is choice (E).

Notes: (1) When we chose our first number we needed to check **every** answer choice. A common mistake would be to choose answer choice (A) because it was the first one to come out true. When we choose our second number we only have to check the answer choices that haven't yet been eliminated.

(2) There are only 3 possibilities for *n*: 13, 26, and 39. Note that each of these 3 numbers is a multiple of 13.

You're doing great! Let's just practice a bit more. Try to solve each of the following problems by using one of the four strategies you just learned. Then, if possible, solve each problem another way. The answers to these problems, followed by full solutions are at the end of this lesson. **Do not** look at the answers until you have attempted these problems yourself. Please remember to mark off any problems you get wrong.

Level 1: Number Theory

5. What is the least integer divisible by the integers 3, 6, 7, 14, and 21?

    (A) 168
    (B) 126
    (C) 84
    (D) 42
    (E) 28

6. Five consecutive integers are listed in increasing order. If their sum is 925, what is the second integer in the list?

Level 3: Number Theory

7. The cost of 5 scarves is d dollars. At this rate, what is the cost, in dollars of 45 scarves?

    (A) $\frac{9d}{5}$
    (B) $\frac{d}{45}$
    (C) $\frac{45}{d}$
    (D) $9d$
    (E) $45d$

8. What is the largest positive integer value of k for which 54^4 is divisible by 3^k ?

    (A) 2
    (B) 4
    (C) 6
    (D) 12
    (E) 14

9. Bill has cows, pigs and chickens on his farm. The number of chickens he has is four times the number of pigs, and the number of pigs he has is three more than the number of cows. Which of the following could be the total number of these animals?

(A) 24
(B) 25
(C) 26
(D) 27
(E) 28

LEVEL 4: NUMBER THEORY

10. If the product of five consecutive integers written in increasing order equals the second integer, what is the greatest of the five integers?

(A) -4
(B) -3
(C) 0
(D) 3
(E) 4

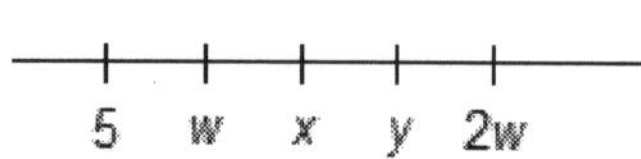

11. If the tick marks are equally spaced on the number line above, what is the value of x?

(A) 14
(B) 13
(C) 12
(D) 11
(E) 10

12. A ball is dropped from 567 centimeters above the ground and after the fourth bounce it rises to a height of 7 centimeters. If the height to which the ball rises after each bounce is always the same fraction of the height reached on its previous bounce, what is this fraction?

(A) $\frac{1}{81}$

(B) $\frac{1}{27}$

(C) $\frac{1}{9}$

(D) $\frac{1}{3}$

(E) $\frac{1}{2}$

Answers

1. E	5. D	9. D
2. E	6. 184	10. D
3. E	7. D	11. E
4. E	8. D	12. D

Note: Full solutions for questions 8 and 9 have been omitted because their solutions are very similar to the solutions for questions 2 and 3, respectively.

Full Solutions

7.

Solution using strategy 4: Let's choose a value for *d*, say *d* = 10. So 5 scarves cost 10 dollars, and therefore each scarf costs 2 dollars. It follows that 45 scarves cost (45)(2) = **90** dollars. **Put a nice big, dark circle around this number so that you can find it easily later.** We now substitute 10 in for *d* into **all** five answer choices.

(A) 90/5 = 18
(B) 10/45
(C) 45/10 = 4.5
(D) 9*10 = 90
(E) 45*10 = 450

Since (D) is the only choice that has become 90, we conclude that (D) is the answer.

Important note: (D) is **not** the correct answer simply because it is equal to 90. It is correct because all 4 of the other choices are **not** 90.

* **Solution using ratios:** We begin by identifying 2 key words. In this case, such a pair of key words is "scarves" and "dollars."

scarves	5	45
dollars	d	x

Notice that we wrote in the number of scarves next to the word scarves, and the cost of the scarves next to the word dollars. Also notice that the cost for 5 scarves is written under the number 5, and the (unknown) cost for 45 scarves is written under the 45. Now draw in the division symbols and equal sign, cross multiply and divide the corresponding ratio to find the unknown quantity x.

$$\frac{5}{d} = \frac{45}{x}$$

$$5x = 45d$$

$$x = 9d$$

So 45 scarves cost $9d$ dollars, choice (D).

For more information on this technique, see **Strategy 14** in ***"The 32 Most Effective SAT Math Strategies."***

10.

* **Solution using strategy 2:** Begin by looking at choice (E) since it is the greatest. If the greatest integer is 4, then the five consecutive integers are 0, 1, 2, 3, 4 and the product is $0 \cdot 1 \cdot 2 \cdot 3 \cdot 4 = 0$. So choice (E) is incorrect, but we can see that if we shift 0 to the right, then the condition will be satisfied.

$$(-1) \cdot 0 \cdot 1 \cdot 2 \cdot 3 = 0.$$

The greatest of the five integers is then 3, choice (D).

Caution: A common mistake in this problem is to pick 0 (choice (C)) as the answer. If you're not careful you might forget that the question is asking for the **greatest** of the five integers.

It's not a bad idea to underline the clause "what is the greatest of the five integers?" prior to solving the problem. This type of error occurs so often that it's worth taking some extra precautions.

Note: There is no real computational advantage here in starting with choice (E), but there is a psychological one. By starting with the greatest value, your mind has consciously registered the word "greatest" and you are less likely to fall into the trap of choosing 0 as mentioned above.

11.

*** Solution using strategy 1:** Begin by looking at choice (C). If $x = 12$, then $w = \frac{5 + 12}{2} = \frac{17}{2} = 8.5$ and $2w = 12 + 7 = 19$ (according to the graph). But $2(8.5) = 17$, so this is incorrect.

Let's try choice (D) next, so that $x = 11$, $w = \frac{5 + 11}{2} = \frac{16}{2} = 8$, and using the graph $2w = 11 + 6 = 17$. But $2(8) = 16$. This is closer, so the answer must be (E).

Let's just verify that the answer is in fact choice (E). If $x = 10$, then it follows that $w = \frac{5 + 10}{2} = \frac{15}{2} = 7.5$. From the graph, $2w = 10 + 5 = 15$ and also $2(7.5) = 15$. Therefore the answer is choice (E).

Algebraic solution: Since w is midway between 5 and x, $w = \frac{5 + x}{2}$, or equivalently $2w = 5 + x$. Also, $x - 5 = 2w - x$, so that $2x - 5 = 2w$. It follows that $5 + x = 2x - 5$, whence $x = 10$, choice (E).

12.

*** Solution using Strategy 1:** Let's begin with choice (C). We divide 567 by 9 four times and get 0.0864197531 which is much too small. So we can eliminate choices (A), (B) and (C). We next try choice (D). If we divide 567 by 3 four times we get 7 so that (D) is the correct answer.

Note: We could have also multiplied 7 by 3 four times to get 567.

An algebraic solution: We want to solve the following equation.

$$567x^4 = 7$$

$$x^4 = \frac{7}{567} = \frac{1}{81}$$

$$x = \frac{1}{3}$$

Thus, the answer is choice (D).

Lesson 2
Algebra

Strategy 16 – Try a Simple Operation

Problems that ask for an expression involving more than one variable often look much harder than they are. By performing a single operation, the problem is usually reduced to one that is very easy to solve. The most common operations to try are addition, subtraction, multiplication and division.

Try to answer the following question using this strategy. **Do not** check the solution until you have attempted this question yourself.

Level 5: Algebra

1. If $rs = 4, st = 7, rt = 63$, and $r > 0$, then $rst =$

Solution

The operation to use here is multiplication.

$$rs = 4$$
$$st = 7$$
$$\underline{rt = 63}$$
$$(rs)(st)(rt) = 4 \cdot 7 \cdot 63$$
$$r^2s^2t^2 = 1764$$

Notice that we multiply all three left hand sides together, and all three right hand sides together. Now just take the square root of each side of the equation to get rst = **42**.

Remark: Whenever we are trying to find an expression that involves multiplication, division, or both, **multiplying or dividing** the given equations usually does the trick.

*** Quick computation:** With a little practice, we can get the solution to this type of problem very quickly. Here, we multiply the three numbers together to get $4 \cdot 7 \cdot 63 = 1764$. We then take the square root of 1764 to get **42**.

Before we go on, try to solve this problem by first finding r, s and t.

Solution

Important note: You should not solve this problem this way on the actual SAT.

Solving the first equation for s gives us $s = \frac{4}{r}$. Substituting this into the second equation gives us $(\frac{4}{r})t = 7$, or equivalently $4t = 7r$. Therefore we have that $t = \frac{7r}{4}$. So the third equation becomes $r(\frac{7r}{4}) = 63$, or equivalently $\frac{7r^2}{4} = 63$. So $r^2 = \frac{63 \cdot 4}{7} = 36$, whence $r = 6$ (because $r > 0$). It follows that $t = \frac{7 \cdot 6}{4} = 10.5$, $s = \frac{4}{6} = \frac{2}{3}$, and $rst = 6 \cdot \left(\frac{2}{3}\right) \cdot 10.5 =$ **42**.

Systems of Linear Equations

There are many different ways to solve a system of linear equations. We will use an example to demonstrate several different methods.

LEVEL 5: ALGEBRA

2. If $2x = 7 - 3y$ and $5y = 5 - 3x$, what is the value of x?

* **Method 1 – elimination:** We begin by making sure that the two equations are "lined up" properly. We do this by adding $3y$ to each side of the first equation, and adding $3x$ to each side of the second equation.

$$2x + 3y = 7$$
$$3x + 5y = 5$$

We will now multiply each side of the first equation by 5, and each side of the second equation by -3.

$$5(2x + 3y) = (7)(5)$$
$$-3(3x + 5y) = (5)(-3)$$

Do not forget to distribute correctly on the left. Add the two equations.

$$\begin{array}{r} 10x + 15y = 35 \\ \underline{-9x - 15y = -15} \\ x \qquad = \mathbf{20} \end{array}$$

Remarks: (1) We chose to use 5 and -3 because multiplying by these numbers makes the y column "match up" so that when we add the two equations in the next step the y term vanishes. We could have also used -5 and 3.

(2) If we wanted to find y instead of x we would multiply the two equations by 3 and -2 (or -3 and 2). In general, if you are only looking for one variable, try to eliminate the one you are **not** looking for.

(3) We chose to multiply by a negative number so that we could add the equations instead of subtracting them. We could have also multiplied the first equation by 5, the second by 3, and subtracted the two equations, but a computational error is more likely to occur this way.

Method 2 – Gauss-Jordan reduction: As in method 1, we first make sure the two equations are "lined up" properly.

$$2x + 3y = 7$$
$$3x + 5y = 5$$

Begin by pushing the MATRIX button (which is 2ND x^{-1}). Scroll over to EDIT and then select [A] (or press 1). We will be inputting a 2×3 matrix, so press 2 ENTER 3 ENTER. We then begin entering the numbers 2, 3, and 7 for the first row, and 3, 5, and 5 for the second row. To do this we can simply type 2 ENTER 3 ENTER 7 ENTER 3 ENTER 5 ENTER 5 ENTER.

Note: What we have just done was create the **augmented matrix** for the system of equations. This is simply an array of numbers which contains the coefficients of the variables together with the right hand sides of the equations.

Now push the QUIT button (2ND MODE) to get a blank screen. Press MATRIX again. This time scroll over to MATH and select rref((or press B). Then press MATRIX again and select [A] (or press 1) and press ENTER.

Note: What we have just done is put the matrix into **reduced row echelon form**. In this form we can read off the solution to the original system of equations.

Warning: Be careful to use the rref(button (2 r's), and not the ref(button (which has only one r).

The display will show the following.

$$\begin{matrix}[\,[1\ 0\ 20] \\ [0\ 1\ -11]\,]\end{matrix}$$

The first line is interpreted as $x = 20$ and the second line as $y = -11$. In particular, $x = \mathbf{20}$.

Method 3 – substitution: We solve the second equation for y and substitute into the first equation.

$5y = 5 - 3x$ implies $y = \frac{5-3x}{5} = \frac{5}{5} - \frac{3x}{5} = 1 - \frac{3x}{5}$. So now using the first equation we have

$$2x = 7 - 3y = 7 - 3(1 - \tfrac{3x}{5}) = 7 - 3 + \tfrac{9x}{5} = 4 + \tfrac{9x}{5}.$$

Multiply each side of this equation by 5 to get rid of the denominator on the right. So we have $10x = 20 + 9x$, and therefore $x = \mathbf{20}$.

Remark: If we wanted to find y instead of x we would solve the first equation for x and substitute into the second equation.

Method 4 – graphical solution: We begin by solving each equation for y.

$2x = 7 - 3y$

$2x - 7 = -3y$

$y = -\frac{2x}{3} + \frac{7}{3}$

$5y = 5 - 3x$

$y = 1 - \frac{3x}{5}$

In your graphing calculator press the Y= button, and enter the following.

Y1 = -2X/3 + 7/3
Y2 = 1 – 3X/5

Now press ZOOM 6 to graph these two lines in a standard window. It looks like the point of intersection of the two lines is off to the right. So we will need to extend the viewing window. Press the WINDOW button, and change Xmax to 50 and Ymin to -20. Then press 2nd TRACE (which is CALC) 5 (or select INTERSECT). Then press ENTER 3 times. You will see that the x-coordinate of the point of intersection of the two lines is **20**.

Remark: The choices made for Xmax and Ymin were just to try to ensure that the point of intersection would appear in the viewing window. Many other windows would work just as well.

You're doing great! Let's just practice a bit more. Try to solve each of the following problems. Use Strategy 16 whenever you can. Then, if possible, solve each problem another way. The answers to these problems, followed by full solutions are at the end of this lesson. **Do not** look at the answers until you have attempted these problems yourself. Please remember to mark off any problems you get wrong.

LEVEL 2: ALGEBRA

3. If $x + 5y = 25$ and $x + 9y = 11$, what is the value of $x + 7y$?

4. If $\frac{a+7}{9} = 10$ and $\frac{a+b}{8} = 25$, what is the value of b?

LEVEL 3: ALGEBRA

5. If $x + y = 5$ and $z + w = 7$, then $xz + xw + yz + yw =$

$$5a + 2y + 3z = 23$$
$$5a + y + 2z = 15$$

6. If the equations above are true, what is the value of $y + z$?

$6z$	$2z$
8	8
$2t$	w
3	3
+9	+9
52	34

7. In the correctly worked addition problems above, what is the value of $4z + 2t - w$?

8. If $ab = 7, bc = \frac{1}{9}, b^2 = 3$, what is the value of ac?

LEVEL 4: ALGEBRA

$$ax + by = 17$$
$$ax + (b + 1)y = 26$$

9. Based on the equations above, which of the following must be true?

   (A) $x = 13.5$
   (B) $x = 18$
   (C) $y = 4.5$
   (D) $y = 9$
   (E) $x - y = 4.5$

LEVEL 5: ALGEBRA AND FUNCTIONS

$$k = a - b + 12$$
$$k = b - c - 17$$
$$k = c - a + 11$$

10. In the system of equations above, what is the value of k ?

11. If $x^{15} = \frac{2}{z}$ and $x^{14} = \frac{2y}{z}$ which of the following is an expression for x in terms of y?

    (A) $3y$
    (B) $2y$
    (C) y
    (D) $\frac{1}{y}$
    (E) $\frac{3}{y}$

12. If $6x = 2 + 4y$ and $7x = 3 - 3y$, what is the value of x?

Answers

1. 42	5. 35	9. D
2. 20	6. 8	10. 2
3. 18	7. 18	11. D
4. 117	8. 7/27 or .259	12. 9/23 or .391

Full Solutions

5.

Solution using strategy 16: The operation to use here is multiplication.

$$\begin{array}{c} x + y = 5 \\ \underline{z + w = 7} \\ (x + y)(z + w) = 35 \\ xz + xw + yz + yw = \mathbf{35} \end{array}$$

* **Quick computation:** Since $(x + y)(z + w) = xz + xw + yz + yw$, the answer is $(5)(7) = \mathbf{35}$.

Solution using strategy 4: Let's choose values for x, y, z, and w that satisfy the given conditions, say $x = 1$, $y = 4$, $z = 2$, $w = 5$. Then we have $xz + xw + yz + yw = (1)(2) + (1)(5) + (4)(2) + (4)(5) = 2 + 5 + 8 + 20 = \mathbf{35}$.

6.

* **Solution using strategy 16:** The operation to use here is subtraction.

$$\begin{array}{c} 5a + 2y + 3z = 23 \\ \underline{5a + y + 2z = 15} \\ y + z = \mathbf{8} \end{array}$$

Remark: Whenever we are trying to find an expression that involves addition, subtraction, or both, **adding or subtracting** the given equations usually does the trick.

7.

Solution using strategy 16: Let's rewrite the equations horizontally since that is how most of us are used to seeing equations.

$$\begin{array}{c} 6z + 8 + 2t + 3 + 9 = 52 \\ 2z + 8 + w + 3 + 9 = 34 \end{array}$$

The operation to use here is subtraction. Let's go ahead and subtract term by term.

$$\begin{array}{c} 6z + 8 + 2t + 3 + 9 = 52 \\ \underline{2z + 8 + w + 3 + 9 = 34} \\ 4z + (2t - w) \qquad = 18 \end{array}$$

So $4z + 2t - w = \mathbf{18}$.

* **Visualizing the answer:** You can save a substantial amount of time by performing the subtraction in your head (left equation minus right equation). Note that above the lines the subtraction yields $4z + 2t - w$. This is exactly what we are looking for. Thus, we need only subtract below the lines to get the answer: $52 - 34 = \mathbf{18}$.

Solution using strategy 4: If we choose any value for z, then t and w will be determined. So, let's set z equal to 0. Then

$$8 + 2t + 3 + 9 = 52 \qquad 8 + w + 3 + 9 = 34$$
$$20 + 2t = 52 \qquad 20 + w = 34$$
$$2t = 32 \qquad w = 14$$
$$t = 16$$

So $4z + 2t - w = 0 + 2(16) - 14 = 32 - 14 =$ **18**.

Remark: Any choice for z will give us the same answer. We could have chosen a value for t or w as well. But once we choose a value for one of the variables the other two are determined.

8.

* **Solution using strategy 16:** The operation to use here is multiplication.

$$ab = 7$$
$$bc = \frac{1}{9}$$
$$(ab)(bc) = (7)\left(\frac{1}{9}\right)$$
$$ab^2c = \frac{7}{9}$$

Now substitute 3 in for b^2. So we have $a(3)c = \frac{7}{9}$. Dividing each side of the equation by 3 gives us $ac = \frac{1}{3} \cdot \frac{7}{9} =$ **7/27** or **.259**.

9.

* **Solution using strategy 16:** First multiply out the second term on the left hand side of the second equation to get $ax + by + y = 26$. Now subtract the first equation from the second equation.

$$ax + by + y = 26$$
$$\underline{ax + by = 17}$$
$$y = 9$$

We see that the answer is choice (D).

10.

* **Solution using strategy 16:** Notice that when we add the three given equations, all the variables on the right hand side add to zero. So we have $3k = 12 - 17 + 11 = 6$. Therefore $k =$ **2**.

11.

* **Solution using strategy 16:** The operation to use here is division. We divide the left hand sides of each equation, and the right hand sides of each equation. First the left: Recall that when we divide expressions with the same base we need to subtract the exponents. So $\frac{x^{15}}{x^{14}} = x^1 = x$. Now for the right: Recall that dividing is the same as multiplying by the reciprocal. So, $\frac{2}{z} \div \frac{2y}{z} = \frac{2}{z} \cdot \frac{z}{2y} = \frac{1}{y}$. Thus, $x = \frac{1}{y}$ and the answer is choice (D).

Alternate Solution: Multiply each side of each equation by z to get

$$zx^{15} = 2 \qquad\qquad zx^{14} = 2y$$

Multiplying each side of the second equation by x yields $zx^{15} = 2xy$. So $2xy = 2$, and thus, $xy = 1$, and therefore $x = \frac{1}{y}$, choice (D).

12.

* **Solution using the elimination method:** Since we are trying to find x, we want to make y go away. So we make the two coefficients of y "match up" by multiplying by the appropriate numbers. We will multiply the first equation by 3 and the second equation by 4.

$$3(6x) = (2 + 4y)(3)$$
$$4(7x) = (3 - 3y)(4)$$

Don't forget to distribute on the right. Then add the two equations.

$$18x = 6 + 12y$$
$$\underline{28x = 12 - 12y}$$
$$46x = 18$$

Now divide each side by 46 to get x = **9/23** or **.391**.

Optional Material

Level 6: Algebra

1. If x and y are positive integers with $x^8 = \frac{z^3}{16}$ and $x^{12} = \frac{z^7}{y^4}$, what is the value of $\frac{xy}{z}$?

2. If $2x + 3y - 4z = 2$, $x - y + 5z = 6$ and $3x + 2y - z = 4$, what is the value of y ?

Solutions

1.

* $x^4 = \frac{x^{12}}{x^8} = \frac{z^7}{y^4} \div \frac{z^3}{16} = \frac{z^7}{y^4} \cdot \frac{16}{z^3} = \frac{16z^4}{y^4}$. So $x = \frac{2z}{y}$, and therefore $\frac{xy}{z}$ = **2**.

2.

* **Solution using Gauss-Jordan reduction:** Push the MATRIX button, scroll over to EDIT and then select [A] (or press 1). We will be inputting a 3×4 matrix, so press 3 ENTER 4 ENTER. Then enter the numbers 2, 3, -4 and 2 for the first row, 1, -1, 5 and 6 for the second row, and 3, 2, -1 and 4 for the third row.

Now push the QUIT button (2ND MODE) to get a blank screen. Press MATRIX again. This time scroll over to MATH and select rref((or press B). Then press MATRIX again and select [A] (or press 1) and press ENTER.

The display will show the following.

$$\begin{matrix}[[1\ 0\ 0 & -.4] \\ [0\ 1\ 0 & 3.6\ ] \\ [0\ 0\ 1 & 2]]\end{matrix}$$

The second line is interpreted as y = **3.6**.

LESSON 3
GEOMETRY

Strategy 28 – Computation of slopes

Slope formulas are not given on the SAT. You should make sure that you know the following.

$$\text{Slope} = m = \frac{rise}{run} = \frac{y_2 - y_1}{x_2 - x_1}$$

Note: Lines with positive slope have graphs that go upwards from left to right. Lines with negative slope have graphs that go downwards from left to right. If the slope of a line is zero, it is horizontal. Vertical lines have **no** slope (this is different from zero slope).

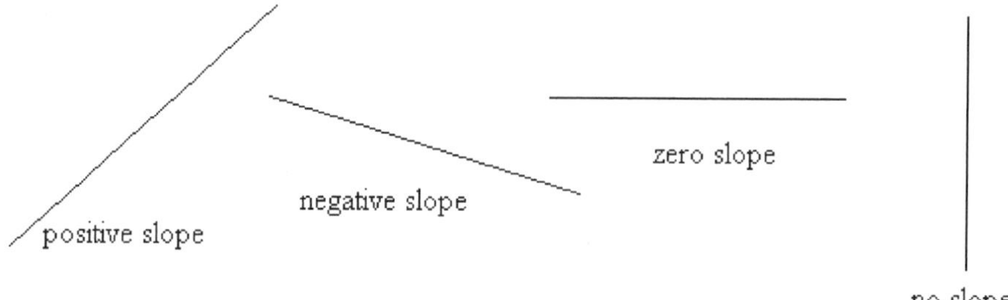

The **slope-intercept form of an equation of a line** is $\boldsymbol{y = mx + b}$ where m is the slope of the line and b is the y-coordinate of the y-intercept, i.e. the point $(0, b)$ is on the line. Note that this point lies on the y-axis.

The **point-slope form of an equation of a line** is $\boldsymbol{y - y_0 = m(x - x_0)}$ where $\boldsymbol{m}$ is the slope of the line and $(\boldsymbol{x_0, y_0})$ is any point on the line.

Try to answer the following question using this strategy together with Strategy 4 from Lesson 1. **Do not** check the solution until you have attempted this question yourself.

LEVEL 4: GEOMETRY

1. If $a > 1$, what is the slope of the line in the xy-plane that passes through the points (a^2, a^4) and (a^3, a^6)?

    (A) $-a^3 + 6a^2$
    (B) $-a^3 + a^2$
    (C) $-a^3 - a^2$
    (D) $a^3 - a^2$
    (E) $a^3 + a^2$

Solution

Let's pick a number for *a*, say *a* = 2. So the two points are (4,16) and (8,64). The slope of the line passing through these two points is

$$m = \frac{64-16}{8-4} = \frac{48}{4} = \mathbf{12}$$

Put a nice big, dark circle around the number 12. We now plug *a* = 2 into each answer choice.

(A) -8 + 6(4) = 16
(B) -8 + 4 = -4
(C) -8 – 4 = -12
(D) 8 – 4 = 4
(E) 8 + 4 = 12

Since choices (A), (B), (C), and (D) all came out incorrect, the answer is choice (E).

Remark: We could have also gotten the slope geometrically by plotting the two points, and noticing that to get from (4,16) to (8,64) we need to travel up 48 units and right 4 units. So the slope is

$$m = \frac{rise}{run} = \frac{48}{4} = \mathbf{12}.$$

Before we go on, try to solve this problem directly (without plugging in numbers).

Solution

Note: Do not worry if you have trouble following this solution. The algebra performed here will be reviewed in Lesson 14.

* Using the slope formula we have

$$m = \frac{a^6-a^4}{a^3-a^2} = \frac{a^4(a^2-1)}{a^2(a-1)} = \frac{a^2(a+1)(a-1)}{a-1} = a^2(a+1) = a^3 + a^2.$$

This is choice (E).

Strategy 5 – Plug in the given point

If the graph of a function or other equation passes through certain points, plug those points into the equation to eliminate answer choices.

Try to answer the following question using this strategy. **Do not** check the solution until you have attempted this question yourself.

LEVEL 4: GEOMETRY

2. Which of the following is an equation of the line in the xy-plane that passes through the point (4,-2) and is perpendicular to the line $y = -4x + 7$?

   (A) $y = -4x - 6$
   (B) $y = -4x - 3$
   (C) $y = -4x + 3$
   (D) $y = \frac{1}{4}x - 3$
   (E) $y = \frac{1}{4}x + 6$

Solution

* Since the point (4,-2) lies on the line, if we substitute 4 in for *x*, we should get **-2** for *y*. Let's substitute 4 in for *x* in each answer choice.

(A) -4*4 – 6 = -16 – 6 = -22
(B) -4*4 – 3 = -16 – 3 = -19
(C) -4*4 + 3 = -16 + 3 = -13
(D) (1/4)*4 – 3 = 1 – 3 = -2
(E) (1/4)*4 + 6 = 1 + 6 = 7

We can eliminate choices (A), (B), (C) and (E) because they did not come out to -2. The answer is therefore choice (D).

Important note: (D) is **not** the correct answer simply because *y* came out to -2. It is correct because all 4 of the other choices did **not** give -2 for *y*.

Before we go on, try to solve this problem using geometry.

Solution

Note that the given line has a slope of -4. Since **perpendicular lines have slopes that are negative reciprocals of each other**, $m = \frac{1}{4}$. Also, we are given that the point $(x_0, y_0) = (4,-2)$ is on the line. We use the point-slope form for the equation of a line $\boldsymbol{y - y_0 = m(x - x_0)}$ to get $y - (-2) = \frac{1}{4}(x - 4)$. Let's solve this equation for *y*.

$$y - (-2) = \frac{1}{4}(x - 4)$$

$$y + 2 = \frac{1}{4}(x - 4)$$

$$y + 2 = \frac{1}{4}x - 1$$

$$y = \frac{1}{4}x - 3$$

Therefore the answer is choice (D).

Note: To get the reciprocal of a number we interchange the numerator and denominator. The number -4 has a "hidden" denominator of 1, so the reciprocal of -4 is $-\frac{1}{4}$. Now to get the negative reciprocal, we simply change the sign of the reciprocal. Thus, the negative reciprocal of -4 is $\frac{1}{4}$.

Now try to solve each of the following problems by using Strategy 5 or 28. Then, if possible, solve each problem another way. The answers to these problems, followed by full solutions are at the end of this lesson. **Do not** look at the answers until you have attempted these problems yourself. Please remember to mark off any problems you get wrong.

Level 1: Geometry

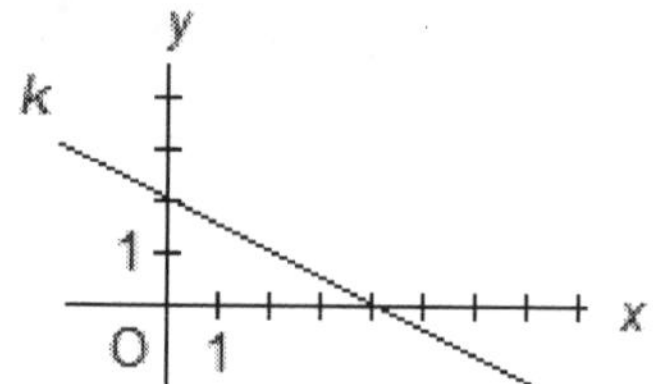

3. What is the equation of line k in the figure above?

   (A) $y = -2x + 2$
   (B) $y = -2x + 4$
   (C) $y = -\frac{1}{2}x + 2$
   (D) $y = -\frac{1}{2}x + 4$
   (E) $y = 2x + 2$

Level 2: Geometry

4. In an xy-coordinate system, point Q is located by beginning at P, moving 6 units up and then moving 4 units to the right. What is the slope of line $\overline{PQ}$?

   (A) 0
   (B) $\frac{2}{3}$
   (C) 1
   (D) $\frac{3}{2}$
   (E) 2

LEVEL 3: GEOMETRY

5. Which of the following is an equation of the line in the xy-plane that passes through the point (0,-5) and is parallel to the line $y = -4x + 7$?

   (A) $y = -4x - 7$
   (B) $y = -4x - 5$
   (C) $y = -4x + 5$
   (D) $y = \frac{1}{4}x + 5$
   (E) $y = \frac{1}{4}x + 7$

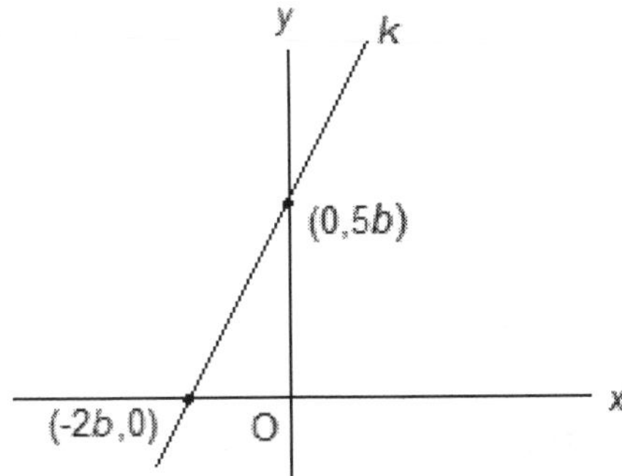

6. In the figure above, what is the slope of line k ?

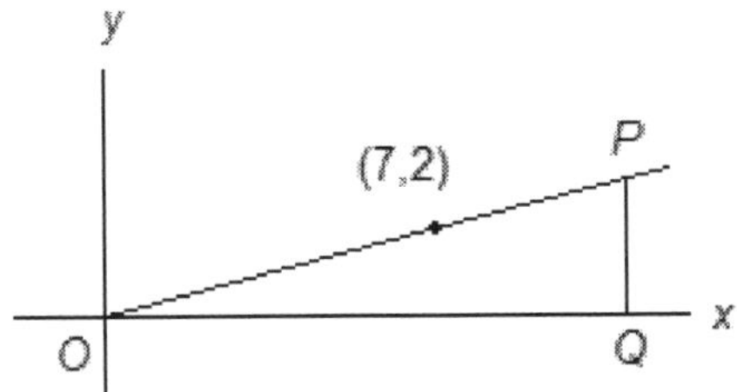

7. Line k (not shown) passes through O and intersects $\overline{PQ}$ between P and Q. What is one possible value of the slope of line k?

8. If $y = 8x$ and the value of x is decreased by 4, then the value of y will be decreased by how much?

   (A) 1
   (B) 8
   (C) 16
   (D) 24
   (E) 32

9. In the xy-coordinate plane, line n passes through the points (0,5) and (-2,0). If line m is perpendicular to line n, what is the slope of line m?

   (A) $-\frac{5}{2}$
   (B) $-\frac{2}{5}$
   (C) 1
   (D) $\frac{2}{5}$
   (E) $\frac{5}{2}$

LEVEL 4: GEOMETRY

10. Which of the following is the equation of a line in the xy-plane that is perpendicular to the line with equation $y = 3$?

    (A) $y = -3$
    (B) $y = -\frac{1}{3}$
    (C) $x = -2$
    (D) $y = -3x$
    (E) $y = -\frac{1}{3}x$

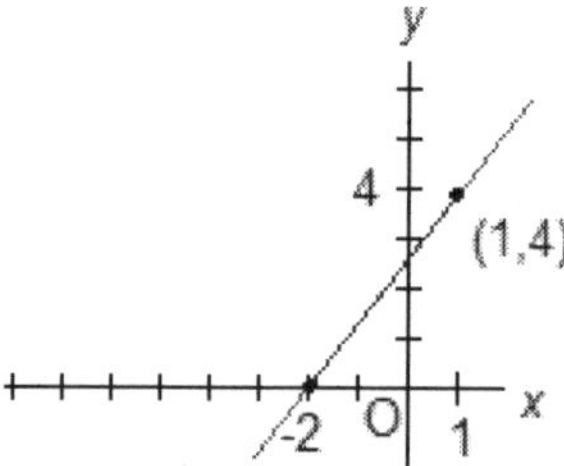

11. The line in the xy-plane above has equation $y = mx + b$, where m and b are constants. What is the value of b?

LEVEL 5: GEOMETRY

12. In the xy-plane, the points $(5, e)$ and $(f, 7)$ are on a line that is perpendicular to the graph of the line $y = -\frac{1}{5}x + 12$. Which of the following represents e in terms of f?

    (A) $5f + 32$
    (B) $-5f + 32$
    (C) $5f + 25$
    (D) $-\frac{1}{5}f + 32$
    (E) $\frac{1}{5}f + 32$

Answers

1. E	5. B	9. B
2. D	6. 5/2 or 2.5	10. C
3. C	7. 0 < m < .259	11. 8/3, 2.66, 2.67
4. D	8. E	12. B

Full Solutions

5.

* **Solution using strategy 5:** Since the point (0,-5) lies on the line, if we substitute 0 in for *x*, we should get -5 for *y*.

(A) -7
(B) -5
(C) 5
(D) 5
(E) 7

We can eliminate choices (A), (C), (D) and (E) because they did not come out to -5. The answer is therefore choice (B).

Solution using strategy 28: We will write an equation of the line in the slope-intercept form ***y* = *mx* + *b***.

(0,-5) is the *y*-intercept of the point. Thus, *b* = -5. The slope of the given line is -4. Since the new line is parallel to this line, its slope is also -4, and the equation of the new line is *y* = -4*x* – 5, choice (B).

6.

Solution using strategies 4 and 28: Let's choose a value for *b*, say *b* = 3. Then the two points are (-6, 0) and (0, 15). Therefore the slope of line *k* is $\frac{15-0}{0-(-6)} = \frac{15}{6}$ = **2.5**.

Remarks: (1) Here we have used the slope formula $m = \frac{y_2 - y_1}{x_2 - x_1}$.
(2) 0 – -6 = 0 + 6 = 6
(3) We could have also found the slope graphically by plotting the two points and observing that to get from (-6, 0) to (0, 15) we need to move up 15 and right 6. Thus the slope is $m = \frac{rise}{run} = \frac{15}{6}$ = 2.5.

* **Solution using strategy 28:** $\frac{5b-0}{0-(-2b)} = \frac{5b}{2b}$ = **5/2** or **2.5**.

7.

* **Solution using strategies 4, 5 and 28:** Let's choose a specific line *k*. The easiest choice is the line passing through (0,0) and (7,1). Now plug these two points into the slope formula to get $\frac{1-0}{7-0}$ = **1/7**.

Remark: If the line *j* passes through the origin (the point (0, 0)) and the point (*a*, *b*) with *a* ≠ 0, then the slope of line *j* is simply $\frac{b}{a}$.

Complete geometric solution: The slope of line $\overline{OP}$ is $\frac{2}{7}$ ~.2587 (see the Remark above) and the slope of line $\overline{OQ}$ is 0. Therefore we can choose any number strictly between 0 and .259 that fits in the answer grid.

8.

* **Solution using strategy 28:** The slope of the line is 8 = $\frac{8}{1}$. So, when *x* is increased by 1, *y* is increased by 8, or equivalently a decrease in *x* by 1 will decrease *y* by 8. So a decrease in *x* by 4 will decrease *y* by (8)(4) = 32, choice (E).

An alternative method: Let's start by plugging in any value for *x*. Let's make *x* = 5. Then *y* = (8)(5) = 40. Now let's decrease *x* by 4. So *x* is now 1. It follows that *y* = (8)(1) = 8. So y decreased by 40 – 8 = 32, choice (E).

9.

* **Solution using strategy 28:** We first compute the slope of line *n*. We can do this by plotting the two points, and computing $\frac{rise}{run} = \frac{5}{2}$ (to get from (-2,0) to (0,5) we go up 5 and right 2). Since line *m* is perpendicular to line *n*, the slope of line *m* is the negative reciprocal of the slope of line *n*. So the answer is $-\frac{2}{5}$, choice (B).

Remark: We can also find the slope of line *n* by using the slope formula $m = \frac{y_2 - y_1}{x_2 - x_1} = \frac{5 - 0}{0 - (-2)} = \frac{5}{2}$.

10.

* **Any equation of the form *y* = *a* for some real number *a* is a horizontal line. Any equation of the form *x* = *c* for some real number *c* is a vertical line. Vertical lines are perpendicular to horizontal lines.** Therefore the answer is choice (C).

11.

* **Solution using strategy 28:** From the graph we can see that the line passes through (-2,0) and (1,4) so that the slope of the line is $\frac{4}{3}$. Let's use the point (1,4) and write an equation of the line in point slope form.

$$y - 4 = \frac{4}{3}(x - 1)$$

We now solve for *y* to get the line into slope-intercept form. We have that $y - 4 = \frac{4}{3}x - \frac{4}{3}$, or equivalently $y = \frac{4}{3}x + \frac{8}{3}$. From the last equation we see that *b* = **8/3**.

Notes: (1) To get the last equation we had to add 4 to $-\frac{4}{3}$.

$$4 - \frac{4}{3} = \frac{12}{3} - \frac{4}{3} = \frac{12 - 4}{3} = \frac{8}{3}.$$

(2) You can also just enter $4 - \frac{4}{3}$ into your calculator and then grid in the decimal **2.66** or **2.67**.

12.

* **Solution using strategy 28:** The given line has a slope of $-\frac{1}{5}$. Since **perpendicular lines have slopes that are negative reciprocals of each other**, we have that the slope of the line containing points (5,*e*) and (*f*,7) is 5 or $\frac{5}{1}$. So $\frac{e - 7}{5 - f} = \frac{5}{1}$. Cross multiplying (or simply multiplying by 5 – *f*) yields *e* – 7 = 5(5 – *f*) = 25 – 5*f* = -5*f* + 25. Adding 7 to each side of this equation gives *e* = -5*f* + 32, choice (B).

LESSON 4
STATISTICS

Strategy 20 – Change averages to sums

A problem involving averages often becomes much easier when we first convert the averages to sums. We can easily change an average to a sum using the following simple formula.

Sum = Average · Number

Many problems with averages involve one or more conversions to sums, followed by a subtraction.

Try to answer the following question using this strategy. **Do not** check the solution until you have attempted this question yourself.

LEVEL 3: STATISTICS

1. The average of $x, y, z,$ and w is 15 and the average of z and w is 11. What is the average of x and y?

Solution

* The Sum of x, y, z, and w is $15 \cdot 4 = 60$. The Sum of z and w is $11 \cdot 2 = 22$. Thus, the Sum of x and y is $60 - 22 = 38$. Finally, the Average of x and y is $\frac{38}{2}$ = **19**.

Notes: (1) We used the formula "**Sum = Average · Number**" twice here.
(2) More formally we have the following.

$$\begin{array}{r} x + y + z + w = 60 \\ \underline{\quad\quad\quad z + w = 22} \\ x + y \quad\quad\quad = 38 \end{array}$$

Thus, $\frac{x+y}{2} = \frac{38}{2}$ = **19**.

Before we go on, try to solve this problem in two other ways.

(1) By "Picking Numbers" (Strategy 4 from Lesson 1).
(2) Algebraically (the way you would do it in school).

Solutions

(1) Let's let $z = w = 11$ and $x = y = 19$. Note that the average of x, y, z, and w is 15 and the average of z and w is 11. Now just observe that the average of x and y is **19**.

Remarks: (1) If all numbers in a list are all equal, then the average of these numbers is that number as well.

(2) When choosing numbers to form a certain average, just "balance" these numbers around the average. In this example we chose z and w to be 11. Since 11 is 4 less than the average, we chose x and y to be 4 greater than the average.

(2) We are given that $\frac{x+y+z+w}{4} = 15$ and $\frac{z+w}{2} = 11$. We multiply each side of the first equation by 4 and each side of the second equation by 2 to eliminate the denominators. Then we subtract the second equation from the first.

$$\begin{array}{r} x + y + z + w = 60 \\ \underline{\qquad\qquad z + w = 22} \\ x + y \qquad\qquad = 38 \end{array}$$

Finally, the average of x and y is $\frac{x+y}{2} = \frac{38}{2} = \mathbf{19}$.

Important note: You should avoid this method on the actual SAT. It is too time consuming.

Now try to solve each of the following problems. Use Strategy 20 whenever possible. The answers to these problems, followed by full solutions are at the end of this lesson. **Do not** look at the answers until you have attempted these problems yourself. Please remember to mark off any problems you get wrong.

LEVEL 1: STATISTICS

2. The average (arithmetic mean) of four numbers is 85. If three of the numbers are 17, 58 and 83, what is the fourth number?

LEVEL 2: STATISTICS

3. The average (arithmetic mean) of z, 2, 16, and 21 is z. What is the value of z?

4. The average (arithmetic mean) of six numbers is 200. If a seventh number, 32, is added to the group, what is the average of the seven numbers?

LEVEL 3: STATISTICS

5. The average (arithmetic mean) of ten numbers is 55. When an eleventh number is added, the average of the eleven numbers is 70. What is the eleventh number?

LEVEL 4: STATISTICS

6. If the average (arithmetic mean) of a, b, and 23 is 12, what is the average of a and b?

   (A) 6.5
   (B) 11
   (C) 13
   (D) 15
   (E) It cannot be determined from the information given.

7. The average (arithmetic mean) age of the people in a certain group was 35 years before one of the members left the group and was replaced by someone who is 12 years older than the person who left. If the average age of the group is now 37 years, how many people are in the group?

8. The average (arithmetic mean) of 11 numbers is j. If one of the numbers is k, what is the average of the remaining 10 numbers in terms of j and k?

(A) $\frac{k}{11}$
(B) $11j + k$
(C) $\frac{10j-k}{11}$
(D) $\frac{11j-k}{10}$
(E) $\frac{11k-j}{10}$

9. The average (arithmetic mean) of a, $2a$, b, and $4b$ is $2a$. What is b in terms of a?

(A) $\frac{a}{4}$
(B) $\frac{a}{2}$
(C) a
(D) $\frac{3a}{2}$
(E) $2a$

LEVEL 5: STATISTICS

10. If $h = a + b + c + d + e + f + g$, what is the average (arithmetic mean) of a, b, c, d, e, f, g and h in terms of h?

(A) $\frac{h}{2}$
(B) $\frac{h}{3}$
(C) $\frac{h}{4}$
(D) $\frac{h}{5}$
(E) $\frac{h}{6}$

11. A group of students takes a test and the average score is 72. One more student takes the test and receives a score of 88 increasing the average score of the group to 76. How many students were in the initial group?

12. The average (arithmetic mean) salary of employees at an advertising firm with P employees in thousands of dollars is 53, and the average salary of employees at an advertising firm with Q employees in thousands of dollars is 95. When the salaries of both firms are combined, the average salary in thousands of dollars is 83. What is the value of $\frac{P}{Q}$?

Answers

1. 19	5. 220	9. C
2. 182	6. A	10. C
3. 13	7. 6	11. 3
4. 176	8. D	12. 2/5 or .4

Full Solutions

5.

* **Solution using strategy 20:** The Sum of the 10 numbers is 55·10 = 550. The Sum of the eleven numbers is 70·11 = 770. So the eleventh number is 770 – 550 = **220**.

6.

* **Solution using strategy 20:** The Sum of the 3 numbers is 12·3 = 36. Thus $a + b + 23 = 36$, and it follows that $a + b = 13$. So the Average of a and b is $\frac{13}{2} = 6.5$, choice (A).

Solution using strategy 4: Let's let $a = 1$ and $b = 12$. We make this choice because 1 and 23 are both 11 units from 12. Then the Average of a and b is $\frac{a+b}{2} = \frac{1+12}{2} = \frac{13}{2} = 6.5$, choice (A).

Remark: Even though we never ruled out choice (E) as the answer in the second solution, Quasi-elimination says that we are probably correct. See **Strategy 10** in ***"The 32 Most Effective SAT Math Strategies"*** for more information.

7.

* **Solution using Strategy 20:** Let n be the number of people in the group. Then originally the sum of the ages of the people in the group was $35n$. After the replacement, the new sum became $37n$. So we have

$$37n = 35n + 12$$
$$2n = 12$$
$$n = \mathbf{6}.$$

8.
* **Solution using strategy 20:** The Sum of the 11 numbers is $11j$. The Sum of the remaining 10 numbers (after removing k) is $11j - k$. So the Average of the remaining 10 numbers is $\frac{11j-k}{10}$, choice (D).

9.
* **Solution using strategy 20:** Converting the Average to a Sum we have that $a + 2a + b + 4b = (2a)(4)$. That is $3a + 5b = 8a$. Subtracting $3a$ from each side of this equation yields $5b = 5a$. Finally, we divide each side of this last equation by 5 to get $b = a$, choice (C).

10.
* The average of a, b, c, d, e, f, g and h is

$$\frac{a+b+c+d+e+f+g+h}{8}$$
$$=\frac{a+b+c+d+e+f+g+a+b+c+d+e+f+g}{8}$$
$$=\frac{2a+2b+2c+2d+2e+2f+2g}{8}$$
$$=\frac{2(a+b+c+d+e+f+g)}{8}$$
$$=\frac{2h}{8}$$
$$=\frac{h}{4}$$

This is choice (C).

Alternate solution by picking numbers: Let's let $a = 1$, $b = 2$, $c = 3$, $d = 4$, $e = 5$, $f = 6$, and $g = 7$. Then $h = 28$, and the average of a, b, c, d, e, f, g and h is $\frac{1+2+3+4+5+6+7+28}{8} = \frac{56}{8} = \mathbf{7}$. Put a nice big, dark circle around this number. Now plug $h = 28$ in to each answer choice.

(A) 14
(B) 9.3333...
(C) 7
(D) 5.6
(E) 4.6666...

Since (A), (B), (D) and (E) are incorrect we can eliminate them. Therefore the answer is choice (C).

11.
* **Solution using strategy 20:** Let n be the number of students in the initial group. Then the Sum of the scores is $72n$.

When we take into account the new student, we can find the new sum in two different ways.

(1) We can add the new score to the old sum to get $72n + 88$.

(2) We can compute the new sum directly using the formula to get $76(n + 1) = 76n + 76$.

We now set these equal to each other and solve for n:

$$72n + 88 = 76n + 76$$
$$12 = 4n$$
$$n = \frac{12}{4} = \mathbf{3}.$$

12.
* The Sum of the salaries of employees at firm P (in thousands) is $53P$. The Sum of the salaries of employees at firm Q (in thousands) is $95Q$.

Adding these we get the Sum of the salaries of all employees (in thousands): $53P + 95Q$.

We can also get this sum directly from the problem.

$$83(P + Q) = 83P + 83Q.$$

So we have that $53P + 95Q = 83P + 83Q$.

We get P to one side of the equation by subtracting $53P$ from each side, and we get Q to the other side by subtracting $83Q$ from each side.

$$12Q = 30P$$

We can get $\frac{P}{Q}$ to one side by performing **cross division.** We do this just like cross multiplication, but we divide instead. Dividing each side of the equation by $30Q$ will do the trick (this way we get rid of Q on the left and 30 on the right).

$$\frac{P}{Q} = \frac{12}{30} = \frac{\mathbf{2}}{\mathbf{5}}$$

So we can grid in **2/5** or **.4**.

OPTIONAL MATERIAL

LEVEL 6: STATISTICS

1. Suppose that the average (arithmetic mean) of a, b, and c is h, the average of b, c, and d is j, and the average of d and e is k. What is the average of a and e?

   (A) $h - j + k$
   (B) $\frac{3h+3j-2k}{2}$
   (C) $\frac{3h-3j+2k}{2}$
   (D) $\frac{3h-3j+2k}{5}$
   (E) $\frac{3h-3j+2k}{8}$

Solution

1.

*** Solution using strategies 16 and 20:** We have that $a + b + c = 3h$, $b + c + d = 3j$, and $d + e = 2k$. If we subtract the second equation from the first, and then add the third equation we get $a + e = 3h - 3j + 2k$. So the average of a and e is $\frac{a+e}{2} = \frac{3h-3j+2k}{2}$, choice (C).

Solution using strategy 4: Let's choose values for a, b, c, d, and e, say $a = 1$, $b = 2$, $c = 3$, $d = 4$, and $e = 6$. Then $h = 2$, $j = 3$, $k = 5$ and the average of a and e is **3.5**. The answer choices become

   (A) 4
   (B) 2.5
   (C) 3.5
   (D) 1.4
   (E) .875

Since (A), (B), (D), and (E) came out incorrect, the answer is choice (C).

Lesson 5
Number Theory

Reminder: Before beginning this lesson remember to redo the problems from Lesson 1 that you have marked off. Do not "unmark" a question unless you get it correct.

Strategy 13 – Remainders in Disguise

To solve a problem that asks to find or use a remainder always begin with a number that is evenly divisible.

Level 4: Number Theory

1. Vincent must inspect 9 electronic components that are arranged in a line and labeled numerically from 1 to 9. He must start with component 1 and proceed in order, returning to the beginning and repeating the process after inspecting component 9, stopping when he encounters a defective component. If the first defective component he encounters is component 6, which of the following could be the total number of components that Vincent inspects (counting repetition), including the defective one?

    (A) 103
    (B) 105
    (C) 107
    (D) 109
    (E) 111

Solution

We have a sequence which repeats in cycles of 9. Component 6 is in the 6th position in this cycle. So we are looking for a number that gives a remainder of 6 when divided by 9. Well, 99 is evenly divisible by 9. Therefore 99 + 6 = 105 gives a remainder of 6 when divided by 9. So the answer is choice (B).

Before we go on, try to solve this problem by "Starting with choice (C)" (Strategy 1 from Lesson 1).

Solution

Let's compute the remainder when 107 is divided by 9. We do the long division by hand (or by using the Calculator Algorithm below). 9 goes into 107 eleven times with a remainder 0f 8. So if we just subtract 2 from 107 we will get a number that gives a remainder of 6 when divided by 9. So the answer is 107 – 2 = 105, choice (B).

Remark: Notice that remainders have a very nice, cyclical pattern. The remainders when you divide ..., 97, 98, 99, 100, 101, 102,.. by 9 are ..., 7, 8, 0, 1, 2, 3,..

Calculator Algorithm for computing a remainder: Although performing division in your calculator never produces a remainder, there is a simple algorithm you can perform which mimics long division. Let's find the remainder when 105 is divided by 9 using this algorithm.

Step 1: Perform the division in your calculator: 105/9 ~ 11.67
Step 2: Multiply the integer part of this answer by the divisor: 11*9 = 99
Step 3: Subtract this result from the dividend to get the remainder:

105 – 99 = **6**.

Prime Factorization

The Fundamental Theorem of Arithmetic: Every integer greater than 1 can be written "uniquely" as a product of primes.

The word "uniquely" is written in quotes because prime factorizations are only unique if we agree to write the primes in increasing order.

For example, 6 can be written as $2 \cdot 3$ or as $3 \cdot 2$. But these two factorizations are the same except that we changed the order of the factors. To make things as simple as possible we always agree to use the **canonical representation**. The word "canonical" is just a fancy name for "natural," and the most natural way to write a prime factorization is in increasing order of primes. So the canonical representation of 6 is $2 \cdot 3$.

As another example, the canonical representation of 18 is 2·3·3. We can tidy this up a bit by rewriting 3·3 as 3^2. So the canonical representation of 18 is $2 \cdot 3^2$.

If you are new to factoring, you may find it helpful to draw a factor tree. For example here is a factor tree for 18:

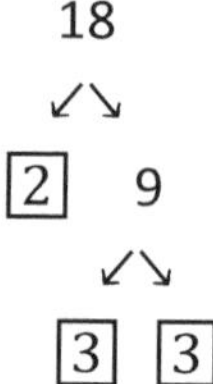

To draw this tree we started by writing 18 as the product 2·9. We put a box around 2 because 2 is prime, and does not need to be factored anymore. We then proceeded to factor 9 as 3·3. We put a box around each 3 because 3 is prime. We now see that we are done, and the prime factorization can be found by multiplying all of the boxed numbers together. Remember that we will usually want the canonical representation, so write the final product in increasing order of primes.

By the Fundamental Theorem of Arithmetic above it does not matter how we factor the number – we will always get the same canonical form. For example, here is a different factor tree for 18:

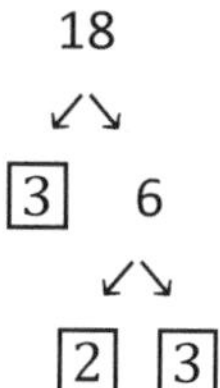

GCD and LCM

The **greatest common divisor (gcd)** of a set of positive integers is the largest positive integer that each integer in the set is divisible by. The **least common multiple (lcm)** of a set of positive integers is the smallest positive integer that is divisible by each integer in the set.

Example 1: Find the gcd and lcm of {9, 15}.

Method 1: The factors of 9 are 1, 3 and 9. The factors of 15 are 1, 3, 5 and 15. So the common factors of 9 and 15 are 1 and 3. So gcd(9,15) = **3**. The multiples of 9 are 9, 18, 27, 36, 45, 54, 63,... and the multiples of 15 are 15, 30, 45,.. We can stop at 45 because 45 is also a multiple of 9. So lcm(9,15) = **45**.

Method 2: The prime factorizations of 9 and 15 are $9 = 3^2$ and $15 = 3 \cdot 5$. To find the gcd we multiply together the smallest powers of each prime from both factorizations, and for the lcm we multiply the highest powers of each prime. So gcd(9,15) = **3** and lcm(9,15) = $3^2 \cdot 5$ = **45**.

Note: If you have trouble seeing where the gcd and lcm are coming from here, it may help to insert the "missing" primes. In this case, 5 is missing from the factorization of 9. So it might help to write $9 = 3^2 \cdot 5^0$. Now we can think of the gcd as $3^1 \cdot 5^0 = 3$.

Method 3: On your TI-84 calculator press MATH, scroll right to NUM. For the gcd press 9, type 9, 15 and press ENTER. You will see an output of **3**. For the lcm press 8, type 9, 15 and press ENTER for an output of **45**.

Example 2: Find the gcd and lcm of {100, 270}.

The prime factorizations of 100 and 270 are $100 = 2^2 \cdot 5^2$ and $270 = 2 \cdot 3^3 \cdot 5$. So gcd(100,270) = $2 \cdot 5$ = **10** and lcm(100,270) = $2^2 \cdot 3^3 \cdot 5^2$ = **2700**.

Note: If we insert the "missing" primes in the prime factorization of 100 we get. $100 = 2^2 \cdot 3^0 \cdot 5^2$. So we can think of the gcd as $2^1 \cdot 3^0 \cdot 5^1 = 10$.

Now try to solve each of the following problems. The answers to these problems, followed by full solutions are at the end of this lesson. **Do not** look at the answers until you have attempted these problems yourself. Please remember to mark off any problems you get wrong.

Level 1: Number Theory

2. What is the greatest positive integer that is a divisor of 14, 21, 49, and 63?

   (A) 1
   (B) 3
   (C) 5
   (D) 7
   (E) 14

Level 2: Number Theory

3. Starting with a blue tile, colored tiles are placed in a row according to the pattern blue, green, yellow, orange, red, purple. If this pattern is repeated, what is the color of the 94th tile?

   (A) Blue
   (B) Green
   (C) Yellow
   (D) Orange
   (E) Red

Level 3: Number Theory

4. If k is divided by 9, the remainder is 7. What is the remainder if $4k$ is divided by 6?

S T A C K S T A C...

5. In the pattern above, the first letter is S and the letters S, T, A, C, and K repeat continually in that order. What is the 97th letter in the pattern?

    (A) S
    (B) T
    (C) A
    (D) C
    (E) K

6. Maggie is making a bracelet. She starts with 3 yellow beads, 5 purple beads, and 4 white beads, in that order, and repeats the pattern until there is no more room on the bracelet. If the last bead is purple, which of the following could be the total number of beads on the bracelet?

    (A) 81
    (B) 85
    (C) 87
    (D) 88
    (E) 93

7. If an integer n is divisible by 3, 7, 21, and 49, what is the next larger integer divisible by these numbers?

    (A) $n + 21$
    (B) $n + 49$
    (C) $n + 73$
    (D) $n + 147$
    (E) $n + 294$

LEVEL 4: NUMBER THEORY

8. What is the least positive integer greater than 7 that leaves a remainder of 6 when divided by both 9 and 15?

9. Cards numbered from 1 through 2012 are distributed, one at a time, into nine stacks. The card numbered 1 is placed on stack 1, card number 2 on stack 2, card number 3 on stack 3, and so on until each stack has one card. If this pattern is repeated, the card numbered 2012 will be placed on the nth stack. What is the value of n?

10. When the positive integer k is divided by 12 the remainder is 3. When the positive integer m is divided by 12 the remainder is 7. What is the remainder when the product km is divided by 6?

Level 5: Number Theory

11. The positive number k is the product of four different positive prime numbers. If the sum of these four prime numbers is a prime number greater than 20, what is the least possible value for k?

12. In the repeating decimal

$$0.\overline{7654321} = 0.765432176543217654321\ldots$$

where the digits 7654321 repeat, which digit is in the 2012th place to the right of the decimal?

Answers

1. B	5. B	9. 5
2. D	6. D	10. 3
3. D	7. D	11.390
4. 4	8. 51	12.5

Full Solutions

4.

Solution using Strategy 4: Let's choose a positive integer *k* whose remainder is 7 when it is divided by 9. A simple way to find such a *k* is to add 9 and 7. So let *k* = 16. Then we have 4*k* = (4)(16) = 64. 6 goes into 64 10 times with a remainder of **4**.

Important: To find a remainder you must perform division **by hand**, or by using the calculator algorithm given in the solution to problem 1. Dividing in your calculator does **not** give you a remainder!

* **Note:** A slightly simpler choice for k is $k = 7$. Indeed, when 7 is divided by 9 we get 0 with 7 left over. Then $4k = 28$, and the remainder when 28 is divided by 6 is **4**.

Note that in general we can get a value for k by starting with any multiple of 9 and adding 7. So $k = 9n + 7$ for some integer n.

Remark: The answer to this problem is independent of our choice for k (assuming that k satisfies the given condition, of course). The method just described does **not** show this. The next method does.

Algebraic solution: Here is a complete algebraic solution that actually demonstrates the independence of choice for k. This solution is quite sophisticated and I do not recommend using it on the actual SAT.

The given condition means that we can write k as $k = 9n + 7$ for some integer n. Then

$$4k = 4(9n + 7) = 36n + 28 = 36n + 24 + 4 = 6(6n + 4) + 4 = 6z + 4$$

where z is the integer $6n + 4$. This shows that when $4k$ is divided by 6 the remainder is **4**.

5.

* **Solution using Strategy 13:** We first find an integer as close as possible to 97 that is divisible by 5 (there are five letters in the pattern). We find that 95 is divisible by 5. Thus, the 96th letter is S. So the 97th letter is T, choice (B).

Remark: Note that the remainder upon dividing 97 by 5 is 2. Therefore the 97th letter in the sequence is the same as the 2nd letter in the sequence, which is T.

Caution: If the remainder is 0, you get the 5th letter in the sequence (there is no 0th letter). For example, the 95th letter in the sequence is K.

6.

* **Solution using Strategy 13:** There are 12 beads before the sequence begins repeating. The 4th, 5th, 6th, 7th and 8th bead are each purple. So when we divide the total number of beads by 12 the remainder should be a number between 4 and 8, inclusive. Since 84 is divisible by 12, 88 gives a remainder of 4 when divided by 12. So the answer is choice (D).

7.

Solution using strategies 2 and 4: Let's choose a value for n satisfying the given condition. If we multiply the given numbers together, then we get n = **24,696**. Starting with choice (A) plug in 24,696 for n, and divide the result by each of the given four numbers.

(A) 24,696 + 21 = 24,717 (not divisible by 49: 24,717/49 ~ 504.4)
(B) 24,696 + 49 = 24,745 (not divisible by 3: 24,745/3 ~ 8248.33)
(C) 24,696 + 73 = 24,769 (not divisible by 3: 24,769/3 ~ 8256.33)
(D) 24,696 + 147 = 24,843 (divisible by all 3)

Since (D) works we can stop here and choose answer choice (D).

Notes:

(a) We only need to check divisibility by 3 and $7^2 = 49$ since these are the highest powers of primes that are factors of the given numbers.
(b) 21 and 49 would work as well (since together they contain the factors 3 and $7^2 = 49$).
(c) A better choice for n is the **least common multiple** of the four given numbers which is $3 \cdot 7^2 = 147$. In this case we get the following:

(A) 147 + 21 = 168 (not divisible by 49: 168/49 ~ 3.4)
(B) 147 + 49 = 196 (not divisible by 3: 196/3 ~ 65.33)
(C) 147+ 73 = 220 (not divisible by all 3: 220/3 ~ 73.33)
(D) 147+ 147 = 294 (divisible by all 3)

Advanced Method: As stated in note (c) above, the least common multiple of the given numbers is 147. We can therefore add any multiple of 147 to n and maintain divisibility by each of the 4 given numbers. So choice (D) is the correct answer.

Note: Choice (E) also always gives an integer divisible by the given 4 numbers. It is not correct because it is not the **next** larger integer.

Remarks: (1) Note that if n is divisible by 147 it can be written as $147k$ for some integer k. Thus $n + 147 = 147k + 147 = 147(k + 1)$. So $n + 147$ is divisible by 147, and thus by any factor of 147 including 3, 7, 21 and 49.

(2) Now that we know the above theory we see that we can get the next larger number divisible by the given numbers by adding the lcm of the given numbers.

* **Quick Solution:** lcm = $3 \cdot 7^2 = 147$. So the answer is $n + 147$, choice (D).

8.

* The lcm of 9 and 15 is 45 (this was done in Example 1 toward the beginning of this lesson). We now simply add the remainder: 45 + 6 = **51**.

9.

Solution using Strategy 13: We first find an integer as close as possible to 2012 that is divisible by 9. We can check this in our calculator.

2012/9 ~ 223.56	2011/9 ~ 223.44	2010/9 ~ 223.33
2009/9 ~ 223.22	2008/9 ~ 223.11	2007/9 = 223

The last computation gave an integer. Therefore 2007 is divisible by 9. So card number 2007 will go on the 9th stack. Card 2008 will go on the 1st stack, card 2009 will go on the 2nd stack, card 2010 will go on the 3rd stack, card 2011 will go on the 4th stack, and card 2012 will go on the 5th stack. Thus, the answer is **5**.

* **Solution using the calculator algorithm:** Divide 2012 by 9 to get 2012/9 ~ 223.56. Now take the integer part of the answer and multiply by 9. We get 223*9 = 2007. Subtract this result from 2012 to get the remainder: 2012 – 2007 = **5**.

10.

* **Solution using Strategy 4:** Using an approach similar to problem 4, we let k = 3 and m = 7. Then km = (3)(7) = 21, and the remainder when 21 is divided by 6 is **3**.

Algebraic solution (not recommended on the actual SAT)**:** The given conditions mean we can write k and m as $k = 12s + 3$ and $m = 12t + 7$ for some integers s and t. Then

$$km = (12s + 3)(12t + 7) = 144st + 84s + 36t + 21$$
$$= 6(24st) + 6(14s) + 6(6t) + 6(3) + 3 = 6(24st + 14s + 6t + 3) + 3 = 6z + 3$$

where z is the integer $24st + 14s + 6t + 3$. This shows that when km is divided by 6 the remainder is **3**.

11.

* Let's begin listing sequences of 4 prime numbers, and checking if their sum is also prime, beginning with the smallest primes.

2, 3, 5, 7	Sum = 17	too small
2, 3, 5, 11	Sum = 21	not prime
2, 3, 7, 11	Sum = 23	prime
2, 3, 5, 13	Sum = 23	prime

Now, (2)(3)(7)(11) = 462, and (2)(3)(5)(13) = 390. Since 390 is smaller, we have *k* = **390**.

12.

* **Solution using Strategy 13:** Since there are exactly 7 digits before repeating we look for the remainder when 2012 is divided by 7. Using one of our standard methods we see that this remainder is 3. So the digit in the 2012th place is the same as the digit in the third place to the right of the decimal point. This is **5**.

OPTIONAL MATERIAL

LEVEL 6: NUMBER THEORY

1. The integer n is equal to k^3 for some integer k. Suppose that n is divisible by 45 and 400. The smallest possible value of n has the form ABC,DEF where A, B, C, D, E, and F are digits. What is the product of A and C?

2. If a and b are positive integers, $\left(a^{\frac{1}{2}}b^{\frac{1}{3}}c^{\frac{1}{5}}\right)^{30} = 41{,}472$, and $abc = 1$, what is the value of ab?

CHALLENGE QUESTION

3. Find the smallest positive integer k such that $\frac{k}{2}$ is a perfect square and $\frac{k}{3}$ is a perfect cube.

Solutions

1.

* We are looking for the smallest perfect cube that is divisible by the least common multiple of 45 and 400. We begin by getting the prime factorizations of 45 and 400 as follows: 45 = $3^2 \cdot 5$, and 400 = $2^4 \cdot 5^2$. So lcm(45,400) = $2^4 \cdot 3^2 \cdot 5^2$. The least perfect cube divisible by this number is $2^6 \cdot 3^3 \cdot 5^3$ = 216,000. So we see that *A* = 2, *C* = 6, and therefore *AC* = **12**.

2.
* $(a^{1/2}b^{1/3}c^{1/5})^{30} = a^{15}b^{10}c^6 = (abc)^6(ab)^4a^5 = (ab)^4a^5$. So we have that $(ab)^4a^5 = 41{,}472$. Since a and b are positive integers, ab must be a positive integer. So let's begin trying positive integer values for ab.

If $ab = 1$, then $a^5 = 41{,}472$. So $a = (41{,}472)^{1/5}$ which is not an integer. Let's try $ab = 2$ next. Then $a^5 = \frac{41{,}472}{2^4} = 2592$. So $a = 2592^{1/2}$ which is also not an integer. Setting ab equal to 3, 4, and 5 also do not work. But if we let $ab = 6$, then $a^5 = \frac{41{,}472}{6^4} = 32$. So $a = 2$, and thus, $b = 3$. So a and b are both integers. Therefore $ab =$ **6**.

Note: It turns out that c is not an integer ($c = \frac{1}{6}$).

3.
Since k is divisible by 2 and 3 and we want the smallest such k, there are positive integers a and b with $k = 2^a3^b$. We have $\frac{k}{2} = 2^{a-1}3^b$ and $\frac{k}{3} = 2^a3^{b-1}$. Since $\frac{k}{2}$ is a perfect square, $a - 1$ and b must be even. Since $\frac{k}{3}$ is a perfect cube, a and $b - 1$ must each be a multiple of 3. So a must be an odd multiple of 3 and b must be even and 1 more than a multiple of 3. The least values of a and b satisfying these conditions are $a = 3$ and $b = 4$. So $k = 2^33^4 =$ **648**.

LESSON 6
ALGEBRA AND FUNCTIONS

Reminder: Before beginning this lesson remember to redo the problems from Lesson 2 that you have marked off. Do not "unmark" a question unless you get it correct.

Direct Variation

The following are all equivalent ways of saying the same thing:

(1) y varies directly as x
(2) y is directly proportional to x
(3) $y = kx$ for some constant k
(4) $\frac{y}{x}$ is constant
(5) the graph of $y = f(x)$ is a nonvertical line through the origin.

For example, in the equation $y = 5x$, y varies directly as x. Here is a partial table of values for this equation.

x	1	2	3	4
y	5	10	15	20

Note that we can tell that this table represents a direct relationship between x and y because $\frac{5}{1} = \frac{10}{2} = \frac{15}{3} = \frac{20}{4}$. Here the **constant of variation** is 5.

Here is a graph of the equation.

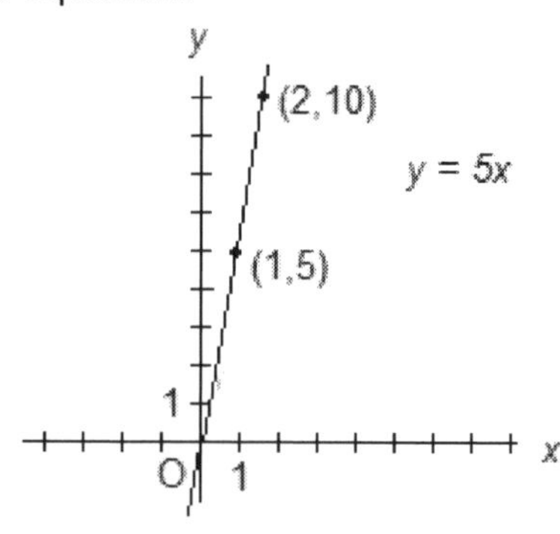

Note that we can tell that this graph represents a direct relationship between x and y because it is a nonvertical line through the origin. The constant of variation is the slope of the line, in this case $m = 5$.

The various equivalent definitions of direct variation lead to several different ways to solve problems.

LEVEL 3: ALGEBRA AND FUNCTIONS

1. If y varies directly as x and $y = 5$ when $x = 8$, then what is y when $x = 24$?

Solutions

(1) Since *y* varies directly as *x*, *y* = *kx* for some constant *k*. We are given that *y* = 5 when *x* = 8, so that 5 = *k*(8), or $k = \frac{5}{8}$. Therefore $y = \frac{5x}{8}$. When *x* = 24, we have $y = \frac{5(24)}{8}$ = **15**.

(2) Since *y* varies directly as *x*, $\frac{y}{x}$ is a constant. So we get the following ratio: $\frac{5}{8} = \frac{y}{24}$. Cross multiplying gives 120 = 8*y*, so that *y* = **15**.

(3) The graph *of y = f(x)* is a line passing through the points (0, 0) and (8, 5). The slope of this line is $\frac{5-0}{8-0} = \frac{5}{8}$. Writing the equation of the line in slope-intercept form we have $y = \frac{5}{8}x$. As in solution 1, when *x* = 24, we have $y = \frac{5(24)}{8}$ = **15**.

* **(4)** To get from *x* = 8 to *x* = 24 we multiply *x* by 3. So we have to also multiply *y* by 3. We get 3(5) = **15**.

Inverse Variation

The following are all equivalent ways of saying the same thing:

(1) y varies inversely as x
(2) y is inversely proportional to x
(3) $y = \frac{k}{x}$ for some constant k
(4) xy is constant

The following is a consequence of (1), (2) (3) or (4).

(5) The graph of $y = f(x)$ is a hyperbola.

Note: (5) is not equivalent to (1), (2), (3) or (4).

For example, in the equation $y = \frac{12}{x}$, y varies inversely as x. Here is a partial table of values for this equation.

x	1	2	3	4
y	12	6	4	3

Note that we can tell that this table represents an inverse relationship between x and y because (1)(12) = (2)(6) = (3)(4) = (4)(3) = 12. Here the **constant of variation** is 12.

Here is a graph of the equation. On the left you can see the full graph. On the right we have a close-up in the first quadrant.

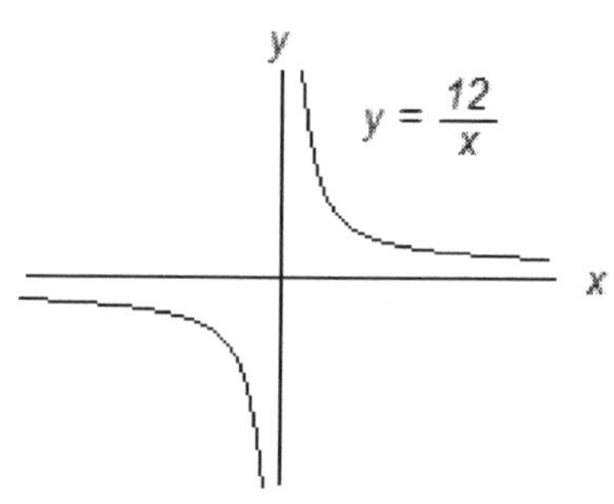

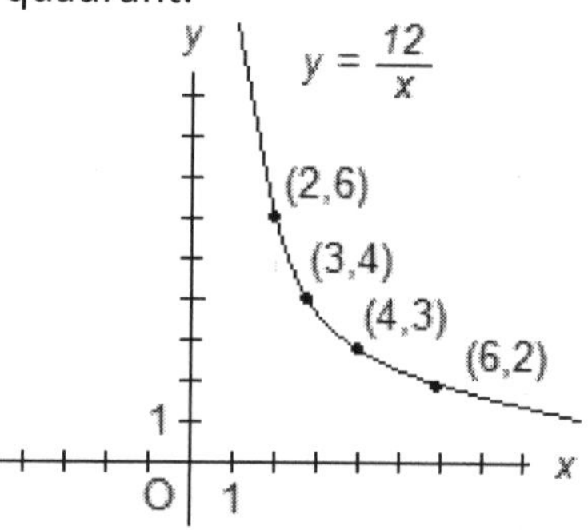

The various equivalent definitions of inverse variation lead to several different ways to solve problems.

Level 3: Algebra and Functions

2. If y varies inversely as x and $y = 8$ when $x = 3$, then what is y when $x = 6$?

Solutions

(1) Since y varies inversely as x, $y = \frac{k}{x}$ for some constant k. We are given that $y = 8$ when $x = 3$, so that $8 = \frac{k}{3}$, or $k = 24$. Thus, $y = \frac{24}{x}$. When $x = 6$, we have $y = \frac{24}{6} = \mathbf{4}$.

(2) Since *y* varies inversely as *x*, *xy* is a constant. So we get the following equation: (3)(8) = 6*y* So 24 = 6*y*, and $y = \frac{24}{6} =$ **4**.

* **(3)** $\frac{(8)(3)}{6}$ = **4**.

.Functions

A function is simply a rule that for each "input" assigns a specific "output." Functions may be given by equations, tables or graphs.

Note about the notation $f(x)$: The variable x is a placeholder. We evaluate the function f at a specific value by substituting that value in for x. For example, if $f(x) = x^3 + 2x$, then $f(-2) = (-2)^3 + 2(-2) = -12$

LEVEL 4: ALGEBRA AND FUNCTIONS

x	$p(x)$	$q(x)$	$r(x)$
-2	-3	4	-3
-1	2	1	2
0	5	-1	-6
1	-7	0	-5

3. The functions p, q and r are defined for all values of x, and certain values of those functions are given in the table above. What is the value of $p(-2) + q(0) - r(1)$?

Solution

* To evaluate *p*(-2), we look at the row corresponding to *x* = -2, and the column corresponding to *p(x)*. We see that the entry there is -3. Therefore *p*(-2) = -3. Similarly, *q*(0) = -1 and *r*(1) = -5. Finally, we have that *p*(-2) + *q*(0) – *r*(1) = -3 – 1 – (-5) = -4 + 5 = **1**.

Try to solve each of the following problems. The answers to these problems, followed by full solutions are at the end of this lesson. **Do not** look at the answers until you have attempted these problems yourself. Please remember to mark off any problems you get wrong.

Level 2: Functions

$$f(x) = 7x - 3$$
$$g(x) = x^2 - 2x + 6$$

4. The functions f and g are defined above. What is the value of $f(11) - g(4)$?

x	$p(x)$	$q(x)$	$r(x)$
1	4	5	9
2	-2	6	-9
3	-5	-9	4
4	-3	-10	-7
5	-5	0	-5

5. The table above gives some values of the functions p, q, and r. At which value of x does $q(x) = p(x) + r(x)$?

Level 3: Functions

6. Let the function g be defined for $x \neq 0$ by $g(x) = \frac{k}{x}$, where k is a constant. If $g(3) = 8$, what is $g(6)$?

7. If y varies inversely as x and $y = 12$ when $x = 5$, then what is y when $x = 15$?

Level 4: Algebra and Functions

8. For all real numbers x, let the function f be defined as $f(x) = 5x - 10$. Which of the following is equal to $f(3) + f(5)$?

   (A) $f(4)$
   (B) $f(6)$
   (C) $f(7)$
   (D) $f(12)$
   (E) $f(20)$

x	$p(x)$	$q(x)$	$r(x)$
-2	-6	-2	-9
-1	-1	5	-10
0	-2	7	-3
1	5	-11	-6
2	-6	0	3

9. The functions p, q and r are defined for all values of x, and certain values of those functions are given in the table above. If the function u is defined by $u(x) = 3p(x) + q(x) - r(x)$ for all values of x, what is the value of $u(-1)$?

$$P(x) = \frac{20x}{98 - x}$$

10. The function P above models the monthly profit, in thousands of dollars, for a company that sells x percent of their inventory for the month. If $90,000 is earned in profit during the month of April, what percent of April's inventory, to the nearest whole percent, has been sold?

    (A) 25%
    (B) 42%
    (C) 56%
    (D) 80%
    (E) 90%

11. If y is directly proportional to x, which of the following could express y in terms of x?

    (A) $7x$
    (B) x^7
    (C) $x + 7$
    (D) $\frac{7}{x}$
    (E) $\frac{x^2}{7}$

LEVEL 5: FUNCTIONS

x	-2	-1	0	1
y	7	a	b	c

12. The values of x and y in the table above are related so that $(y - 2)$ is directly proportional to $(x + 3)$. What is the value of $2a - 3b + 5c$?

Answers

1. 15	5. 4	9. 12
2. 4	6. 4	10. D
3. 1	7. 4	11. A
4. 60	8. B	12. 83

Full Solutions

6.

By substituting 3 in for x in the function g we see that $g(3) = \frac{k}{3}$. We are also given that $g(3) = 8$. So $\frac{k}{3} = 8$. Thus, $k = (8)(3) = 24$. Therefore we have $g(x) = \frac{24}{x}$, and so $g(6) = \frac{24}{6} =$ **4**.

Remark: This is actually an inverse variation question. In fact, it is **exactly** the same question as problem 2 above. Therefore any of those three solutions will work as well.

*** Quickest solution:** $\frac{(8)(3)}{6} =$ **4**.

8.

Solution using strategy 1: First note that $f(3) = 5(3) - 10 = 5$ and $f(5) = 5(5) - 10 = 15$, so that $f(3) + f(5) = 5 + 15 =$ **20**.

Now, beginning with choice (C) we see that $f(7) = 5(7) - 10 = 25$. This is a bit too big. So let's try choice (B). We have $f(6) = 5(6) - 10 = 20$. This is correct. Thus, the answer is choice (B).

Warning: Many students will compute $f(3) + f(5) = 20$ and immediately choose choice (E). Do not fall into this trap!

* **Algebraic solution:** As in the previous solution, direct computation gives $f(3) + f(5) = 20$. Setting $f(x) = 20$ yields $5x - 10 = 20$, so that $5x = 30$, and thus, $x = \frac{30}{5} = 6$. In other words, $f(6) = 20 = f(3) + f(5)$, choice (B).

9.

* $u(-1) = 3p(-1) + q(-1) - r(-1) = 3(-1) + (5) - (-10) = -3 + 5 + 10 =$ **12**.

10.

Solution using strategy 1: We are given that $P(x) = 90$, and being asked to approximate x. So we have $\frac{20x}{98 - x} = 90$. Let's begin with choice (C) and plug in 56 for x. We have 20(56)/(98 – 56) ~ 26.67, too small.

Let's try choice (D) next. So 20(80)/(98 – 80) ~ 88.89. This is close, so the answer is probably choice (D). To be safe we should check the other answer choices.

(A) 20(25)/(98 – 25) ~ 6.85
(B) 20(42)/(98 – 42) = 15
(E) 20(90)/(98 – 90) = 225

So the answer must be choice (D).

* **Algebraic solution:**

$$\frac{20x}{98 - x} = 90$$
$$20x = 90(98 - x)$$
$$20x = 8820 - 90x$$
$$110x = 8820$$
$$x = \frac{8820}{110} \sim 80.18$$

The final answer, to the nearest percent, is 80%, choice (D).

11.

* Simply recall that y is directly proportional to x is equivalent to $y = kx$ for some constant k. The answer is choice (A).

12.

* Beginning with the first column we see that $y - 2 = 5$ and $x + 3 = 1$. So the constant of proportionality is 5 (because $5 \cdot 1 = 5$). Thus, for each of the other columns we multiply $(x + 3)$ by 5 to get $(y - 2)$. So we have

$5(-1 + 3) = a - 2$, or equivalently, $a = 12$
$5(0 + 3) = b - 2$, or equivalently, $b = 17$
$5(1 + 3) = c - 2$, or equivalently, $c = 22$

Thus, $2a - 3b + 5c = 2(12) - 3(17) + 5(22) = \mathbf{83}$.

A more formal algebraic solution: $y - 2 = k(x + 3)$ for some constant k. To find k we use the first column:

$$7 - 2 = k(-2 + 3), \text{ or } 5 = k.$$

Thus, $y - 2 = 5(x + 3)$, or equivalently $y = 5x + 17$. So,

$$\text{when } x = -1,\ a = 5(-1) + 17 = 12$$
$$\text{when } x = 0,\ b = 5(0) + 17 = 17$$
$$\text{when } x = 1,\ c = 5(1) + 17 = 22.$$

As before, $2a - 3b + 5c = 2(12) - 3(17) + 5(22) = \mathbf{83}$.

OPTIONAL MATERIAL

LEVEL 6: ALGEBRA AND FUNCTIONS

1. Let f be a linear function such that $f(5) = -2$ and $f(11) = 28$. What is the value of $\frac{f(9)-f(7)}{2}$?

2. Suppose that z varies directly as x^2 and inversely as y^3. If $z = 9$ when $x = 3$ and $y = 2$, what is y when $z = 4.5$ and $x = 6$?

Solutions

1.

* The graph of f is a line with slope

$$\frac{f(11) - f(5)}{11 - 5} = \frac{28 - (-2)}{6} = \frac{30}{6} = 5.$$

But the slope of the line is also $\frac{f(9) - f(7)}{9 - 7} = \frac{f(9) - f(7)}{2}$. So the answer is **5**.

2.

* We are given that $z = \frac{kx^2}{y^3}$ for some constant k. Since $z = 9$ when $x = 3$ and $y = 2$, we have $9 = \frac{k(3)^2}{2^3} = \frac{9k}{8}$. So $k = 8$, and $z = \frac{8x^2}{y^3}$. We now substitute $z = 4.5$ and $x = 6$ to get $4.5 = \frac{8(6)^2}{y^3}$. So $y^3 = \frac{8(36)}{4.5} = 64$, and therefore $y = \mathbf{4}$.

LESSON 7
GEOMETRY

Reminder: Before beginning this lesson remember to redo the problems from Lesson 3 that you have marked off. Do not "unmark" a question unless you get it correct.

The Triangle Rule

The triangle rule states that the length of the third side of a triangle is between the sum and difference of the lengths of the other two sides.

Example: If a triangle has sides of length 2, 5, and x, then we have that $5 - 2 < x < 5 + 2$. That is, $3 < x < 7$.

The Pythagorean Theorem and its Converse

The Pythagorean Theorem says that if a right triangle has legs of length a and b, and a hypotenuse of length c, then $c^2 = a^2 + b^2$. Note that the Pythagorean Theorem is one of the formulas given to you in the beginning of each math section.

The converse of the Pythagorean Theorem is also true: If a triangle has sides with length a, b, and c satisfying $c^2 = a^2 + b^2$, then the triangle is a right triangle.

More specifically, we have the following.

$c^2 > a^2 + b^2$ if and only if the angle opposite the side of length c is greater than 90 degrees.

$c^2 < a^2 + b^2$ if and only if the angle opposite the side of length c is less than 90 degrees.

Try to answer the following question using the converse of the Pythagorean Theorem together with the Triangle Rule. **Do not** check the solution until you have attempted this question yourself.

LEVEL 4: GEOMETRY

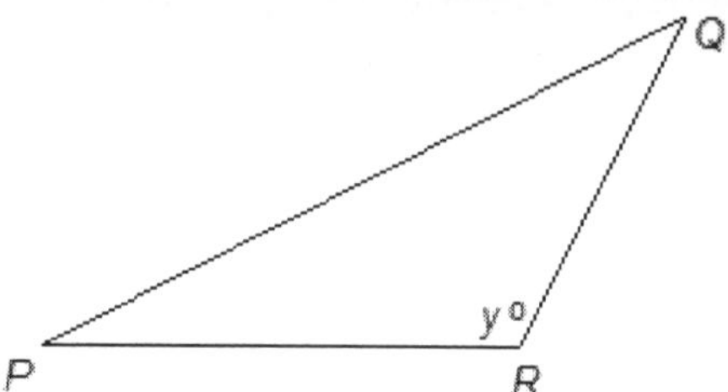

1. In the figure above, $PR = 12$ and $RQ = 9$. If $y > 90$, what is one possible length of $\overline{PQ}$?

Solution

We have 12 – 9 = 3 and 12 + 9 = 21. So by the **Triangle Rule**, 3 < *PQ* < 21.

Using the **converse of the Pythagorean Theorem**, $(PQ)^2 > (PR)^2 + (RQ)^2$. So we have $(PQ)^2 > 12^2 + 9^2 = 144 + 81 = 225$, and therefore *PQ* > 15.

Putting the two rules together we have **15 < *PQ* < 21**.

For example, we can grid in **16**.

Now try to solve each of the following problems. The answers to these problems, followed by full solutions are at the end of this lesson. **Do not** look at the answers until you have attempted these problems yourself. Please remember to mark off any problems you get wrong.

LEVEL 3: GEOMETRY

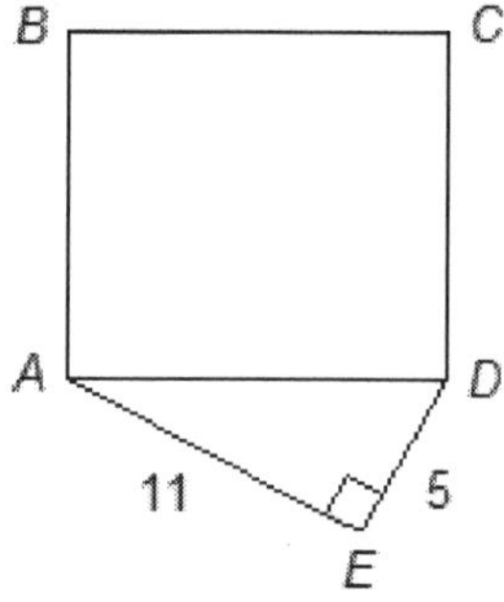

2. In the figure above, what is the area of square $ABCD$?

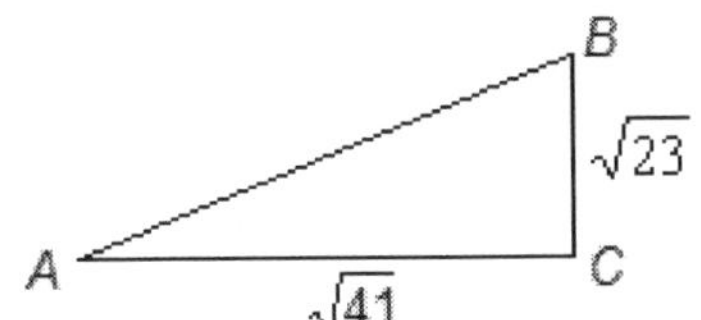

Note: Figure not drawn to scale.

3. In right triangle ABC above, what is the length of side $\overline{AB}$?

LEVEL 4: GEOMETRY

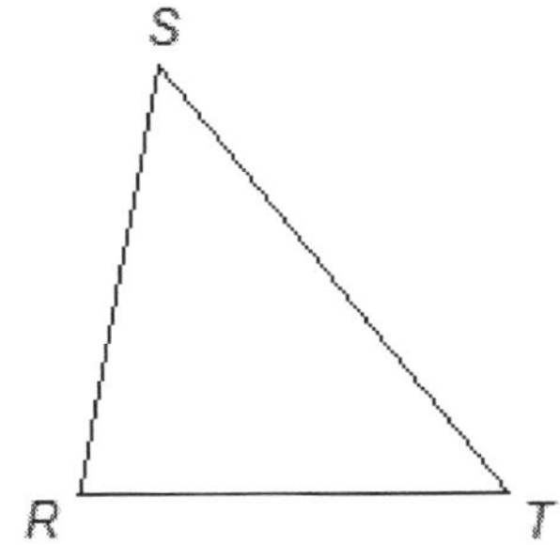

Note: Figure not drawn to scale.

4. In the triangle above, $RS = RT = 26$ and $ST = 20$. What is the area of the triangle?

LEVEL 5: GEOMETRY

5. If x is an integer less than 6, how many different triangles are there with sides of length 5, 9 and x ?

    (A) One
    (B) Two
    (C) Three
    (D) Four
    (E) Five

6. The lengths of the sides of a triangle are x, 16 and 31, where x is the shortest side. If the triangle is not isosceles, what is a possible value of x?

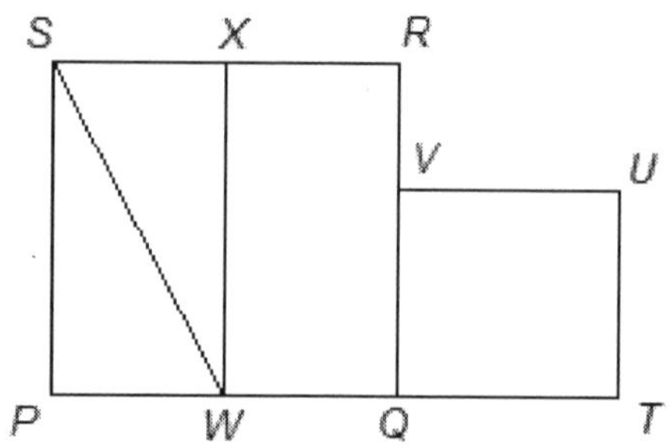

Note: Figure not drawn to scale.

7. In the figure above, $PQRS$ and $QTUV$ are squares, W and X are the midpoints of $\overline{PQ}$ and $\overline{RS}$, respectively, and $TW = SW$. If $RX = \frac{1}{2}$, what is the length of $\overline{UV}$?

(A) $\frac{\sqrt{5}-1}{2}$
(B) $\frac{\sqrt{3}-1}{2}$
(C) $\frac{\sqrt{5}}{2}$
(D) $\frac{\sqrt{3}}{2}$
(E) $\frac{2}{3}$

8. Points Q, R and S lie in a plane. If the distance between Q and R is 18 and the distance between R and S is 11, which of the following could be the distance between Q and S ?

I. 7
II. 28
III. 29

(A) I only
(B) II only
(C) III only
(D) I and III only
(E) I, II, and III

9. The lengths of the sides of an isosceles triangle are 22, m, and m. If m is an integer, what is the smallest possible perimeter of the triangle?

   (A) 30
   (B) 31
   (C) 32
   (D) 34
   (E) 46

10. In ΔABC, the length of side $\overline{BC}$ is 16 and the length of side $\overline{AC}$ is 17. What is the least possible integer length of side $\overline{AB}$?

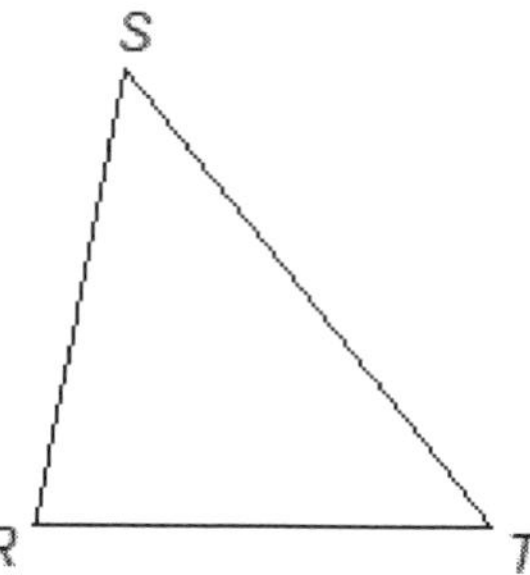

Note: Figure not drawn to scale.

11. In the triangle above, $RS = 6$ and $ST = 9$. Point U lies on RT between R and T so that $SU \perp RT$. Which of the following cannot be the length of SU?

   (A) 1
   (B) 2
   (C) 3
   (D) 5
   (E) 7

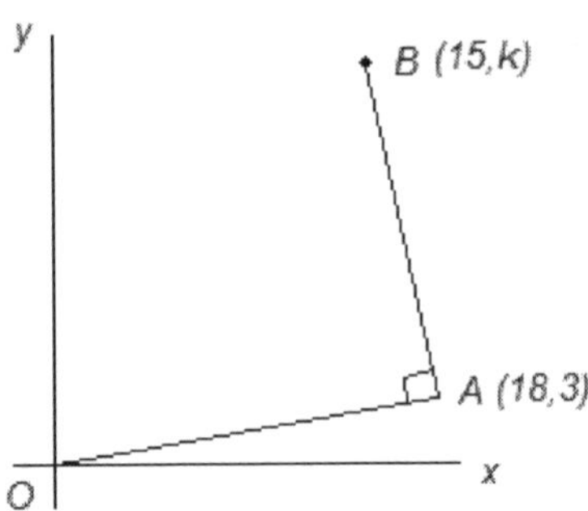

12. In the xy-plane above $OA = AB$. What is the value of k?

Answers

1. $15 < PQ < 21$	5. A	9. E
2. 146	6. $15 < x < 16$	10. 2
3. 8	7. A	11. E
4. 240	8. E	12. 21

Full Solutions

2.
* **Solution using the Pythagorean Theorem:** Let x be the length of a side of the square. So $AD = x$. By the Pythagorean Theorem

$$x^2 = 11^2 + 5^2 = 121 + 25 = 146.$$

But x^2 is precisely the area of the square. Therefore the answer is **146**.

3.
* **Solution using the Pythagorean Theorem:** $c^2 = a^2 + b^2 = 23 + 41 = 64$. Therefore $AB = c =$ **8**.

4.
* We choose ST as the base, and draw altitude RP from vertex R to base ST.

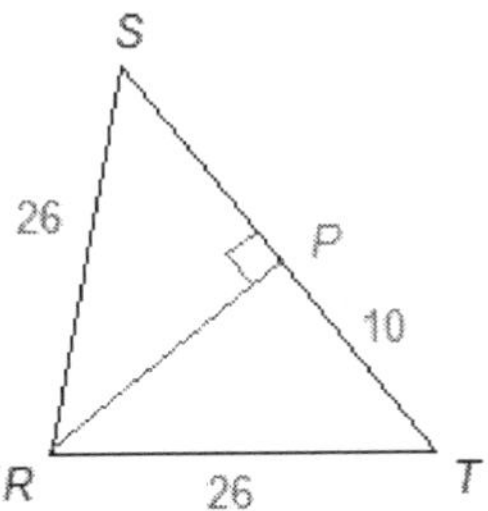

In an isosceles triangle the altitude is equal to the median. It follows that $TP = \frac{1}{2}ST = 10$. Note that $10 = 2\cdot5$ and $26 = 2\cdot13$. Using the Pythagorean triple 5, 12, 13, we have that $RP = 2\cdot12 = 24$.

Area = $(\frac{1}{2})bh = (\frac{1}{2})(20)(24) =$ **240**.

Remarks:

(1) An **altitude** of a triangle is perpendicular to the base. A **median** of a triangle splits the base into two equal parts. In an isosceles triangle, the altitude and median are equal (when you choose the base that is **not** one of the equal sides).

(2) We chose ST to be the base because it is the side that is not one of the equal sides.

(3) 3, 4, 5 and 5, 12, 13 are the two most common Pythagorean triples. These sets of numbers satisfy the Pythagorean Theorem.

(4) If you do not remember the Pythagorean triples it is no big deal. Just use the Pythagorean Theorem. In this case,

$$10^2 + b^2 = 26^2$$
$$100 + b^2 = 676$$
$$b^2 = 676 - 100 = 576$$
$$b = 24.$$

5.

* **Solution using the triangle rule:** By the triangle rule, $9 - 5 < x < 9 + 5$. That is, $4 < x < 14$. Since x is an integer less than 6, x can only be 5. So there is **one** possibility, choice (A).

6.

* **Solution using the triangle rule:** By the triangle rule, x lies between $31 - 16 = 15$ and $31 + 16 = 47$. That is, we have $15 < x < 47$.

But we are also given that x is the length of the shortest side of the triangle. So $x < 16$.Therefore we can grid in any number between 15 and 16. For example, we can grid in **15.1**.

7.

* Let's label the given figure with what we know.

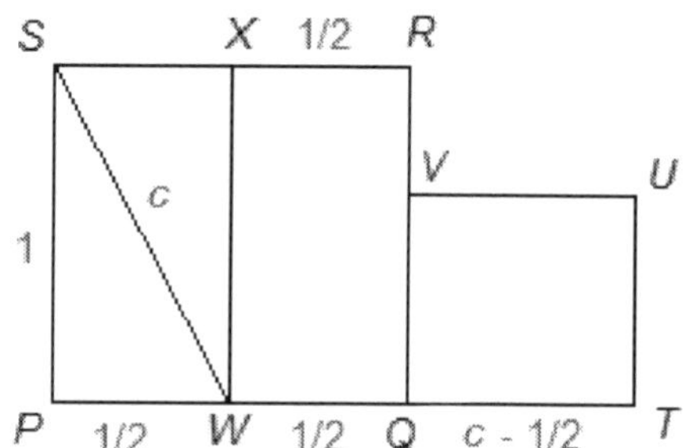

By the Pythagorean Theorem, $c^2 = 1^2 + (\frac{1}{2})^2 = 1 + \frac{1}{4} = \frac{5}{4}$. So $c = \sqrt{\frac{5}{4}} = \frac{\sqrt{5}}{2}$.

Then $UV = QT = c - \frac{1}{2} = \frac{\sqrt{5}}{2} - \frac{1}{2} = \frac{\sqrt{5}-1}{2}$, choice (A).

8.

* **Solution using the triangle rule:** In this case, if Q, R and S form a triangle, then the length of QS is between $18 - 11 = 7$ and $18 + 11 = 29$. The extreme cases 7 and 29 form straight lines. In this problem that is fine, so the distance between Q and S is between 7 and 29, inclusive. Thus, the answer is choice (E).

9.

Solution using the triangle rule: Using the triangle rule we have that $m - m < 22 < m + m$. That is, $0 < 22 < 2m$. So $m > \frac{22}{2} = 11$. Therefore the smallest integer that m can be is $m = 12$, and it follows that the smallest possible perimeter of the triangle is $22 + 12 + 12 = 46$, choice (E).

* **A slightly quicker solution:** For this particular question we actually only need that the third side of the triangle is less than the sum of the other two sides. So we have that $22 < m + m = 2m$, and so $m > \frac{22}{2} = 11$. Once again, it follows that we should let $m = 12$, and thus the perimeter is $22 + 12 + 12 = 46$, choice (E).

10.

*** Solution using the triangle rule:** By the triangle rule, we have that $17 - 16 < AB < 17 + 16$. That is, $1 < AB < 33$. Therefore the least possible integer length of side *AB* is **2**.

11.

*Let's draw *SU*.

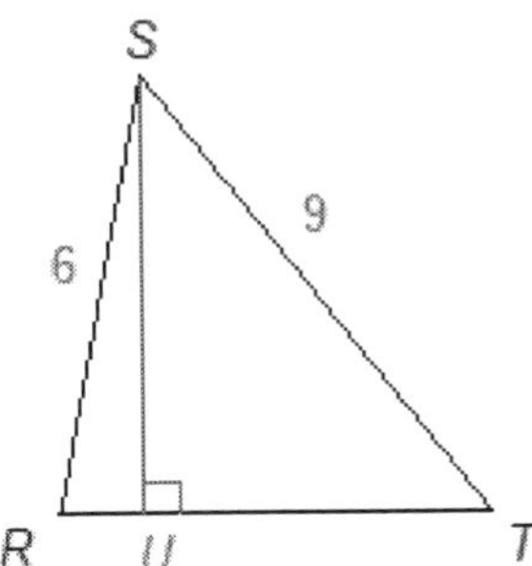

Note: Figure not drawn to scale.

Now just note that *RS* is the hypotenuse of triangle *RSU*. Thus *SU* must be less than 6. So *SU* cannot be 7, and the answer is choice (E).

12.

*** Solution using strategy 28:** To get from *O* to *A* we go up 3 units, right 18 units. So the slope of *OA* is $\frac{3}{18} = \frac{1}{6}$. Since *AB* is perpendicular to *OA*, we have that the slope of *AB* is $-6 = -\frac{6}{1}$. Thus, for every unit we move right along *AB*, we must move down 6 units. Equivalently, for every unit we move left along *AB*, we must move up 6 units. To get from 18 to 15 we must move left 3 units. Therefore we must move up $3 \cdot 6 = 18$ units. Since we are starting at 3, $k = 3 + 18 =$ **21**.

An algebraic solution using slopes: We can do all of this algebraically using the slope formula as follows.

The slope of *OA* is $\frac{3}{18} = \frac{1}{6}$ (see the remark at the end of the first solution to problem 7 from Lesson 3). So the slope of *AB* is -6 because *OA* and *AB* are perpendicular. We can also compute the slope of *AB* using the slope formula as follows.

$$m_{AB} = \frac{k-3}{15-18} = \frac{k-3}{-3}$$

Now set these equal to each other and solve for k (or guess and check).

$$\frac{k-3}{-3} = -6$$
$$k - 3 = 18$$
$$k = \mathbf{21}$$

A solution using two applications of the Pythagorean Theorem: We form two right triangles and use the given points to write down three lengths as shown in the picture below.

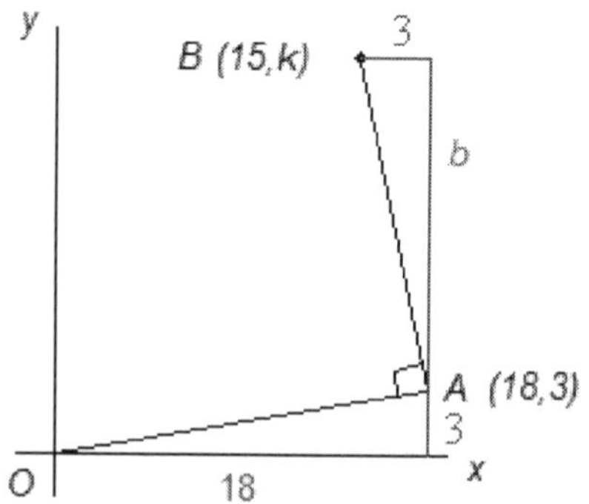

We can now find OA using the Pythagorean Theorem.

$$OA^2 = 18^2 + 3^2 = 333.$$

So $OA = \sqrt{333}$, and therefore $AB = \sqrt{333}$ also since $OA = AB$ is given. Finally, we can use the Pythagorean Theorem one more time to find b.

$$3^2 + b^2 = AB^2$$
$$9 + b^2 = 333$$
$$b^2 = 324$$
$$b = 18$$

So $k = 3 + 18 = \mathbf{21}$.

Lesson 8
Counting

Reminder: Before beginning this lesson remember to redo the problems from Lesson 4 that you have marked off. Do not "unmark" a question unless you get it correct.

Strategy 21 – Writing a list

Sometimes the easiest way to count the number of possibilities is to simply list them all. When doing this it is important that we have a systematic way of forming our list. This will reduce the likelihood of missing something, or listing something twice.

Try to answer the following question by writing a list. **Do not** check the solution until you have attempted this question yourself.

Level 5: Counting

1. How many integers between 3000 and 4000 have digits that are all different and that increase from left to right?

Solution

* Let's form a list:

3456	3567
7	8
8	9
9	78
67	9
8	89
9	678
78	9
9	89
89	789

There are **20** integers in this list.

Remarks: (1) Notice that we only wrote down the necessary information when forming our list. For example, the second entry was just written "7" instead of "3457." This will save a substantial amount of time.

(2) A clear and definite pattern was used in forming this list. In this case the list was written in increasing order. This will minimize the risk of duplicating or leaving out entries.

Counting Principle

The **counting principle** says that if one event is followed by a second independent event, the number of possibilities is multiplied.

More generally, if $E_1, E_2, \ldots, E_n$ are n independent events with $m_1, m_2, \ldots, m_n$ possibilities, respectively, then event E_1 followed by event E_2, followed by event E_3, ..., followed by event E_n has $m_1 \cdot m_2 \cdots m_n$ possibilities.

Try to answer the following question by using the counting principle. **Do not** check the solution until you have attempted this question yourself.

LEVEL 3: COUNTING

2. How many integers between 9 and 300 have the tens digit equal to 2, 3, or 4 and the units digit (ones digit) equal to 5 or 6?

Solution

* There are 2 possibilities for the ones digit (5 or 6). There are 3 possibilities for the tens digit (2, 3, or 4). There are 3 possibilities for the hundreds digit (0, 1, or 2).

The counting principle says that we multiply the possibilities to get (2)(3)(3) = **18**.

Before we go on try to also solve this problem by writing a list.

Solution

Let's try to list the numbers in **increasing order**.

25	26	35	36	45	46
125	126	135	136	145	146
225	226	235	236	245	246

And that's it. We see that the answer is **18**.

Permutations and Combinations

The **factorial** of a positive integer n, written $n!$, is the product of all positive integers less than or equal to n.

$$n! = 1 \cdot 2 \cdot 3 \cdots n$$

0! is defined to be 1, so that $n!$ is defined for all nonnegative integers n.

A **permutation** is just an arrangement of elements from a set. The number of permutations of n things taken r at a time is ${}_nP_r = \frac{n!}{(n-r)!}$. For example, the number of permutations of {1, 2, 3} taken 2 at a time is ${}_3P_2 = \frac{3!}{1!} = 6$. These permutations are 12, 21, 13, 31, 23, and 32.

Note that on the SAT you **do not** need to know the permutation formula. You can do this computation very quickly on your graphing calculator. To compute ${}_3P_2$, type 3 into your calculator, then in the **Math** menu scroll over to **Prb** and select **nPr** (or press **2**). Then type 2 and press **Enter**. You will get an answer of 6.

A **combination** is just a subset containing a specific number of the elements of a particular set. The number of combinations of *n* things taken *r* at a time is ${}_nC_r = \frac{n!}{r!(n-r)!}$. For example, the number of combinations of {1, 2, 3} taken 2 at a time is ${}_3C_2 = \frac{3!}{2!1!} = 3$. These combinations are 12, 13, and 23.

Note that on the SAT you **do not** need to know the combination formula. You can do this computation very quickly on your graphing calculator. To compute ${}_3C_2$, type 3 into your calculator, then in the **Math** menu scroll over to **Prb** and select **nCr** (or press **3**). Then type 2 and press **Enter**. You will get an answer of 3.

Note that 12 and 21 are different permutations, but the same combination.

Example: Compute the number of permutations and combinations of elements from {a, b, c, d} taken (a) 2 at a time, and (b) 4 at a time.

${}_4P_2 = 4!/2! = \mathbf{12}$, ${}_4C_2 = 4!/(2!2!) = \mathbf{6}$, ${}_4P_4 = 4!/0! = \mathbf{24}$, ${}_4C_4 = 4!/(4!0!) = \mathbf{1}$

Notes: (1) The permutations taken 2 at a time are *ab, ba, ac, ca, ad, da, bc, cb, bd, db, cd,* and *dc.*

(2) The combinations taken 2 at a time are *ab, ac, ad, bc, bd,* and *cd.*

Now see if you can list all 24 permutations of {*a*, *b*, *c*, *d*} taken 4 at a time. Note that all 24 of these permutations represent the same combination.

Example: How many committees of 4 people can be formed from a group of 9?

The order in which we choose the 4 people does not matter. Therefore this is the combination ${}_9C_4 = \mathbf{126}$.

LEVEL 1: COUNTING

3. A menu lists 7 meals and 5 drinks. How many different meal-drink combinations are possible from this menu?

LEVEL 2: COUNTING

4. Five different books are to be stacked in a pile. In how many different orders can the books be placed on the stack?

Level 3: Counting

5. A chemist is testing 9 different liquids. For each test, the chemist chooses 4 of the liquids and mixes them together. What is the least number of tests that must be done so that every possible combination of liquids is tested?

6. Nine different books are to be stacked in a pile. One book is chosen for the bottom of the pile and another book is chosen for the top of the pile. In how many different orders can the remaining books be placed on the stack?

Level 4: Counting

7. Any 2 points determine a line. If there are 18 points in a plane, no 3 of which lie on the same line, how many lines are determined by pairs of these 18 points?

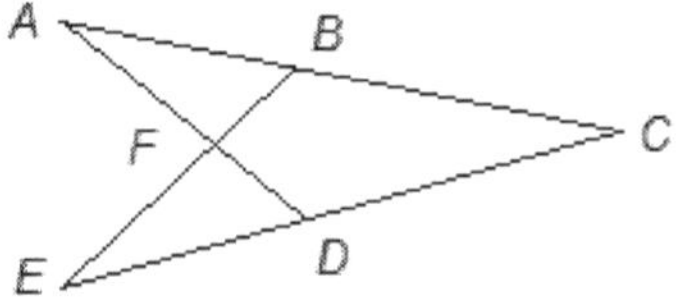

8. Segments $\overline{AC}$, $\overline{AD}$, $\overline{BE}$, and $\overline{EC}$ intersect at the labeled points as shown in the figure above. Define two points as "dependent" if they lie on the same segment in the figure. Of the labeled points in the figure, how many pairs of dependent points are there?

    (A) None
    (B) Three
    (C) Six
    (D) Nine
    (E) Twelve

9. A wall is to be painted one color with a stripe of a different color running through the middle. If 9 different colors are available, how many color combinations are possible?

LEVEL 5: COUNTING

10. A six digit number is to be formed using each of the digits 1, 2, 3, 4, 5 and 6 exactly once. How many such numbers are there in which the digits 2 and 3 are next to each other?

11. If seven cards, each of a different color are placed in a row so that the green one is placed at an end, how many different arrangements are possible?

12. How many positive integers less than 4,000 are multiples of 5 and are equal to 13 times an even integer?

Answers

1. 20	5. 126	9. 72
2. 18	6. 5040	10. 240
3. 35	7. 153	11. 1440
4. 120	8. E	12. 30

Full Solutions

5.

* **Solution using combinations:** We are counting the number of ways to choose 4 of the 9 liquids. This is ${}_9C_4$ = **126**.

6.

* There are seven books left to stack. Therefore we see that there are 7! = (7)(6)(5)(4)(3)(2)(1) = **5040** ways to stack these books.

Calculator remark: You can compute 7! in your calculator as follows. After typing 7, simply press MATH, scroll to PRB and then select ! (or press 4)

7.

* **Solution using combinations:** We need to count the number of ways to choose 2 points from 18. This is the combination ${}_{18}C_2$ = **153**.

8.

* **Solution using strategy 21:** Let's list the dependent pairs of points.

A,F	F,D	A,D	E,F	F,B	E,B
A,B	B,C	A,C	E,D	D,C	E,C

So there are twelve pairs of dependent points, choice (E).

Note: Notice that our list follows a definite pattern. Here we took one long segment at a time, and listed first the two pairs of points adjoining the two shorter segments, and then the pair adjoining the long segment.

* **Solution using combinations:** We can count the pairs without actually making a list. There are 4 line segments, each with 3 points. So each segment has ${}_3C_2 = 3$ pairs of dependent points. So there are $4 \cdot 3 = 12$ pairs of dependent points all together, choice (E).

9.

* **Solution using the counting principle:** There are 9 ways to choose a color for the wall. Once this color is chosen there are now 8 ways to choose a color for the stripe. Therefore there are (9)(8) = **72** possibilities.

Solution using permutations: There are ${}_9P_2$ = **72** ways to choose 2 colors from 9, and place them in a specific order.

Important note: Don't let the word "combinations" in the problem itself trick you. This is **not** a combination in the mathematical sense. If you paint the wall red and the stripe blue, then this is a **different** choice from painting the wall blue and the stripe red.

10.

* **Solution using the counting principle:** Let's start by counting the number of ways we can place 2 and 3 with 2 to the **left** of 3. Well, 2 can go in the first, second, third, fourth, or fifth position. So there are 5 ways.

Now, there are 5 additional ways we can place 2 and 3 with 2 to the **right** of 3. So all together there are 5 + 5 = 10 ways to place 2 and 3 so that these two numbers are next to each other. Once we place 2 and 3, there are four places left. So now there are 4 ways to place 1, 3 ways to place 4, 2 ways to place 5, and 1 way to place 6.

Using the counting principle, we see that the final answer is (10)(4)(3)(2)(1) = **240**.

11.

* **Solution using the counting principle:** There are 2 ways to place the green card. Once the green card is placed, there are 6 ways to place the next card, 5 ways to place the card after that, then 4, then 3, then 2, and finally 1 way to place the last card. By the counting principle there are (2)(6)(5)(4)(3)(2)(1) = **1440** different arrangements.

12.

* Note that 13 times an even integer is just a multiple of (13)(2) = 26. So we are looking for positive integers less than 4,000 that are multiples of both 5 and 26. Since 5 and 26 have no prime factors in common, we are just looking for multiples of (5)(26) = 130 that are less than 4000. The answer is just the integer part of $\frac{4000}{130}$ ~ 30.7692. So we grid in **30**.

OPTIONAL MATERIAL

CHALLENGE QUESTION

1. Let j and k be positive integers with $j \leq k$. In how many ways can k be written as a sum of j positive integers?

Solution

Let's begin with some simple examples. Let's try j = 2, k = 3. Then we have 3 = 1 + 2 = 2 + 1. So there are 2 possibilities.

Now let's try j = 3, k = 5. We have

5 = 1 + 1 + 3 = 1 + 3 + 1 = 3 + 1 + 1 = 1 + 2 + 2 = 2 + 1 + 2 = 2 + 2 + 1.

Let's think about what we did here. Think of 5 as 1 + 1 + 1 + 1 + 1, and notice that there are 4 plus signs. We can think of adding two adjacent ones as "choosing" a plus sign. For example if we choose the first plus sign we get 2 + 1 + 1 + 1. It's not enough to choose just 1 plus sign. We need to choose 2 of them (in this example). If we choose the last two plus signs we get 1 + 1 + 3. If we choose the first and last plus sign we get 2 + 1 + 2, and so on. In other words we are counting the number of ways to choose 2 of the plus signs from the 4 plus signs. Also, note that the number of plus signs is 1 less than 5, and the number we need to choose is 1 less than 3.

For general j and k with $j \leq k$, we have $k - 1$ plus signs, and we need to choose $j - 1$ of them. So the answer is ${}_{k-1}C_{j-1}$.

LESSON 9
NUMBER THEORY

Reminder: Before beginning this lesson remember to redo the problems from Lessons 1 and 5 that you have marked off. Do not "unmark" a question unless you get it correct.

Strategy 15 – Change fractions to decimals

Decimals are often easier to work with than fractions, especially since you have a calculator. To change a fraction to a decimal you simply perform the division in your calculator.

Try to answer the following question using this strategy. **Do not** check the solution until you have attempted this question yourself.

LEVEL 4: NUMBER THEORY

1. What is one possible value of x for which $\frac{5}{16} < x < \frac{2}{5}$?

Solution

We divide 5 by 16, and 2 by 5 in our calculator: $\frac{5}{16}$ =.3125 and $\frac{2}{5}$ = .4. So **.32** is a possible answer.

Note: We can grid in any number between .312 and .4 (but .312 and .4 will both be marked wrong).

Strategy 18 – Change fractional parts to wholes

We can often change fractional parts to wholes by making the total equal to some multiple of the least common denominator of the fractions involved. If the problem is multiple-choice use the denominators in the answer choices as a guide.

Try to answer the following question using this strategy. **Do not** check the solution until you have attempted this question yourself.

Level 5: Number Theory

2. A business is owned by 1 man and 5 women, each of whom has an equal share. If one of the women sells $\frac{2}{5}$ of her share to the man, and another of the women keeps $\frac{1}{4}$ of her share and sells the rest to the man, what fraction of the business will the man own?

   (A) $\frac{9}{40}$
   (B) $\frac{37}{120}$
   (C) $\frac{2}{3}$
   (D) $\frac{43}{120}$
   (E) $\frac{3}{8}$

Solution

Using the answer choices as a guide we will split the business into 120 parts, so that each person has $\frac{120}{6} = 20$ parts. We have $(\frac{2}{5})(20) = 8$ and $(\frac{3}{4})(20) = 15$. So after both sales the man has $20 + 8 + 15 = 43$ parts out of 120 parts total. Thus, the answer is choice (D).

Remark: The number 120 comes from multiplying the least common denominator of the two fractions ($5 \cdot 4 = 20$) by the number of people (6).

Before we go on, try to solve this problem with a single computation.

Solution

* This is quick, but a bit tricky. Each of the 6 people begins with $\frac{1}{6}$ of the business. The first woman sells $(\frac{2}{5})(\frac{1}{6})$ of the business, and the second woman sells $(\frac{3}{4})(\frac{1}{6})$ of the business (if she keeps $\frac{1}{4}$, then she sells $\frac{3}{4}$). Therefore we can get the answer by doing the following single computation in our calculator:

$$\frac{1}{6} + (\frac{2}{5})(\frac{1}{6}) + (\frac{3}{4})(\frac{1}{6}) = \frac{43}{120}, \text{ choice (D).}$$

Strategy 32 – To make something large make something else small (and vice versa)

Try to answer the following question using this strategy. **Do not** check the solution until you have attempted this question yourself.

LEVEL 5: NUMBER THEORY

3. If $14 \leq x \leq 18$ and $9 \leq y \leq 11$, what is the greatest possible value of $\frac{6}{x-y}$?

Solution

* To make a fraction as large as possible, we make the denominator of the fraction as small as possible (while keeping it positive). So we want to make $x - y$ as small as possible (but positive). To make $x - y$ small, we make x as small as possible and y as large as possible. So we let $x = 14$ and $y = 11$. Then $x - y = 14 - 11 = 3$. Thus, $\frac{6}{x-y} = \frac{6}{3} = \mathbf{2}$.

If you ever get confused as to where the biggest and smallest numbers get plugged in, you can simply **try all the extremes**. Try to solve the problem this way as well.

Solution

We compute $\frac{6}{x-y}$ when x and y are equal to each of the extreme values in the given ranges. The extreme values for x are 14 and 18. The extreme values for y are 9 and 11.

x	y	$x - y$	$\frac{6}{x-y}$
14	9	5	$\frac{6}{5}$
14	11	3	$\frac{6}{3} = 2$
18	9	9	$\frac{6}{9} = \frac{2}{3}$
18	11	7	$\frac{6}{7}$

Notice that we tried all four possibilities using the extreme values for x and y. The last column shows that the greatest possible value of $\frac{6}{x-y}$ is **2**.

The Pigeonhole Principle

If n pigeons are put into m pigeonholes with $n > m$, then at least one pigeonhole must contain more than one pigeon.

In the picture above there are $n = 5$ pigeons in $m = 4$ holes. Since 5 > 4, the pigeonhole principle says that at least one hole has more than one pigeon.

Try to answer the following question using the pigeonhole principle. **Do not** check the solution until you have attempted this question yourself.

Level 4: Number Theory

4. The integers 1 through 15 are written on each of fifteen boxes. A boy has placed 44 marbles into these boxes so that the 4th box has the greatest number of marbles. What is the least number of marbles that can be in the 4th box?

Solution

For the first 30 marbles we can place 2 in each box. We have 14 marbles left. If we only place 1 more in the 4th box for a total of 3, then at least one other box will have at least 3 as well, and the 4th box will not have the greatest number of marbles. So we must place 2 more marbles in the 4th box for a total of 4 marbles. We can now disperse the remaining 12 marbles evenly throughout 12 of the other boxes. Each of the other boxes will now have at most 3 marbles, while the 4th box has **4**.

Now try to solve each of the following problems. The answers to these problems, followed by full solutions are at the end of this lesson. **Do not** look at the answers until you have attempted these problems yourself. Please remember to mark off any problems you get wrong.

LEVEL 1: NUMBER THEORY

5. Which of the following numbers is between $\frac{1}{9}$ and $\frac{1}{8}$?

    (A) 0.10
    (B) 0.12
    (C) 0.14
    (D) 0.16
    (E) 0.18

LEVEL 2: NUMBER THEORY

6. A group of 286 parents is to be divided into committees with 3 or more parents on each committee. If each committee must have the same number of parents and every parent must be on a committee what is the maximum number of committees possible?

LEVEL 4: NUMBER THEORY

$$a^b = 6561$$

7. In the equation above, a and b are positive integers. What is the greatest possible value of $a - b$?

8. What is the greatest total number of Sundays there could be in February and March of the same year? (Assume that it is not a leap year so that February has 28 days and March has 31 days).

9. There are 6 red, 6 brown, 6 yellow, and 6 gray scarves packaged in 24 identical, unmarked boxes, 1 scarf per box. What is the least number of boxes that must be selected in order to be sure that among the boxes selected 3 or more contain scarves of the same color?

10. The sum of 15 positive odd integers is 67. Some of these integers are equal to each other. What is the greatest possible value of one of these integers?

11. The set P consists of m integers, and the difference between the greatest integer in P and the least integer in P is 455. A new set of m integers, set Q, is formed by multiplying each integer in P by 5 and then adding 3 to the product. What is the difference between the greatest integer in Q and the least integer in Q?

Level 5: Number Theory

12. If $9 \leq x \leq 15$ and $3 \leq y \leq 5$, what is the greatest possible value of $\frac{7}{x-y}$?

Answers

1. .312 < x < .4	5. B	9. 9
2. D	6. 26	10. 53
3. 2	7. 6560	11. 2275
4. 4	8. 9	12. 7/4 or 1.75

Note: The full solution for question 12 has been omitted because its solution is very similar to the solution for question 3.

Full Solutions

7.

* **Solution using strategy 32:** To make $a - b$ as large as possible, we make a large and b small. So just let $a = 6561$ and $b = 1$. Then $a^b = 6561$, and $a - b = 6561 - 1 =$ **6560**.

8.

* There are 59 days total. To maximize the number of Sundays, let's assume that day 1 is a Sunday. It follows that the Sundays are days 1, 8, 15, 22, 29, 36, 43, 50, and 57. So there are **9** Sundays.

Remark: We listed all the values that give a remainder of 1 when divided by 7.

Warning: Dividing 59 by 7 gives approximately 8.4. This may lead you to believe that there can be at most 8 Sundays. But that is incorrect.

9.

*** Solution using the pigeonhole principle:** If you were to pick 4 boxes, then you COULD get 1 scarf of each color (this is the worst case scenario). If you were to pick 8 boxes, then you COULD get 2 scarfs of each color (again, worst case scenario). In other words, choosing 8 boxes will not GUARANTEE that you will get 3 scarves of the same color. But if you pick 9 boxes, then because there are only 4 colors, at least one of the three colors has to be selected 3 times. So the answer is **9**.

10.

*** Solution using strategy 32:** To make one of the integers as large as possible we will make the other fourteen as small as possible. The smallest odd positive integer is 1, so we make 14 of the integers 1. Thus, the 15th integer is $67 - 14 = \mathbf{53}$.

11.

*** Solution using strategy 4:** The question implies that any choice for k will produce the same answer. So, let's choose $k = 2$, and let $P = \{0, 455\}$. Then $Q = \{3, 2278\}$, and the difference between the greatest and least integer in Q is $2278 - 3 = \mathbf{2275}$.

Algebraic solution: Let x and y be the least and greatest integers in set P, respectively. Then the least and greatest integers in set Q are $5x + 3$ and $5y + 3$. So the difference between the greatest and least integer in Q is

$$(5y + 3) - (5x + 3) = 5y + 3 - 5x - 3 = 5y - 5x = 5(y - x) = 5(455) = \mathbf{2275}.$$

Caution: A common mistake is to distribute the minus sign incorrectly. The following computation is **wrong**.

$$(5y + 3) - (5x + 3) = 5y + 3 - 5x + 3$$

Optional Material

Challenge Questions

1. Given a list of 50 positive integers, each no bigger than 98, show that at least one integer in the list is divisible by another integer in the list.

2. Show that $\sqrt{5}-\sqrt{9-4\sqrt{5}}$ is an integer.

Solutions

1.

Any integer can be written as *mn*, where *m* is a power of 2 and *n* is odd. Let's call *m* the "even part" and *n* the "odd part" of the integer. There are $\frac{98}{2}$ = 49 odd integers less than 98. By the pigeonhole principle, there must be two integers in the list with the same odd part *n*, let's call these two integers $j = 2^a n$, and $k = 2^b n$. If $a \leq b$, then *k* is divisible by *j*. Otherwise *j* is divisible by *k*.

2.

$$\sqrt{5}-\sqrt{9-4\sqrt{5}}=\sqrt{5}-\sqrt{5-4\sqrt{5}+4}=\sqrt{5}-\sqrt{\left(\sqrt{5}-2\right)^2}$$
$$=\sqrt{5}-\left(\sqrt{5}-2\right)=\sqrt{5}-\sqrt{5}+2=2$$

LESSON 10
ALGEBRA

Reminder: Before beginning this lesson remember to redo the problems from Lessons 2 and 6 that you have marked off. Do not "unmark" a question unless you get it correct.

Absolute Value

Here are a few basic things you might want to know about absolute value for the SAT.

The **absolute value** of x, written $|x|$ is simply x if x is nonnegative, and $-x$ if x is negative. Put simply, $|x|$ just removes the minus sign if one is there.

Examples: |3| = 3, and |-3| = 3. Also, |0| = 0.

Geometrically, $|x-y|$ is the distance between x and y. In particular, $|x-y|=|y-x|$.

Examples: |5 – 3| = |3 – 5| = 2 because the distance between 3 and 5 is 2.

If $|x-3|=7$, then the distance between x and 3 is 7. So there are two possible values for x. They are 3 + 7 = 10, and 3 – 7 = -4. See the figure below for clarification.

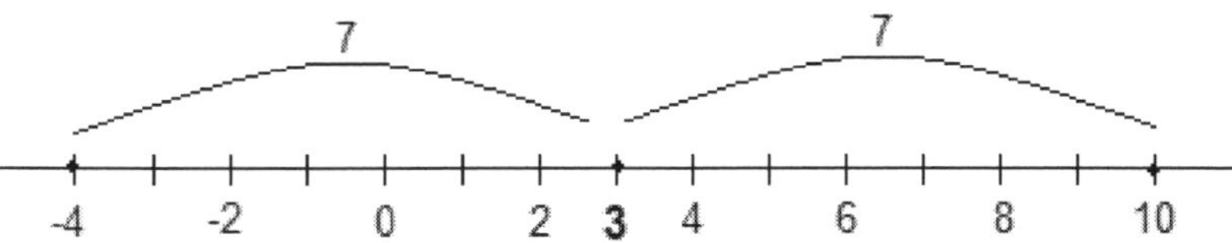

If $|x-3|<7$, then the distance between x and 3 is less than 7. If you look at the above figure you should be able to see that this is all x satisfying $-4<x<10$.

If $|x-3|>7$, then the distance between x and 3 is greater than 7. If you look at the above figure you should be able to see that this is all x satisfying $x<-4$ or $x>10$

Algebraically, we have the following. For $c > 0$,

$$|x| = c \text{ is equivalent to } x = c \text{ or } x = -c$$

$$|x| < c \text{ is equivalent to } -c < x < c$$

$$|x| > c \text{ is equivalent to } x < -c \text{ or } x > c.$$

Let's look at the same examples as before algebraically.

Examples: If $|x - 3| = 7$, then $x - 3 = 7$ or $x - 3 = -7$. So $x = 10$ or $x = -4$.

If $|x - 3| < 7$, then $-7 < x - 3 < 7$. So $-4 < x < 10$.

If $|x - 3| > 7$, then $x - 3 < -7$ or $x - 3 > 7$. So $x < -4$ or $x > 10$.

Try to answer the following question involving absolute value by "Starting with choice (C)" (Strategy 1 from Lesson 1). **Do not** check the solution until you have attempted this question yourself.

LEVEL 3: ALGEBRA

1. If the exact weight of an item is X pounds and the estimated weight of the item is Y pounds, then the error, in pounds, is given by $|X - Y|$. Which of the following could be the exact weight, in pounds, of an object with an estimated weight of 6.2 pounds and with an error of less than 0.02 pounds?

   (A) 6.215
   (B) 6.221
   (C) 6.23
   (D) 6.3
   (E) 6.33

Solution

Begin by looking at choice (C). So we are assuming that the exact weight of the object is $X = 6.23$. It follows that $|X - Y| = |6.23 - 6.2| = .03$ which is too large. So we want X to be **closer** in value to Y.

Let's try choice (B) next. In this case $|X - Y| = |6.221 - 6.2| = .021$. This is still a bit too large.

Let's try choice (A). So $|X - Y| = |6.215 - 6.2| = .015$. This is less than .02. Therefore the answer is choice (A).

Before we go on, try to solve this problem in two other ways.

(1) Algebraically
(2) Geometrically

Solutions

* **(1)** We are given $Y = 6.2$, so we have

$$|X - 6.2| < .02$$
$$-.02 < X - 6.2 < .02$$
$$6.18 < X < 6.22$$

The only answer choice with a number that satisfies this inequality is choice (A).

(2) We are given that the distance between X and 6.2 is less than .02. Let's draw a figure.

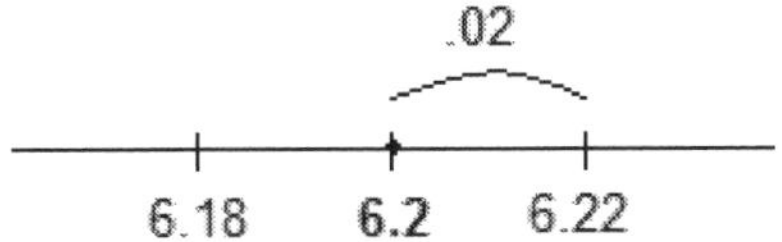

From this picture we see that 6.215 is in the given range, choice (A).

Try to solve each of the following problems. The answers to these problems, followed by full solutions are at the end of this lesson. **Do not** look at the answers until you have attempted these problems yourself. Please remember to mark off any problems you get wrong.

LEVEL 1: ALGEBRA

2. If $3c + 2 < 11$, which of the following cannot be equal to c?

(A) -1
(B) 0
(C) 1
(D) 2
(E) 3

3. For which of the following values of k will the value of $11k - 12$ be greater than 21?

(A) 0
(B) 1
(C) 2
(D) 3
(E) 4

LEVEL 3: ALGEBRA

4. Let h be a function such that $h(x) = |5x| + c$ where c is a constant. If $h(4) = -2$, what is the value of $h(-9)$?

5. If $|-2x + 3| < 1$, what is one possible value of x?

6. If $rs = 3$ and $r - s = 6$, what is the value of $r^2s - rs^2$?

LEVEL 4: ALGEBRA

7. If r and s are positive numbers, then the inequality $r\sqrt{7} < s\sqrt{2}$ is equivalent to which of the following?

(A) $r^2 > \frac{2}{7}s^2$

(B) $r^2 < \frac{2}{7}s^2$

(C) $r > \frac{4}{49}s$

(D) $r > \frac{2}{7}s$

(E) $r < \frac{2}{7}s$

8. If $15 < |b - 11| < 16$ and $b < 0$, what is one possible value of $|b|$?

9. In a certain game a player can attain a score that is a real number between 0 and 100. The player is said to be in scoring range D if his or her score is between 65 and 83. If John has a score of x, and John is in scoring range D, which of the following represents all possible values of x?

(A) $|x + 74| < 9$

(B) $|x - 74| < 9$

(C) $|x + 74| = 9$

(D) $|x - 74| > 9$

(E) $|x - 74| = 9$

LEVEL 5: ALGEBRA

10. On the number line, the distance between the point whose coordinate is s and the point whose coordinate is t is greater than 500. Which of the following must be true?

I. $|s| \cdot |t| > 500$
II. $|s - t| > 500$
III. $t - s > 500$

(A) I only
(B) II only
(C) III only
(D) I and II only
(E) I, II, and III

11. If $|-3a + 9| = 6$ and $|-2b + 10| = 20$, what is the greatest possible value of ab?

12. If $f(x) = x^2 - 5$, which of the following is <u>not</u> true?

(A) $f(-3) = |f(-3)|$

(B) $f(-2) = -|f(2)|$

(C) $f(1) < |f(-1)|$

(D) $f(0) = |f(0)|$

(E) $f(2) < |f(2)|$

Answers

1. A	5. $1 < x < 2$	9. B
2. E	6. 18	10. B
3. E	7. B	11. 75
4. 23	8. $4 < \|b\| < 5$	12. D

Full Solutions

4.

* $h(4) = |5(4)| + c = |20| + c = 20 + c$. But it is given that $h(4) = -2$. Thus, $20 + c = -2$, and therefore $c = -22$. So $h(x) = |5x| - 22$. Finally,

$$h(-9) = |5(-9)| - 22 = |-45| - 22 = 45 - 22 = \mathbf{23}.$$

Calculator remark: You can take absolute values in your graphing calculator by pressing MATH, scrolling right to NUM and pressing ENTER (or 1). The display will say abs(. For example, in this problem to compute $h(-9)$ you can simply type abs(5*-9) – 22, and the output will read **23**.

5.

Solution using strategy 3: Let's try to guess a value for x, say $x = 1$. Then we have that $|-2(1) + 3| = |1| = 1$. Almost! Let's try $x = 1.5$. Then we have $|-2(1.5) + 3| = |-3 + 3| = |0| = 0$. This works. So we can grid in **1.5.**

Remark: The number 1.5 is a really nice guess because it makes the expression under the absolute value 0, and certainly $|0| = 0 < 1$.

* **Quick solution:** Just solve the equation $-2x + 3 = 0$. So $2x = 3$, and therefore $x =$ **3/2** or **1.5**.

Algebraic solution: Remember that $|-2x + 3| < 1$ is equivalent to the inequality $-1 < -2x + 3 < 1$. Let's solve this.

$$-1 < -2x + 3 < 1$$
$$-4 < -2x < -2$$
$$2 > x > 1$$
$$1 < x < 2$$

So we can grid in any number between 1 and 2 (but be careful! The numbers 1 or 2 will be marked wrong!).

Caution: Note that in going from the second to the third step above we divided by -2. Dividing by a negative number reverses the inequality.

6.

* $r^2s - rs^2 = rs(r - s) = (3)(6) =$ **18**.

7.

* Since r and s are positive, each side of the given inequality is positive. Therefore if we square each side of the inequality, the order is maintained. Now $(r\sqrt{7})^2 = r^2{\cdot}7$, and $(s\sqrt{2})^2 = s^2{\cdot}2$. So we have $7r^2 < 2s^2$. We divide each side of this inequality by 7 to get $r^2 < (\frac{2}{7})s^2$, choice (B).

8.

Solution using strategy 3: A bit of guessing and checking should lead you to something close to $b = -4.5$. Indeed, $|-4.5 - 11| = |-15.5| = 15.5$. So we see that $b = -4.5$ satisfies both conditions, and therefore we can grid in $|b| =$ **4.5**.

* **Quick solution:** Just solve the equation $b - 11 = -15.5$, to get $b = -4.5$. So we have $|b| =$ **4.5**.

Algebraic solution: This is a bit tricky. Since b must be negative we want to solve the inequality $-16 < b - 11 < -15$. Adding 11 to each part gives us $-5 < b < -4$. So $4 < |b| < 5$. Therefore we can grid in any number between 4 and 5 (but 4 or 5 will be marked wrong!).

9.

Solution using strategy 4: Let's pick a value for x that is in scoring range D and try to eliminate answer choices. A good choice is a number close to one of the extremes. So let's try $x = 66$, and substitute this value into each answer choice.

(A) $|66 + 74| = |140| = 140$ and $140 < 9$ is False
(B) $|66 - 74| = |-8| = 8$ and $8 < 9$ is True
(C) $|66 + 74| = |140| = 140$ and $140 = 9$ is False
(D) $|66 - 74| = |-8| = 8$ and $8 > 9$ is False
(E) $|66 - 74| = |-8| = 8$ and $8 = 9$ is False

Since choices (A), (C), (D), and (E) came out false we can eliminate them, and the answer is choice (B).

* **Algebraic solution:** We are given that x is between 65 and 83. That is, $65 < x < 83$. Using the answer choices as a guide, let us subtract 74 from each part of this inequality. We have that $65 - 74 = -9$ and $83 - 74 = 9$. Therefore we have $-9 < x - 74 < 9$. This is equivalent to $|x - 74| < 9$, choice (B).

10.
* The first sentence is precisely the statement of II. Letting $s = 1000$ and $t = 0$ gives a counterexample for both I and III. The answer is choice (B).

11.
* The first equation is equivalent to $-3a + 9 = 6$ or $-3a + 9 = -6$. These two equations have solutions $a = 1$ and $a = 5$, respectively. Similarly, the second equation is equivalent to $-2b + 10 = 20$ or $-2b + 10 = -20$. These two equations have solutions $b = -5$ and $b = 15$, respectively. Finally, we get the greatest value of ab by multiplying the greatest value of a with the greatest value of b. So $ab = (5)(15) =$ **75**.

12.
* **Solution using strategy 1:** Let's start with choice (C). We have that $f(1) = 1^2 - 5 = -4$ and $|f(-1)| = |(-1)^2 - 5| = |1 - 5| = |-4| = 4$. Since $-4 < 4$, the inequality in choice (C) is true.

Let's try choice (D) next. Now $f(0) = 0^2 - 5 = -5$ and $|f(0)| = |-5| = 5$. Since $f(0)$ is different from $|f(0)|$, the equation in choice (D) is false. Therefore the answer is choice (D).

Remark: The other three computations are similar. If you struggled with the computations in choices (C) and (D), you may want to do the other computations for practice.

LESSON 11
GEOMETRY

Reminder: Before beginning this lesson remember to redo the problems from Lessons 3 and 7 that you have marked off. Do not "unmark" a question unless you get it correct.

Similarity

Two triangles are **similar** if their angles are congruent. Note that similar triangles **do not** have to be the same size. Also note that to show that two triangles are similar we need only show that two pairs of angles are congruent. We get the third pair for free because all triangles have 180 degrees.

Example:

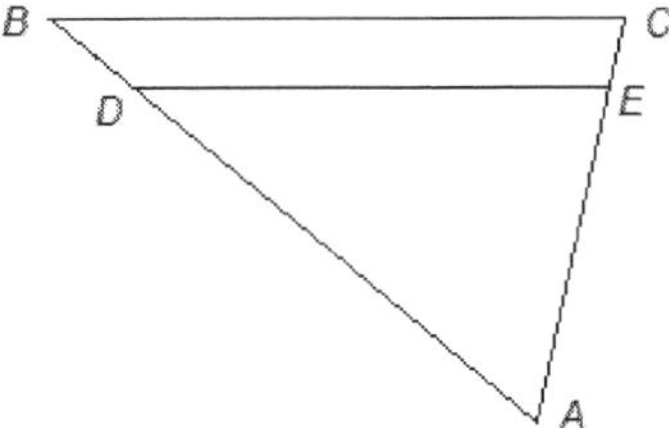

In the figure above, assume that $\overline{BC}$ is parallel to $\overline{DE}$. It then follows that angles *ADE* and *ABC* are congruent (alternate interior angles). Since triangles *ADE* and *ABC* share angle *A*, the two triangles are similar.

Note that **corresponding sides of similar triangles are in proportion**. So for example, in the figure above $\frac{AD}{AB} = \frac{DE}{BC}$.

Now consider the following figure.

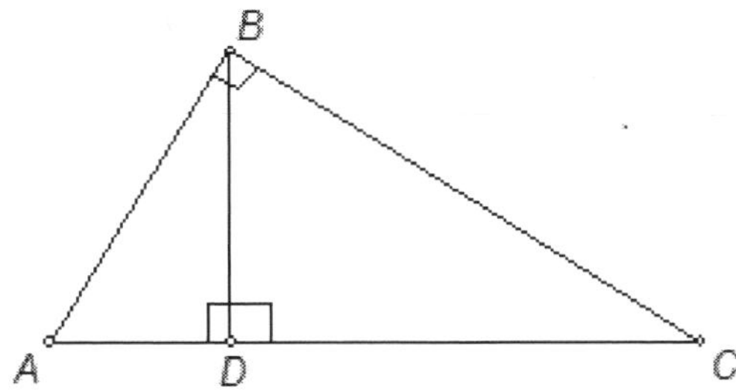

We have a right triangle with an **altitude** drawn from the right angle to the hypotenuse. In this figure triangles BDC, ADB and ABC are similar to each other. When solving a problem involving this figure I strongly recommend redrawing all 3 triangles next to each other so that congruent angles match up. The 3 figures will look like this.

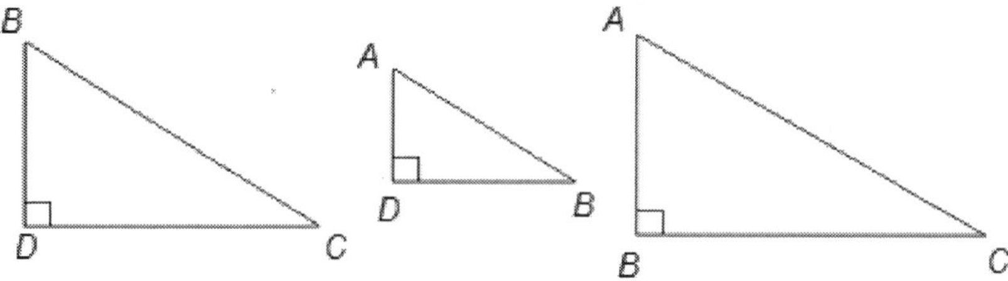

As an example, let's find h in the following figure.

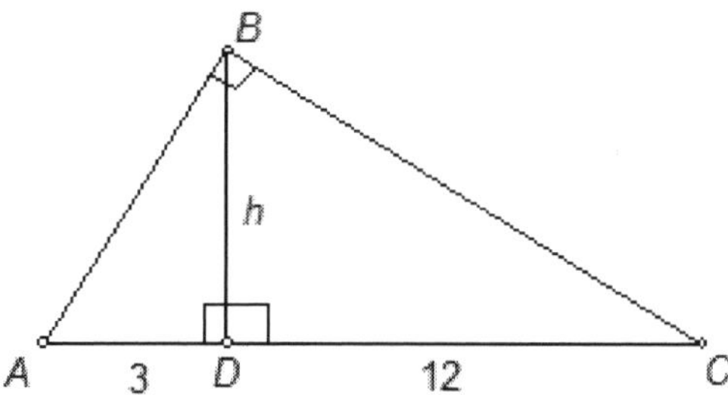

Solution: We redraw the three triangles next to each other so that congruent angles match up.

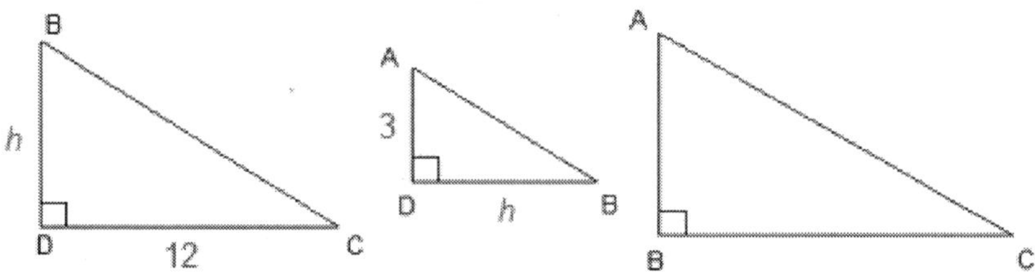

We now set up a ratio, cross multiply, and divide: $\frac{h}{12} = \frac{3}{h}$. So $h^2 = 36$, and therefore h = **6**.

Remark: Clearly we didn't need to redraw the third triangle, but I suggest drawing all three until you get the hang of this.

Strategy 30 – The Measure of an Exterior Angle of a Triangle is the Sum of the Measures of the Two Opposite Interior Angles of the Triangle.

Try to answer the following question using this strategy. **Do not** check the solution until you have attempted this question yourself.

LEVEL 2: GEOMETRY

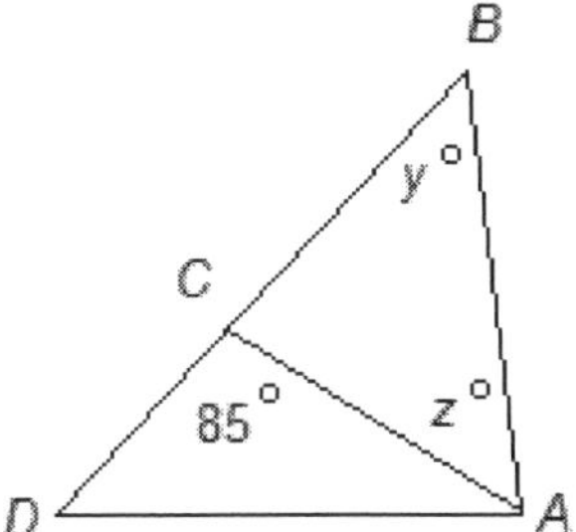

1. In ΔABD above, if $y = 39$, what is the value of z ?

Solutions

*** Solution using Strategy 30:** 85 = 39 + *z*, and therefore *z* = 85 – 39 = **46**.

Alternate method: Angles *ACD* and *ACB* form a **linear pair** and are therefore **supplementary**. So angle *ACB* has measure 180 – 85 = 95 degrees. Since the angles of a triangle add up to 180 degrees, it follows that *z* = 180 – 39 – 95 = **46**.

Special Right Triangles

Recall that the following two special right triangles are given to you on the SAT.

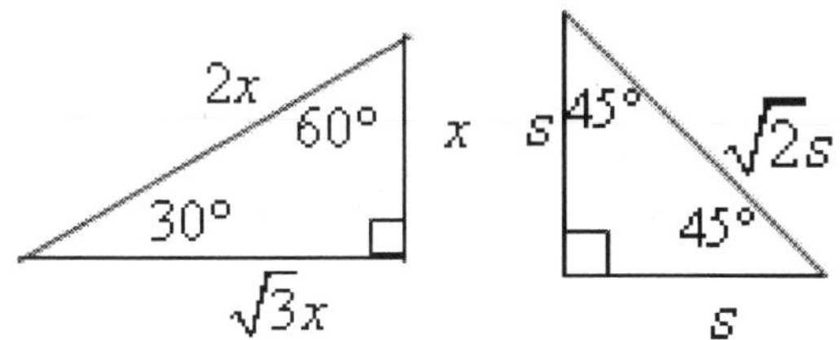

Now try to answer the following question. **Do not** check the solution until you have attempted this question yourself.

LEVEL 4: GEOMETRY

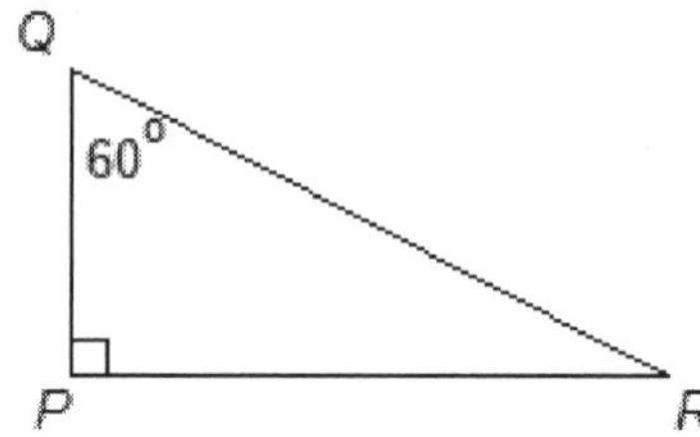

2. In the triangle above, $QR = 8$. What is the area of ΔPQR?

(A) $32\sqrt{3}$
(B) 32
(C) $16\sqrt{3}$
(D) 16
(E) $8\sqrt{3}$

Solution

Using the special 30, 60, 90 triangle we can label each side with its length as follows.

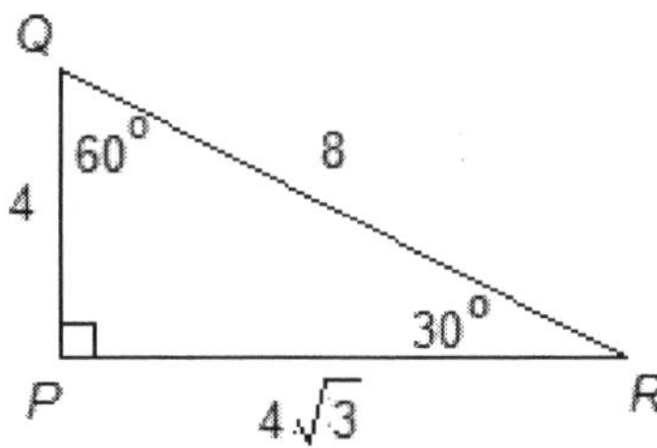

The area is $A = \frac{1}{2}bh = \frac{1}{2}(4)\cdot 4\sqrt{3} = 8\sqrt{3}$, choice (E).

Note: The hypotenuse of a 30, 60, 90 triangle is always twice the length of the side opposite the 30 degree angle.

Also, if we always think of a side as going with its opposite angle, there will never be any confusion, even if our picture is facing a different direction than the triangle on the SAT. This is actually good advice for any triangle problem. Always think of a side in terms of its opposite angle and vice versa.

Angles of Regular Polygons

A **regular** polygon is a polygon with all sides equal in length, and all angles equal in measure.

The total number of degrees in the interior of an n-sided polygon is

$$\boldsymbol{(n-2)\cdot 180}$$

For example, a six-sided polygon (or hexagon) has

(6 – 2)·180 = 4·180 = **720** degrees

in its interior. Therefore each angle of a **regular** hexagon has

$\frac{720}{6}$ = **120** degrees.

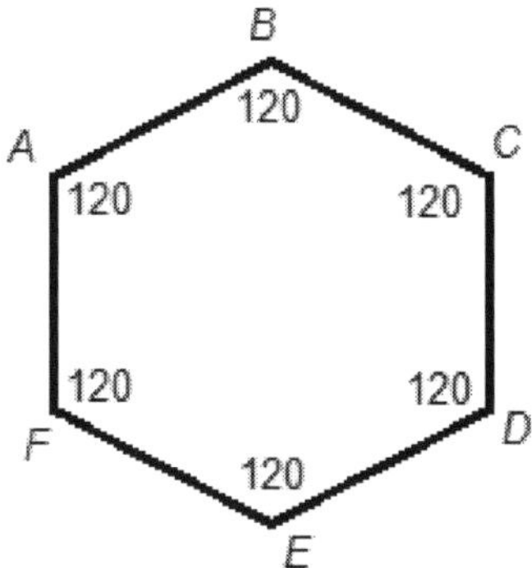

For those of us that do not like to memorize formulas, there is a quick visual way to determine the total number of degrees in the interior of an n-sided polygon. Simply split the polygon up into triangles and quadrilaterals by drawing nonintersecting line segments between vertices. Then add 180 degrees for each triangle and 360 degrees for each quadrilateral. For example, here is one way to do it for a hexagon.

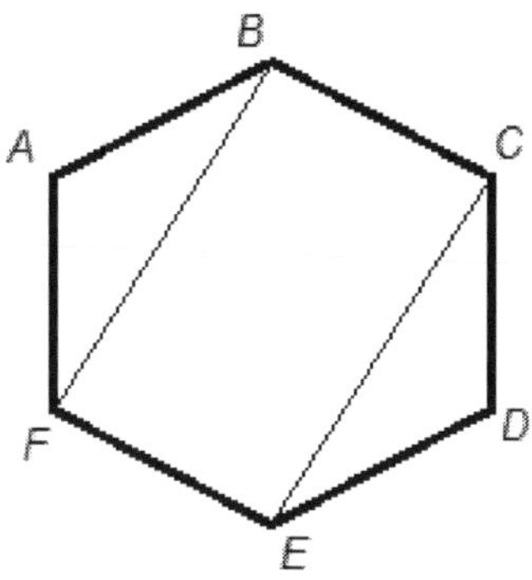

Since the hexagon has been split up into 2 triangles and 1 quadrilateral, the hexagon has 2(180) + 360 = **720** degrees. This is the same number we got from the formula.

To avoid potential mistakes, let me give a picture that would be incorrect.

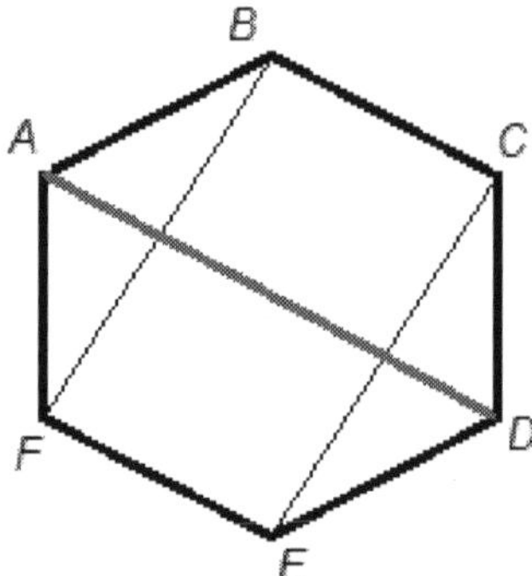

The above figure **cannot** be used to compute the number of interior angles in the hexagon because segment $\overline{AD}$ is "crossing through" segment $\overline{BF}$.

Now let's draw a segment from the center of the hexagon to each vertex of the hexagon.

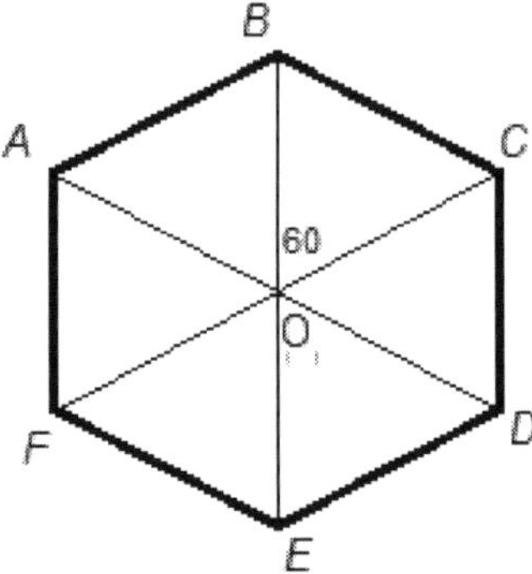

We see that the central angles formed must add up to 360 degrees. Therefore each central angle is 60 degrees as shown in the figure above.

In general, the number of degrees in a central angle of an n-sided polygon is $\frac{360}{n}$.

It is worth looking at a regular hexagon in a bit more detail.

Each of the segments just drawn in the previous figure is a radius of the circumscribed circle of this hexagon, and therefore they are all congruent. This means that each triangle is isosceles, and so the measure of each of the other two angles of any of these triangles is $\frac{180-60}{2} = 60$. Therefore each of these triangles is equilateral. This fact is worth committing to memory.

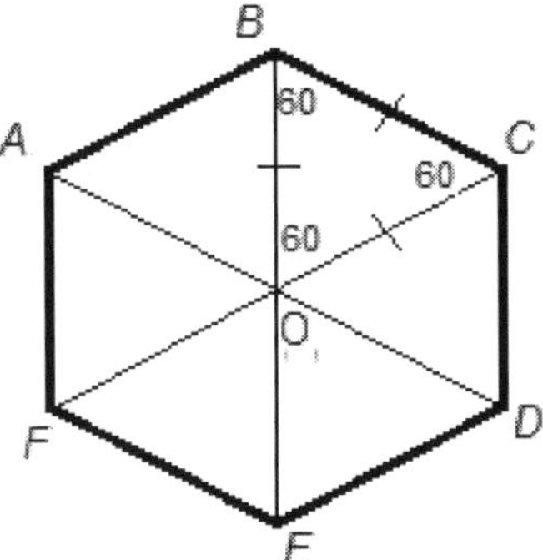

Now try to solve each of the following problems. The answers to these problems, followed by full solutions are at the end of this lesson. **Do not** look at the answers until you have attempted these problems yourself. Please remember to mark off any problems you get wrong.

LEVEL 2: GEOMETRY

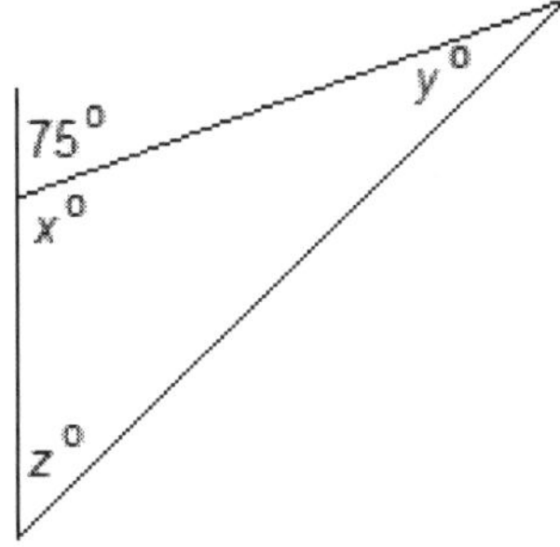

3. In the figure above, one side of a triangle is extended. Which of the following is true?

   (A) $y = 75$
   (B) $z = 75$
   (C) $z - y = 75$
   (D) $y + z = 75$
   (E) $x = y + z$

LEVEL 4: GEOMETRY

4. If a square has a side of length $x + 5$ and a diagonal of length $x + 10$, what is the value of x ?

   (A) 5
   (B) 10
   (C) 20
   (D) $5\sqrt{2}$
   (E) $10\sqrt{2}$

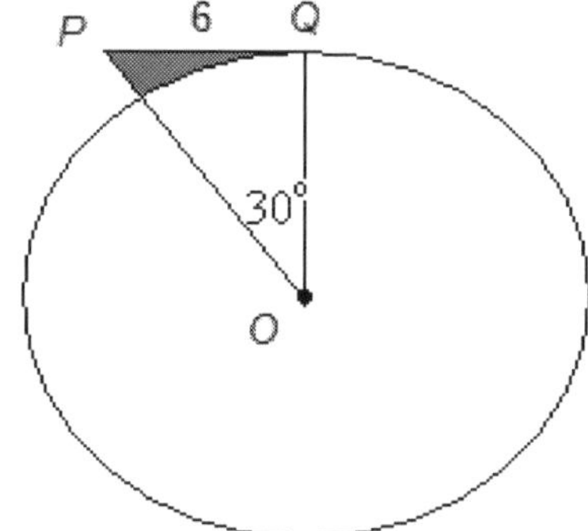

5. In the figure above, the center of the circle is O and $\overline{PQ}$ is tangent to the circle at Q. What is the area of the shaded region to the nearest tenth?

6. What is the area of a square whose diagonal has length $5\sqrt{2}$?

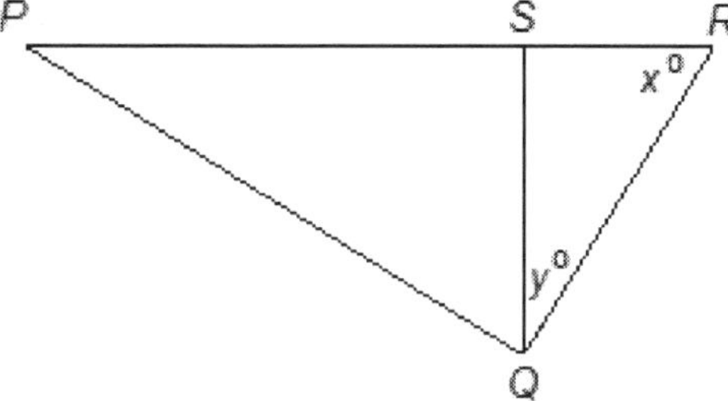

Note: Figure not drawn to scale.

7. In the figure above, if $x = 35$, $PQ \perp QR$, and $PQ = PS$, what is the value of y ?

Level 5: Geometry

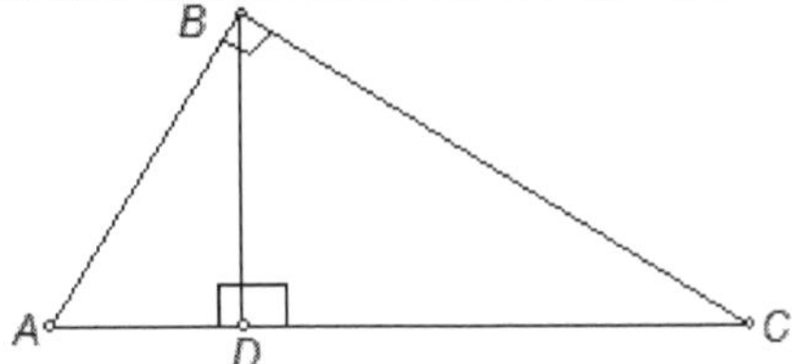

8. In the triangle above, $DC = 3$ and $BC = 6$. What is the value of AC ?

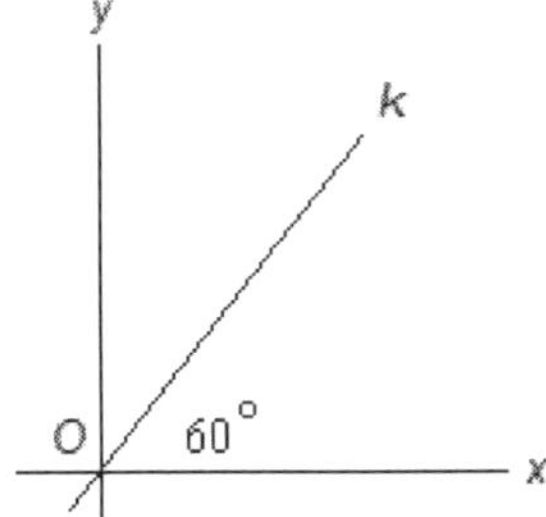

9. In the figure above, what is the equation of line k?

   (A) $y = \frac{x}{2}$
   (B) $y = \frac{x}{\sqrt{2}}$
   (C) $y = \frac{x}{\sqrt{3}}$
   (D) $y = \sqrt{2}x$
   (E) $y = \sqrt{3}x$

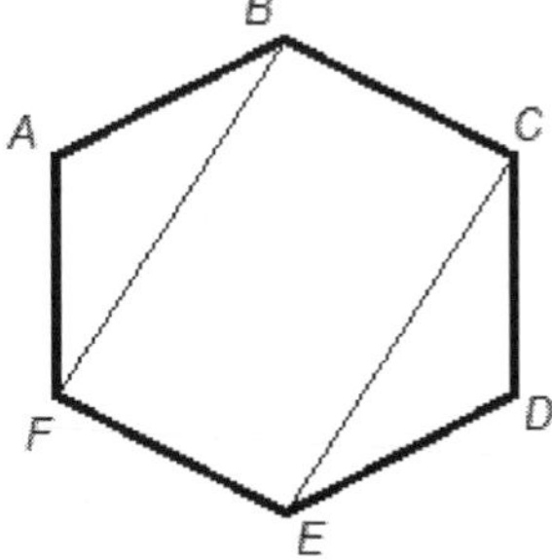

10. In the figure above, $ABCDEF$ is a regular hexagon and $CD = 6$. What is the perimeter of rectangle $BCEF$ to the nearest tenth?

11. A diagonal of a rectangle forms an angle of measure $30°$ with each of the two longer sides of the rectangle. If the length of the shorter side of the rectangle is 12, what is the length of the diagonal?

    (A) 26
    (B) 24
    (C) 18
    (D) $12\sqrt{3}$
    (E) $12\sqrt{2}$

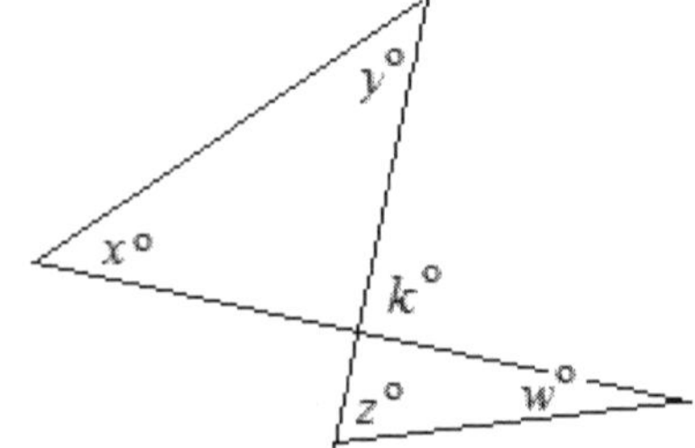

12. In the figure above, what is $xw + xz + yw + yz$ in terms of k?

    (A) $\frac{k^2}{4}$
    (B) $\frac{k}{2}$
    (C) k
    (D) k^2
    (E) $4k^2$

Answers

1. 46	5. 2.9	9. E
2. E	6. 25	10. 32.8
3. D	7. 27.5	11. B
4. D	8. 12	12. D

Full Solutions

4.

* We begin by drawing a picture

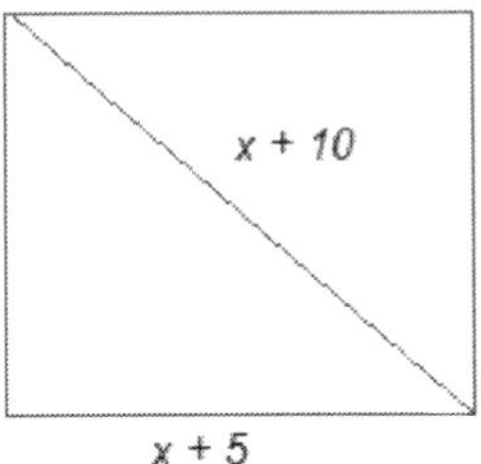

Solution using a 45, 45, 90 triangle: Note that since the sides of a square are congruent, each triangle is an isosceles right triangle. This is the same as a 45, 45, 90 right triangle. So we need $x + 10 = \sqrt{2}(x + 5)$. We can now either solve this algebraically or by starting with choice (C) and using our calculator. We will do the more difficult algebraic method and leave the second method to the reader.

$$x + 10 = \sqrt{2}(x + 5)$$
$$x + 10 = x\sqrt{2} + 5\sqrt{2}$$
$$x\sqrt{2} - x = 10 - 5\sqrt{2}$$
$$x(\sqrt{2} - 1) = 10 - 5\sqrt{2}$$
$$x = \frac{10 - 5\sqrt{2}}{\sqrt{2}-1} \sim 7.07$$

Putting $5\sqrt{2}$ into your calculator gives the same output. So the answer is choice (D).

Solution using the Pythagorean Theorem: We have

$$(x + 5)^2 + (x + 5)^2 = (x + 10)^2$$
$$x^2 + 10x + 25 + x^2 + 10x + 25 = x^2 + 20x + 100$$
$$2x^2 + 20x + 50 = x^2 + 20x + 100$$
$$x^2 = 50$$
$$x = \sqrt{50} = \sqrt{25 \cdot 2} = \sqrt{25} \cdot \sqrt{2} = 5\sqrt{2}, \text{ choice (D).}$$

Some clarification: $(x + 5)^2 = (x + 5)(x + 5) = x^2 + 5x + 5x + 25$. Therefore $(x + 5)^2 = x^2 + 10x + 25$.

5.

*** A tangent line to a circle is perpendicular to the radius** so that the triangle is a 30, 60, 90 right triangle. Since the side opposite 30 is 6, the side opposite 60 is $6\sqrt{3}$. In a right triangle we can think of the two legs as the base and the height. So the area of the triangle is

$$A = \frac{1}{2}bh = \frac{1}{2}(6)\cdot 6\sqrt{3}. = 18\sqrt{3}.$$

We already found that the radius of the circle is $6\sqrt{3}$. Thus the area of the circle is

$$A = \pi r^2 = \pi(6\sqrt{3})^2 = \pi \cdot 36 \cdot 3 = 108\pi.$$

The sector shown is $\frac{1}{12}$ of the entire circle. So the area of the sector is

$$A = (\frac{1}{12}) \cdot 108\pi = 9\pi.$$

The area of the shaded region is the area of the triangle minus the area of the sector.

$$A = 18\sqrt{3} - 9\pi \sim 2.90258065$$

Rounding to the nearest tenth gives us **2.9**.

Remarks: (1) We know that the sector is $\frac{1}{12}$ of the circle because there are 360 degrees in a circle and $\frac{30}{360} = \frac{1}{12}$.

(2) We can more formally find the area of the sector by using the following ratio:

	Sector	Circle
Angle	30	360
Area	x	108π

$$\frac{30}{x} = \frac{360}{108\pi}$$

$$3240\pi = 360x$$

$$x = \frac{3240\pi}{360} = 9\pi$$

See Lesson 19 for more details.

6.
We begin by drawing a picture

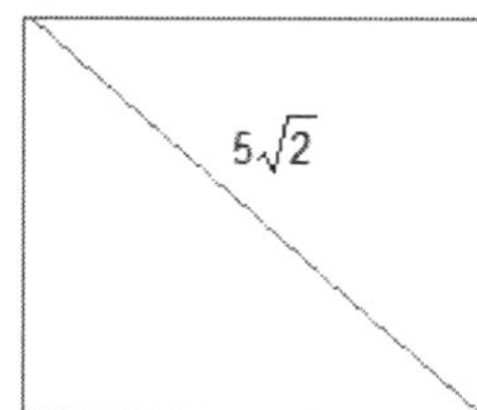

Solution using a 45, 45, 90 triangle: Since all sides of a square have equal length, an isosceles right triangle is formed. An isosceles right triangle is the same as a 45, 45, 90 triangle. So we can get the length of a side of the triangle just by looking at the formula for a 45, 45, 90 right triangle. Here $s = 5$. The area of the square is then $A = s^2 = 5^2 = \mathbf{25}$.

Solution using the Pythagorean Theorem: If we let s be the length of a side of the square, then by the Pythagorean Theorem

$$s^2 + s^2 = (5\sqrt{2})^2$$
$$2s^2 = 50$$
$$s^2 = 25$$
$$s = 5$$

Thus, the area of the square is $A = s^2 = 5^2 = \mathbf{25}$.

Remark: We did a bit more work than we had to here. The area of the square is $A = s^2$. We already found that $s^2 = 25$. There was no need to solve this equation for s.

* **Using an area formula:** The area of a square is $\boldsymbol{A = \frac{d^2}{2}}$ where d is the length of the diagonal of the square. Therefore in this problem

$$A = \frac{d^2}{2} = \frac{(5\sqrt{2})^2}{2} = \frac{50}{2} = \mathbf{25}.$$

7.

* We are given that $\overline{PQ}$ is perpendicular to $\overline{QR}$. It follows that the measure of angle PQR is 90 degrees. Since $x = 35$, the measure of angle QPR is $180 - 90 - 35 = 55$. Now, since $PQ = PS$, the angles opposite these sides are congruent. So angle PQS has measure $\frac{180-55}{2} = 62.5$. Therefore $y = 90 - 62.5 = \mathbf{27.5}$.

Here is a picture of the triangle with some of the angles filled in.

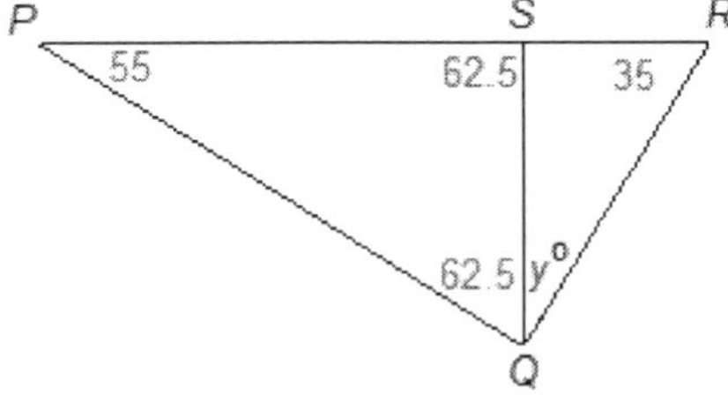

8.

Solution: We redraw the three triangles next to each other so that congruent angles match up.

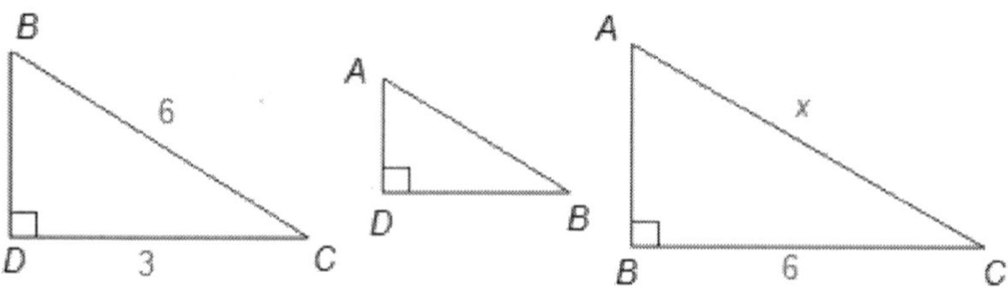

We now set up a ratio, cross multiply, and divide: $\frac{6}{3} = \frac{x}{6}$. So 36 = 3x, and therefore x = **12**.

9.

* We begin by forming a 30, 60, 90 triangle. If we let $x = 1$ in the special triangle given to us at the beginning of each math section of the SAT we get the following picture.

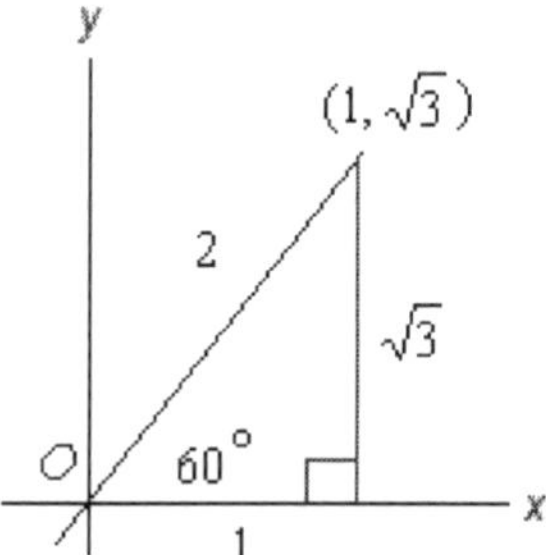

Note that we plotted the point by going right 1, then up $\sqrt{3}$. The slope of the line is $m = \frac{\sqrt{3}}{1} = \sqrt{3}$. Since the line passes through the origin, we have $b = 0$. Thus, the equation of the line in slope-intercept form is

$$y = mx + b = \sqrt{3}x + 0.$$

So $y = \sqrt{3}x$, choice (E).

10.

* Since the hexagon is regular, $BC = EF = CD = 6$. Now let's add a bit to the picture.

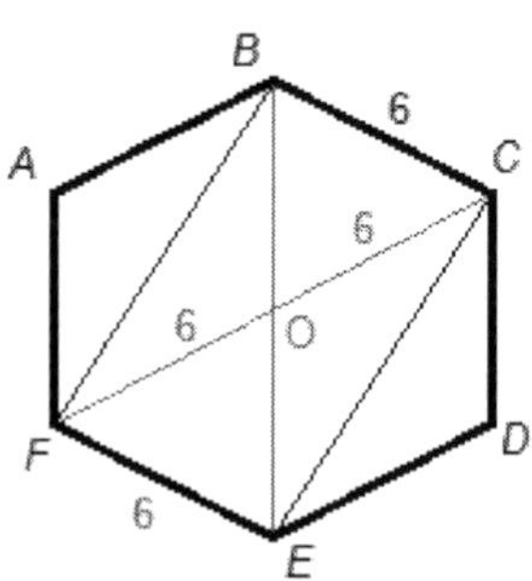

Again, note that the hexagon is regular. So each angle of triangle *BOC* is 60 degrees. Thus, triangle *BOC* is equilateral. Therefore $OF = OC = BC = 6$. Since $EF = 6$ and $FC = 12$, triangle *CEF* is a 30, 60, 90 triangle. It follows that $CE = 6\sqrt{2}$. Since BCEF is a rectangle, $BF = 6\sqrt{3}$ as well. Therefore the perimeter of rectangle is $6 + 6 + 6\sqrt{3} + 63 = 12 + 12\sqrt{3} \sim 32.78$. To the nearest tenth the answer is **32.8**.

11.

* We begin by drawing a picture.

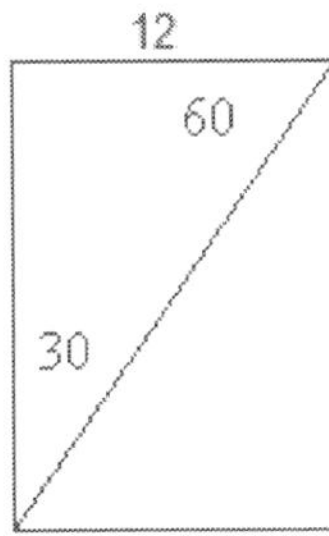

The side opposite the 30 degree angle has length 12. Thus, the hypotenuse has length 24, choice (B).

12.

* **Solution using Strategy 30:** First note that

$$xw + xz + yw + yz = x(w + z) + y(w + z) = (x + y)(w + z).$$

Now, $k = x + y$, $k = w + z$, and so $(x + y)(w + z) = k \cdot k = k^2$. So the answer is choice (D).

Remark: Note that the angle labeled *k* is an exterior angle of both triangles. We have used Strategy 30 twice here, once for each triangle.

Solution using strategy 4: Let's choose values for *x*, *y* and *z*, say $x = 40$, $y = 50$, and $z = 30$. Each unlabeled interior angle is $180 - 40 - 50 = 90$, and so $w = 180 - 90 - 30 = 60$. Now,

$$xw + xz + yw + yz = (40)(60) + (40)(30) + (50)(60) + (50)(30) = \mathbf{8100}$$

Since the angle labeled with *k* is supplementary with the unlabeled angle, $k = 180 - 90 = 90$. So let's plug $k = 90$ into each answer choice.

(A) 2025
(B) 45
(C) 90
(D) 8100
(E) 32,400

Since (A), (B), (C), and (E) came out incorrect, the answer is choice (D).

OPTIONAL MATERIAL

LEVEL 6: GEOMETRY

1. Suppose that quadrilateral $PQRS$ has four congruent sides and satisfies $PQ = PR$. What is the value of $\frac{QS}{PR}$?

Solution

1.

* Note that the quadrilateral is a rhombus. Let's draw a picture.

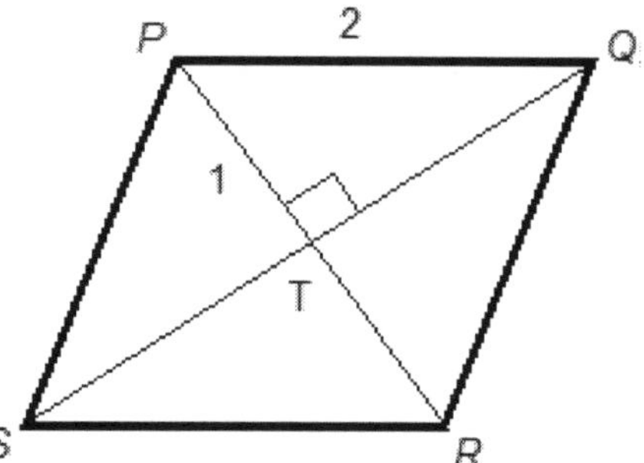

Now, let's choose a value for *PQ*, say *PQ* = 2. Since *PQ* = *PR*, *PR* = 2 as well. In a rhombus, the diagonals bisect each other, and are perpendicular to each other. It follows that *PT* = 1 and angle *PTQ* is a right angle. So triangle *PTQ* is a 30, 60, 90 triangle, and *QT* = $\sqrt{3}$. Thus, *QS* = $2\sqrt{3}$, and it follows that $\frac{QS}{PR}$ = $\frac{2\sqrt{3}}{2}$ = $\sqrt{3}$ ~ 1.73205. If this were an actual grid in question we would grid in **1.73**.

Note: If we let *PT* = *x*, then *PQ* = 2*x*, and by a similar argument to the solution above *PR* = 2*x* and *QS* = $2x\sqrt{3}$. So $\frac{QS}{PR}$ = $\frac{2x\sqrt{3}}{2x}$ = $\sqrt{3}$, as before.

LESSON 12
PROBABILITY

Reminder: Before beginning this lesson remember to redo the problems from Lessons 4 and 8 that you have marked off. Do not "unmark" a question unless you get it correct.

Simple Probability Principle

To compute a simple probability where all outcomes are equally likely, divide the number of "successes" by the total number of outcomes.

Try to answer the following question using the simple probability principle. **Do not** check the solution until you have attempted this question yourself.

LEVEL 4: PROBABILITY

1. If one of the positive factors of 60 is to be chosen at random, what is the probability that the chosen factor will not be a multiple of 15?

Solution

* Let's begin by listing all the positive factors of 60.

1, 2, 3, 4, 5, 6, 10, 12, 15, 20, 30, 60

The total number of factors is 12. Of these factors, 9 are **not** multiples of 15. By the simple probability principle, the probability is $\frac{9}{12}$ = **3/4** or **.75**.

Note: Since factors come in pairs, it is not too difficult to ensure that we have listed them all. The factor pairs in this example are 1 and 60, 2 and 30, 3 and 20, 4 and 15, 5 and 12, and 6 and 10.

Now try to solve each of the following problems. The answers to these problems, followed by full solutions are at the end of this lesson. **Do not** look at the answers until you have attempted these problems yourself. Please remember to mark off any problems you get wrong.

LEVEL 1: PROBABILITY

2. In a jar there are exactly 72 marbles, each of which is yellow, purple, or blue. The probability of randomly selecting a yellow marble from the jar is $\frac{5}{9}$ and the probability of randomly selecting a purple marble from the jar is $\frac{3}{9}$. How many marbles in the jar are blue?

LEVEL 2: PROBABILITY

3. Of the marbles in a jar, 21 are red. Joseph randomly takes one marble out of the jar. If the probability is $\frac{7}{15}$ that the marble he chooses is red, how many marbles are in the jar?

LEVEL 3: PROBABILITY

4. If the numbers from 1 through 6, inclusive, are to be randomly ordered, what is the probability that the numbers will appear in the order 6, 5, 4, 3, 2, 1?

LEVEL 4: PROBABILITY

5. Jennifer has 7 shirts and 7 pairs of shoes, and each shirt matches a different pair of shoes. If she chooses one of these shirts and one pair of shoes at random, what is the probability that they will <u>not</u> match?

6. A jar contains a number of gems of which 75 are blue, 19 are red, and the remainder are white. If the probability of picking a white gem from this jar at random is $\frac{1}{3}$, how many white gems are in the jar?

7. The x- and y-coordinates of point A are each to be chosen at random from the set of integers -2 through 10. What is the probability that A will be in quadrant III?

8. A pet store has a white dog, a black dog, and a grey dog. The store also has three cats – one white, one black, and one grey – and three birds – one white, one black, and one grey. If Philip chooses one dog, one cat, and one bird at random, what is the probability that he chooses one of each color?

9. Exactly 5 musicians try out to play 5 different instruments for a particular performance. If each musician can play each of the 5 instruments, and each musician is assigned an instrument, what is the probability that Gary will play the piano?

LEVEL 5: PROBABILITY

10. The integers 1 through 6 are written on each of six cards. The cards are shuffled and one card is drawn at random. That card is then replaced, the cards are shuffled again and another card is drawn at random. This procedure is repeated one more time (for a total of three times). What is the probability that the product of the numbers on the three cards drawn was between 5 and 8, inclusive?

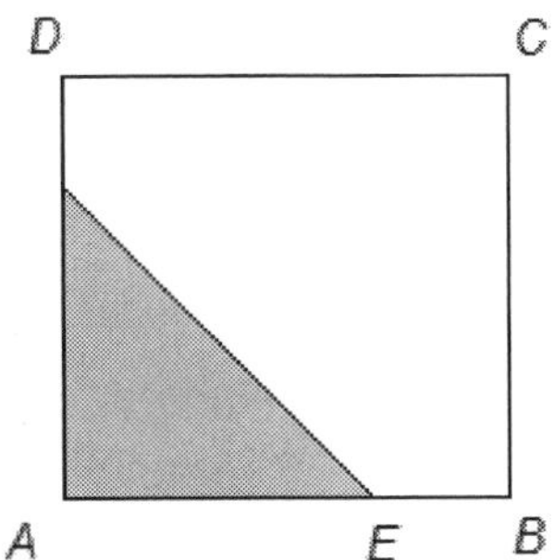

Note: Figure not drawn to scale.

11. In the figure above, $ABCD$ is a square, the triangle is isosceles, $EB = 10 - 2c$, and $AD = 10$. A point in square $ABCD$ is to be chosen at random. If the probability that the point will be in the shaded triangle is $\frac{2}{25}$, what is the value of c?

12. A set of marbles contains only black marbles, white marbles, and yellow marbles. If the probability of randomly choosing a black marble is $\frac{1}{14}$ and the probability of randomly choosing a white marble is $\frac{3}{4}$, what is the probability of randomly choosing a yellow marble?

Answers

1. 3/4 or .75	5. 6/7 or .857	9. 1/5 or .2
2. 8	6. 47	10. .087 or .088
3. 45	7. .023 or .024	11. 2
4. .001	8. 2/9 or .222	12. 5/28, .178, .179

Full Solutions

4.

* The total number of arrangements of the numbers from 1 through 6 is $6! = (6)(5)(4)(3)(2)(1) = 720$. Only one of these results is 6, 5, 4, 3, 2, 1. Therefore the probability is $\frac{1}{720}$ which is approximately .00138888. So we grid in **.001**.

Remark: If you are having trouble counting the total number of arrangements in this problem, go back and review Lesson 8.

5.

* By the counting principle there are $(7)(7) = 49$ shirt/shoe combinations. 7 of these combinations are matching. Therefore there are $49 - 7 = 42$ nonmatching combinations. So the probability the shirt and shoes will not match is $\frac{42}{49}$ = **6/7** (or **.857**).

6.

* **Quick solution:** There are $75 + 19 = 94$ gems that are not white. Also we have that $1 - \frac{1}{3} = \frac{2}{3}$ of the gems are not white. It follows that $\frac{2}{3}$ of the total number of gems is 94. So $\frac{1}{3}$ of the total number of gems is $\frac{94}{2}$ = **47**.

Algebraic solution: Let x be the total number of gems. Then we have $\frac{2}{3} \cdot x = 75 + 19 = 94$. So $x = 94(\frac{3}{2}) = 141$. The number of white gems is then $(\frac{1}{3})(141)$ = **47**.

Remark: Instead of solving for *x*, and then multiplying by $\frac{1}{3}$, we can solve for $\frac{x}{3}$ right away. Once we have $\frac{2}{3}x = 94$, simply divide each side of this equation by 2 to get $\frac{1}{3}x = 47$.

7.

* There are 13 integers from -2 through 10 (see note below). By the counting principle, there are (13)(13) = 169 points in total. For a point to be in quadrant III both coordinates must be negative. There are 4 possibilities: (-1,-1), (-1,-2), (-2,-1), (-2,-2). So the desired probability is $\frac{4}{169} \sim .0236686$. So we grid in **.023** or **.024**.

Note: There are several ways to count the integers from -2 through 10.

(1) List them: -2, -1, 0, 1, 2, 3, 4, 5, 6, 7, 8, 9, 10.
(2) Note that there are 10 integers from 1 through 10, 2 integers from -2 to -1, and add one more for 0.
(3) Use the **fence-post formula** (see Lesson 13) to get 10 – (-2) + 1 = 13.

8.

* By the counting principle there are (3)(3)(3) = 27 ways to choose one of each of the 3 animals. The number of ways to choose one of each animal so that each is a different color is ${}_3P_3 = 3! =$ **6**. So the desired probability is $\frac{6}{27}$ = **2/9** or **.222**.

9.

* The number of possible assignments is ${}_5P_5 = 5! = 120$. The number of assignments which have Gary playing the piano is ${}_4P_4 = 4! = 24$. So the probability that Gary will play the piano is $\frac{24}{120}$ = **1/5** or **.2**.

10.

* The total number of possibilities for the three cards is (6)(6)(6) = 216. Now let us list all possibilities so that the product of the numbers on the three cards drawn was between 5 and 8.

(1)(1)(5) = 5 (1)(5)(1) = 5 (5)(1)(1) = 5

(1)(1)(6) = 6 (1)(6)(1) = 6 (6)(1)(1) = 6

(1)(2)(3) = 6 (1)(3)(2) = 6 (2)(1)(3) = 6
(2)(3)(1) = 6 (3)(1)(2) = 6 (3)(2)(1) = 6

(1)(2)(4) = 8 (1)(4)(2) = 8 (2)(1)(4) = 8
(2)(4)(1) = 8 (4)(1)(2) = 8 (4)(2)(1) = 8

(2)(2)(2) = 8

Thus there are 19 possibilities that give the desired product. The probability is therefore $\frac{19}{216} \sim .087962963$. So we grid in **.087** or **.088**.

Note: We can save time by just listing one representative of each of the groups above, and then counting the number of distinct permutations of the factors in the product.

(1)(1)(5) 3 distinct permutations
(1)(2)(3) 6 distinct permutations
(2)(2)(2) 1 distinct permutation
(1)(1)(6) 3 distinct permutations
(1)(2)(4) 6 distinct permutations

Total = 3 + 3 + 6 + 6 + 1 = 19.

11.

* $AE = 10 - (10 - 2c) = 10 - 10 + 2c = 2c$. So the area of the triangle is

$$(\tfrac{1}{2})(2c)(2c) = 2c^2.$$

The area of the square is (10)(10) = 100. Thus the probability of choosing a point in the triangle is $\frac{2c^2}{100} = \frac{c^2}{50}$. We are given that this is equal to $\frac{2}{25}$. We cross multiply and divide to get $25c^2 = 100$. So $c^2 = 4$, and thus, $c =$ **2**.

12.

* **Quick solution:** Since probabilities add up to one, the probability of randomly choosing a yellow marble is $1 - \frac{1}{14} - \frac{3}{4} \sim .1785714286$ (this computation was done in a calculator). Thus, we can grid in **.178**, **.179**, or the fraction **5/28**.

Solution using strategy 18: The least common denominator of the two fractions is 28, so we will assume that there are 28 marbles total. Then there are $(\frac{1}{14})(28) = 2$ black marbles, and $(\frac{3}{4})(28) = 21$ white marbles. So there are 28 – 2 – 21 = 5 yellow marbles, and the probability of choosing a yellow marble is **5/28**.

Note: Instead of using the least common denominator we could have simply multiplied the denominators together to get (14)(4) = 56. There would then be $(\frac{1}{14})(56) = 4$ black marbles, $(\frac{3}{4})(56) = 42$ white marbles, and therefore 56 – 4 – 42 = 10 yellow marbles. Thus, the probability of choosing a yellow marble is $\frac{10}{56}$. Since there are too many symbols to grid in, we must reduce this fraction or change it to a decimal.

Remark: The **least common denominator** is simply the **least common multiple** of the denominators. See Lesson 5 for more on least common multiples.

OPTIONAL MATERIAL

CHALLENGE QUESTION

10. If 2 real numbers are randomly chosen from a line segment of length 10, what is the probability that the distance between them is at least 7?

Solution

We may assume that the two real numbers, a and b are chosen to be between 0 and 10. Consider the following picture.

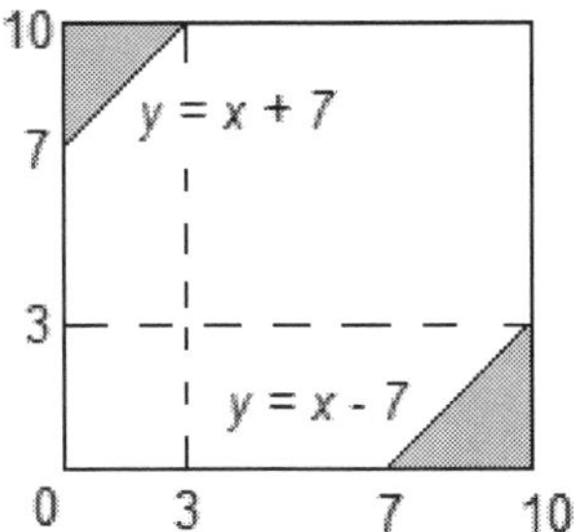

Note that we are trying to compute the probability that $|a - b| \geq 7$. This is equivalent to the two inequalities $a - b \leq -7$ and $a - b \geq 7$. Solving each of these inequalities for b gives $b \geq a + 7$ and $b \leq a - 7$. These inequalities correspond to the two shaded triangles in the figure above. The area of the shaded region is $2(\frac{1}{2})(3)(3) = 9$ and the area of the whole square is $10^2 = 100$. Therefore the probability we are looking for is $\frac{9}{100}$ = **.09**.

LESSON 13
NUMBER THEORY

Reminder: Before beginning this lesson remember to redo the problems from Lessons 1, 5 and 9 that you have marked off. Do not "unmark" a question unless you get it correct.

Arithmetic Sequences

An **arithmetic sequence** is a sequence of numbers such that the difference $\boldsymbol{d}$ between consecutive terms is constant. The number $\boldsymbol{d}$ is called the **common difference** of the arithmetic sequence.

Here is a simple example of an arithmetic sequence: 1, 3, 5, 7, 9, 11,...
In this example the common difference is $d = 2$.

Arithmetic sequence formula: $\boldsymbol{a_n = a_1 + (n-1)d}$

In the above formula, a_n is the nth term of the sequence. For example, a_1 is the first term of the sequence.

Example: In the arithmetic sequence 1, 3, 5, 7, 9, 11,... note that $a_1 = 1$ and $d = 2$. Therefore $a_n = 1 + (n-1)(2) = 1 + (2n-2) = 2n-1$.

Linear equations and arithmetic sequences: Questions about arithmetic sequences can easily be thought of as questions about lines and linear equations. We can identify terms of the sequence with points on a line where the *x*-coordinate is the term number and the *y*-coordinate is the term itself.

In the example above, since the first term of the sequence is 1, we can identify this term with the point (1,1). Since the second term of the sequence is 3, we can identify this with the point (2,3). Note that the common difference d is just the slope of the line that passes through these two points, i.e. $d = \frac{3-1}{2-1} = 2$.

If we were to write an equation of the line passing through (1,1) with slope 2 in point-slope form we get $y - 1 = 2(x - 1)$ (see Lesson 3 if you need to review this). Distributing the 2 and adding 1 to each side of the equation gives $y = 2x - 1$. Compare this to the expression $a_n = 2n - 1$ that we arrived at earlier. They are the same except for the names of the unknowns!

Try to solve the following problem in two ways.

(1) Using the arithmetic sequence formula
(2) Using geometry

LEVEL 4: NUMBER THEORY

1. Each term of a certain sequence is greater than the term before it. The difference between any two consecutive terms in the sequence is always the same number. If the fifth and ninth terms of the sequence are 33 and 97, respectively, what is the twelfth term?

Solutions

(1) Substituting 5 in for n and 33 in for a_n into the arithmetic sequence formula gives us $33 = a_1 + 4d$.

Similarly, substituting 9 in for n and 97 in for a_n into the arithmetic sequence formula gives us $97 = a_1 + 8d$.

So we solve the following system of equations to find d.

$$\begin{aligned} 97 &= a_1 + 8d \\ \underline{33} &\underline{= a_1 + 4d} \\ 64 &= \quad\;\; 4d \end{aligned}$$

The last equation comes from subtraction. We now divide each side of this last equation by 4 to get $d = 16$.

Finally, we add 16 to 97 three times to get $97 + 16(3) =$ **145**.

Remarks: (1) We used the elimination method to find d here. This method (as well as others) was described in Lesson 2.

(2) Once we have that $d = 16$, we can substitute this into either of the original equations to find a_1. For example, we have $33 = a_1 + 4(16)$, so that $a_1 = 33 - 64 = -31$. The nth term of the sequence is then

$$a_n = -31 + (n - 1)(16) = -31 + 16n - 16 = 16n - 47$$

In particular, $a_{12} = 16(12) - 47 =$ **145**.

* **(2)** We identify the two given terms with the points (5,33) and (9,97). The common difference is then $d = \frac{97-33}{9-5} = \frac{64}{4} = 16$. As in the previous solution, the twelfth term is 97 + 16(3) = 1**45**.

Remark: If we want to write the equation of the line in point-slope form we get $y - 33 = 16(x - 5)$. We can then find the twelfth term by plugging in a 12 for x: $y - 33 = 16(12 - 5) = 16(7) = 112$. So $y = 112 + 33 =$ **145**.

If we were to use the point (9,97) instead of (5,33) we would get the same answer.

Fence-Post Formula

The number of integers from a to b, inclusive, is $\boldsymbol{b - a + 1}$.

For example, let's count the number of integers from 5 to 12, inclusive. They are 5, 6, 7, 8, 9, 10, 11, 12, and we see that there are 8 of them. Now 12 – 5 = 7 which is not the correct amount, but 12 – 5 + 1 = 8 which is the correct amount.

If you ever happen to forget this little formula test it out on a small list of numbers as I just did. But it's nice to have this one committed to memory so that it is there for you when you need it.

Remark: If you put up a fence that is 10 feet long, and put up fence-posts every foot, then there are 10 – 0 + 1 = 11 fence-posts.

Try to answer the following question using the fence-post formula. **Do not** check the solution until you have attempted this question yourself.

LEVEL 5: NUMBER THEORY

2. How many numbers between 72 and 356 can be expressed as $5x + 3$, where x is an integer?

Solution

* Let's keep guessing x-values until we find the smallest and largest values of x satisfying $72 < 5x + 3 < 356$. Since we have $5(13) + 3 = 68$ and $5(14) + 3 = 73$ we see that 14 is the smallest value of x satisfying the inequality. Since $5(70) + 3 = 353$ and $5(71) + 3 = 358$ we see that 70 is the largest value of x satisfying the inequality. Therefore it follows that the answer is $70 - 14 + 1 =$ **57**.

Remarks: (1) We used the fence-post formula together with Strategy 3 from Lesson 1 here.

(2) We could have also found the two extreme x-values algebraically as follows.

$$72 < 5x + 3 < 356$$
$$69 < 5x < 353$$
$$69/5 < x < 353/5$$
$$13.8 < x < 70.6$$
$$14 \leq x \leq 70$$

We get the last inequality because x must be an integer. Notice that this last inequality is **not** strict.

Strategy 11 – Differences of large sums

The quickest way to subtract two large sums is to follow these steps:

(1) Write out each sum formally.
(2) Figure out how to line them up properly.
(3) Subtract term by term.
(4) Finish the computation.

Try to answer the following question using this strategy. **Do not** check the solution until you have attempted this question yourself.

LEVEL 5: NUMBER THEORY

3. If x denotes the sum of the integers from 10 to 70 inclusive, and y denotes the sum of the integers from 80 to 140 inclusive, what is the value of $y - x$?

Solution

* We write out each sum formally and line them up with *y* above *x*.

$$\begin{array}{c} 80 + 81 + 82 + \ldots + 140 \\ 10 + 11 + 12 + \ldots + 70 \end{array}$$

Now subtract term by term.

$$\begin{array}{c} 80 + 81 + 82 + \ldots + 140 \\ \underline{10 + 11 + 12 + \ldots + 70} \\ 70 + 70 + 70 + \ldots + 70 \end{array}$$

Now notice that we're adding 70 to itself 70 – 10 + 1 = 61 times (by the fence-post formula). This is the same as multiplying 70 by 61. So we get (70)(61) = **4270**.

Remark: Although it is possible to get the answer by performing these long computations in your calculator, this is not recommended. Most students do not get the correct answer this way due to computational error. Also, a lot of time is wasted.

You can also use the sum feature on your graphing calculator to solve this problem as follows.

Solution

Press the **2nd** button followed by the **List** button (same as **Stat** button).
Go to **Math** and select **5: sum(** or press **5**.
Press **2nd** followed by **List** again.
Go to **Ops** and select **5: seq(** or press **5**.
Enter **x, x, 10, 70))**.
The display should look like this:

sum(seq(x, x, 10, 70))

Press **Enter** and you should get the answer **2440.**

Next enter **sum(seq(x, x, 80, 140))** and you should get the answer **6710**. Finally, $y - x = 6710 - 2440 =$ **4270**.

Time-Saving Remark: After entering **sum(seq(x, x, 10, 70))** and getting an answer of 2440, you can press the **2**[nd] button followed by the **Enter** button to bring **sum(seq(x, x, 10, 70))** back up in your calculator. Then move the cursor back, change the 10 to an 80 and the 70 to 140 and press **Enter** again.

Also, you do not need to type the closing parentheses. For example, it is okay to enter **sum(seq(x, x, 10, 70** instead of **sum(seq(x, x, 10, 70)).**

Although I do not recommend the next solution for use on the SAT, I will include it for completeness.

Solution

The sum of the terms of a sequence is called a **series**. A series is **arithmetic** if any two consecutive terms have the same difference. There is a simple formula for the sum of an arithmetic series:

$\boldsymbol{A_n = n \cdot m}$ where $\boldsymbol{n}$ is the number of terms and $\boldsymbol{m}$ is the average (arithmetic mean) of the first and last term.

The sum of the integers from 10 to 70 inclusive is $61(\frac{10+70}{2}) = 2440$, and the sum from 80 to 140 inclusive is $61(\frac{80+140}{2}) = 6710$. It follows that $y - x = 6710 - 2440 =$ **4270**.

Remark: We used the fence-post formula to get that $n = 61$.

See the optional material at the end of this lesson for a derivation of the arithmetic series formula.

Now try to solve each of the following problems. The answers to these problems, followed by full solutions are at the end of this lesson. **Do not** look at the answers until you have attempted these problems yourself. Please remember to mark off any problems you get wrong.

Level 1: Number Theory

48, 35, 22, ...

4. The first term of the sequence above is 48. Each term after the first is 13 less than the previous term. What is the first negative number in the sequence?

   (A) -1
   (B) -2
   (C) -3
   (D) -4
   (E) -5

Level 2: Number Theory

35, 20, 57, 31, 18, ...

5. In the sequence above, 35 is the first term and each term thereafter is obtained by using the following rules.

- If the previous term is even, multiply it by 3 and then subtract 3.
- If the previous term is odd, add 5 to it and then divide by 2.

What is the seventh term of the sequence?

Level 5: Number Theory

6. A 700 foot long fence is constructed. Fence-posts are placed at each end and also placed every 10 feet along the fence. How many fence-posts are there in all in the 700 foot stretch?

7. If x denotes the sum of the integers from 1 to 40 inclusive, and y denotes the sum of the integers from 41 to 80 inclusive, what is the value of $y - x$?

$$\frac{51}{(2)(3)}, \frac{51}{(3)(4)}, \frac{51}{(4)(5)}, \frac{51}{(5)(6)}$$

8. The first four terms of a sequence are given above. The nth term of the sequence is $\frac{51}{(n+1)(n+2)}$, which is equal to $\frac{51}{n+1} - \frac{51}{n+2}$. What is the sum of the first 100 terms of this sequence?

   (A) $\frac{51}{2}$
   (B) 25
   (C) $\frac{2499}{50}$
   (D) $\frac{1224}{50}$
   (E) $\frac{1}{50}$

9. In a certain sequence, each term after the second is the product of the two preceding terms. If the sixth term is 32 and the seventh term is 512, what is the second term of this sequence?

10. The sum of the positive odd integers less than 200 is subtracted from the sum of the positive even integers less than or equal to 200. What is the resulting difference?

$$3, 9, 27, \ldots$$

11. The first term of the sequence above is 3, and each term after the first is three times the preceding term. Which of the following expressions represents the nth term of the sequence?

   (A) $3n$
   (B) $(n-1)^3$
   (C) n^3
   (D) 3^{n-1}
   (E) 3^n

12. 125 blank cards are lined up in one long row. In the upper left hand corner of each card a number is written beginning with 1 on the first card, 2 on the second card, and so on until 125 is written in the upper left hand corner of the last card in the row. Now another number is written in the lower right hand corner of each card, this time beginning with 125 on the first card, 124 on the second card, and so on until 1 is written in the lower right hand corner of the last card. Which of the following is a pair of numbers written on the same card?

    (A) 71 and 57
    (B) 70 and 56
    (C) 69 and 55
    (D) 68 and 54
    (E) 67 and 53

Answers

1. 145	5. 28	9. 1/4 or .25
2. 57	6. 71	10. 100
3. 4270	7. 1600	11. E
4. D	8. B	12. B

Full Solutions

6.

* **Solution using the fence-post formula:** Since $\frac{700}{10} = 70$, we can identify the posts with the integers from 0 to 70, inclusive. By the fence-post formula, the number of fence-posts is 70 – 0 + 1 = **71**.

8.

* The second form of the sequence is much nicer to work with. We get the first term by substituting in a 1 for *n*. So the 1st term of the sequence is $\frac{51}{2} - \frac{51}{3}$. Similarly, the 2nd term of the sequence is $\frac{51}{3} - \frac{51}{4}$. Continuing in this fashion we get that the 100th term of the sequence is $\frac{51}{101} - \frac{51}{102}$. When we add all these up we get the following.

$$\left(\frac{51}{2} - \frac{51}{3}\right) + \left(\frac{51}{3} - \frac{51}{4}\right) + \left(\frac{51}{4} - \frac{51}{5}\right) + \cdots + \left(\frac{51}{101} - \frac{51}{102}\right).$$

This is called a **telescoping sum**. These sums are nice because a lot of cancellation takes place. Notice that everything goes away except for $\frac{51}{2} - \frac{51}{102}$. Type this into your calculator to get 25, choice (B).

9.

* The fifth term is $\frac{512}{32}$ = 16. The fourth term is $\frac{32}{16}$ = 2. The third term is $\frac{16}{2}$ = 8. The second term is $\frac{2}{8}$ = **1/4** or **.25**.

10.

Solution using strategy 11: We write out each sum formally, line them up, and subtract term by term.

$$\begin{array}{r} 2+4+6+\ldots+200 \\ \underline{1+3+5+\ldots+199} \\ 1+1+1+\ldots+\quad 1 \end{array}$$

Now notice that we're adding 1 to itself 100 times. So the answer is **100**.

Note: It is easiest to see that we are adding 100 ones by looking at the sum of the positive even integers less than or equal to 200. There are $\frac{200}{2}$ = 100 terms in this sum.

* **Quick computation:** Once you get a little practice with this type of problem you can simply compute 100·1 = **100**.

Solution using the sum feature on your graphing calculator: Press the **2nd** button followed by the **List** button (same as **Stat** button).
Go to **Math** and select **5: sum(** or press **5**.
Press **2nd** followed by **List** again.
Go to **Ops** and select **5: seq(** or press **5**.
Enter **x, x, 1, 199, 2))**.
The display should look like this: **sum(seq(x, x, 1, 199, 2))**.
Press **Enter** and you should get the answer **10,000.**
Next enter **sum(seq(x, x, 2, 200, 2))** and you should get the answer **10,100**. Finally, 10,100 – 10,000 = **100**.

Note: In the expression **sum(seq(x, x, 2, 200, 2))** the last 2 indicates the **step size**. Here we are adding every other number.

See the solution to problem 3 for a time-saving remark, and a third solution using the Arithmetic Series formula.

11.
* **Solution using strategy 4:** Let's choose a value for n, say $n = 2$. We see that the 2nd term of the sequence is **9**. **Put a nice big circle around this number.** Now substitute $n = 2$ into each answer choice.

(A) 6
(B) 1
(C) 8
(D) 3
(E) 9

Since (A), (B), (C) and (D) are incorrect we can eliminate them. Therefore the answer is choice (E).

* **Complete solution:** We can rewrite the sequence as $3^1, 3^2, 3^3,...$

Note that the 1st term is 3^1, the 2nd term is 3^2, the 3rd term is 3^3, etc. Thus, the nth term is is 3^n, choice (E).

12.
* Note that the sum of the numbers on the first card is 1 + 125 = 126, the sum of the numbers on the second card is 2 + 124 = 126, etc. So we are looking for two numbers that add to 126. Since 70 + 56 = 126, the answer is choice (B).

OPTIONAL MATERIAL

LEVEL 6: NUMBER THEORY

1. If $10x$ is the sum of the integers from 24 to 276 inclusive, $x =$

CHALLENGE QUESTION

2. Show that the sum of an arithmetic series is $A_n = n \cdot m$ where n is the number of terms and m is the average (arithmetic mean) of the first and last term.

Solutions

1.

*** Solution using strategy 11:** We formally write out this sum forward and backward, and then add.

$$\begin{array}{c} 24 + 25 + \ldots + 275 + 276 \\ \underline{276 + 275 + \ldots + 25 + 24} \\ 300 + 300 + \ldots + 300 + 300 \end{array}$$

By the fence-post formula we are adding 300 to itself 276 – 24 + 1 = 253 times. This gives 300(253) = 75,900. Since we added the sum twice we now divide by 2 to get $10x = 37{,}950$, so that $x =$ **3795**.

2.

Let a be the first term of the series and let d be the common difference.

$$\begin{array}{llllll} A_n = & a & + \; (a + d) & + \; (a + 2d) & + \ldots + & (a + (n-1)d) \\ \underline{A_n = } & \underline{(a + (n-1)d)} & \underline{+ \; (a + (n-2)d)} & \underline{+ \; (a + (n-3)d)} & \underline{+ \ldots +} & \underline{a} \\ 2A_n = & (2a + (n-1)d) & + \; (2a + (n-1)d) & + \; (2a + (n-1)d) & + \ldots + & (2a + (n-1)d) \end{array}$$

$$2A_n = n(2a + (n-1)d) = n(a + a + (n-1)d) = n(a + a_n).$$

$$A_n = n\left(\frac{a + a_n}{2}\right) = n \cdot m.$$

Remarks: Recall that $a_n = a + (n - 1)d$ where a is the first term of the arithmetic sequence, d is the common difference, and a_n is the nth term of the arithmetic sequence. In the first equation we are formally writing out the sum of the first n terms of the arithmetic sequence. Note that to get from one term to the next we simply add the common difference d. We form the second equation by reversing the order in which the terms were written in the first equation. Note that we add the equations term by term. Each term gives the same sum of $2a + (n - 1)d$. Since this expression is repeated n times, the sum is equal to $n(2a + (n - 1)d)$. We then use the arithmetic sequence formula to replace $a + (n - 1)d$ by a_n. Finally, recall that $m = \frac{a + a_n}{2}$, the average of the first and last term.

Lesson 14
Algebra and Functions

Reminder: Before beginning this lesson remember to redo the problems from Lessons 2, 6 and 10 that you have marked off. Do not "unmark" a question unless you get it correct.

Laws of Exponents

Law	Example
$x^0 = 1$	$3^0 = 1$
$x^1 = x$	$9^1 = 9$
$x^a x^b = x^{a+b}$	$x^3 x^5 = x^8$
$x^a/x^b = x^{a-b}$	$x^{11}/x^4 = x^7$
$(x^a)^b = x^{ab}$	$(x^5)^3 = x^{15}$
$(xy)^a = x^a y^a$	$(xy)^4 = x^4 y^4$
$(x/y)^a = x^a/y^a$	$(x/y)^6 = x^6/y^6$
$x^{-1} = 1/x$	$3^{-1} = 1/3$
$x^{-a} = 1/x^a$	$9^{-2} = 1/81$
$x^{1/n} = \sqrt[n]{x}$	$x^{1/3} = \sqrt[3]{x}$
$x^{m/n} = \sqrt[n]{x^m} = \left(\sqrt[n]{x}\right)^m$	$x^{9/2} = \sqrt{x^9} = \left(\sqrt{x}\right)^9$

Now let's practice. Simplify the following expressions using the basic laws of exponents. Get rid of all negative and fractional exponents.

1. $5^2 \cdot 5^3$
2. $\frac{5^3}{5^2}$
3. $\frac{x^5 \cdot x^3}{x^8}$
4. $(2^3)^4$
5. $\frac{(xy)^7(yz)^2}{y^9}$
6. $(\frac{2}{3})^3(\frac{9}{4})^2$
7. $\frac{x^4+x^2}{x^2}$
8. $\frac{(x^{10}+x^9+x^8)(y^5+y^4)}{y^4(x^2+x+1)}$
9. 7^{-1}
10. $\frac{5^2}{5^5}$
11. $\frac{x^{-5} \cdot x^{-3}}{x^{-4}}$
12. $5^{\frac{1}{2}}$
13. $5^{-\frac{1}{2}}$
14. $7^{-\frac{11}{3}}$
15. $\frac{x^{-\frac{5}{2}} \cdot x^{-1}}{x^{-\frac{4}{3}}}$

Answers

1. $5^5 = 3125$

2. $5^1 = 5$

3. $\frac{x^8}{x^8} = 1$

4. $2^{12} = 4096$

5. $\frac{x^7y^7y^2z^2}{y^9} = \frac{x^7y^9z^2}{y^9} = x^7z^2$

6. $\frac{2^3}{3^3} \cdot \frac{9^2}{4^2} = \frac{2^3}{3^3} \cdot \frac{(3^2)^2}{(2^2)^2} = \frac{2^3}{3^3} \cdot \frac{3^4}{2^4} = \frac{3^1}{2^1} = \frac{3}{2}$

7. $\frac{x^2(x^2+1)}{x^2} = x^2 + 1$

8. $\frac{x^8(x^2+x+1)y^4(y+1)}{y^4(x^2+x+1)} = x^8(y + 1)$

9. $\frac{1}{7}$

10. $5^{-3} = \frac{1}{5^3} = \frac{1}{125}$

11. $\frac{x^{-8}}{x^{-4}} = x^{-4} = \frac{1}{x^4}$

12. $\sqrt{5}$

13. $\frac{1}{5^{\frac{1}{2}}} = \frac{1}{\sqrt{5}}$

14. $\frac{1}{7^{\frac{11}{3}}} = \frac{1}{\sqrt[3]{7^{11}}}$

15. $\frac{x^{-\frac{7}{2}}}{x^{-\frac{4}{3}}} = x^{-\frac{13}{6}} = \frac{1}{x^{\frac{13}{6}}} = \frac{1}{\sqrt[6]{x^{13}}}$

Now try to solve each of the following problems. The answers to these problems, followed by full solutions are at the end of this lesson. **Do not** look at the answers until you have attempted these problems yourself. Please remember to mark off any problems you get wrong.

Level 1: Algebra

1. If $9^2 = 3^z$, then $z =$

Level 2: Algebra

2. If $8^{x+1} = 4096$, what is the value of x ?

Level 3: Algebra

3. If $7^x = 6$, then $7^{3x} =$

4. If $(\sqrt{x})^y = 5$, what is the value of $\frac{1}{x^{2y}}$?

Level 4: Algebra and Functions

$$2^{9x} = 27z^3$$

5. In the equation above, x is a positive integer and $z > 0$. If $8^x = nz$, what is the value of n?

6. If $y = 7^x$, which of the following expressions is equivalent to $49^x - 7^{x+2}$ for all positive integer values of x ?

(A) $7y - 7$
(B) y^2
(C) $y^2 - y$
(D) $y^2 - 7y$
(E) $y^2 - 49y$

x	-3	0	3
$g(x)$	$\frac{7}{27}$	7	189

7. The table above shows some values for the function g. If $g(x) = ab^x$ for some positive constants a and b, what is the value of b?

8. If $a^{\frac{2}{5}} = b$, what does a^6 equal in terms of b?

(A) b^2
(B) $b^{\frac{12}{5}}$
(C) b^5
(D) b^{15}
(E) b^{16}

9. Positive integers $a, b,$ and c satisfy the equations $a^{-b} = \frac{1}{64}$ and $b^c = 216$. If $a < b$, what is the value of abc ?

10. If $a \neq 13$ and $\frac{a^2-169}{a-13} = b^2$, what does a equal in terms of b ?

(A) $b^2 - 13$
(B) $b^2 + 13$
(C) $\sqrt{b} - \sqrt{13}$
(D) $b - \sqrt{13}$
(E) $b + \sqrt{13}$

LEVEL 5: ALGEBRA

11. If a and b are positive integers, which of the following is equivalent to $(7a)^{5b} - (7a)^{2b}$?

    (A) $(7a)^{3b}$
    (B) $7^b(a^5 - a^2)$
    (C) $(7a)^{2b}[(7a)^{3b} - 1]$
    (D) $(7a)^{2b}[49a^b - 1]$
    (E) $(7a)^{2b}[(7a)^5 - 1]$

12. Let $x \therefore y$ be defined as the sum of all integers between x and y. For example, $1 \therefore 4 = 2 + 3 = 5$. What is the value of $(60 \therefore 900) - (63 \therefore 898)$?

Answers

1. 4	5. 3	9. 36
2. 3	6. E	10. A
3. 216	7. 3	11. C
4. .001 or .002	8. D	12. 1983

Full Solutions

3.

* $7^{3x} = (7^x)^3 = 6^3 =$ **216**.

4.

* **Solution using strategy 4:** The nature of the question implies that every choice of *y* will lead to the same answer (see the exception below). So choose *y* = 1. Then we have

$$\sqrt{x} = 5, \text{ so that } x = 5^2 = 25.$$

Then $1/x^{2y} = 1/x^2 = 1/625 = .0016$. So we grid in **.001** or **.002**.

Exception: We cannot choose *y* = 0 because the left side would then become 1 making the given equation 1 = 5 which is false.

Algebraic solution: $(\sqrt{x})^y = x^{y/2}$, so that the given equation is equivalent to $x^{y/2} = 5$. We raise each side to the fourth power to get that $x^{2y} = 625$. So $\frac{1}{x^{2y}} = \frac{1}{625} = .0016$. So grid in **.001** or **.002**.

5.

* $2^{9x} = (2^3)^{3x} = 8^{3x} = (8^x)^3 = (nz)^3 = n^3z^3$. So $n^3 = 27$, and therefore n = **3**.

6.

Solution using strategy 4: Let's choose a value for x, say $x = 2$. Then we have $y = 7^2 = 49$, and $49^x - 7^{x+2} = 49^2 - 7^4 =$ **0**. **Put a nice big dark circle around the number 0.** Now substitute $y = 49$ into each answer choice.

(A) $7*49 - 7 = 63 - 7 = 56$
(B) $49^2 = 2401$
(C) $49^2 - 49 = 2401 - 49 = 2352$
(D) $49^2 - 7*49 = 2401 - 343 = 2058$
(E) $49^2 - 49*49 = 2401 - 2401 = 0$

Since (A), (B), (C) and (D) are incorrect we can eliminate them. Therefore the answer is choice (E)

* **Algebraic solution:** $49^x - 7^{x+2} = (7^2)^x - 7^x7^2 = (7^x)^2 - 49(7^x) = y^2 - 49y$. This is choice (E).

7.

* Let's start with the easiest point (0, 7). Equivalently, $7 = f(0) = ab^0 = a$. So the function is now $f(x) = 7b^x$. Let's use the point (3, 189) to find b. Equivalently, $189 = f(3) = 7b^3$ so that $b^3 = 27$ and b = **3** (since $b > 0$).

Note: Be careful with order of operations here. Exponentiation is always done before multiplication. So ab^x means raise b to the x power, and **then** multiply by a. **Do not** multiply a times b first.

8.

Solution using strategy 4: Let's choose a value for a, say $a = 3$. Then using our calculator we have $b = a^{2/5} = 3^{2/5} \sim 1.5518$. Also a^6 = **729**. **Put a nice big, dark circle around this number so that you can find it easily later.** We now substitute 1.5518 in for b into **all** five answer choices.

(A) 2.408
(B) 2.8708
(C) 8.9987
(D) 728.6789
(E) 1130.764

The answer is choice (D).

Notes: (1) The number in choice (D) didn't come out to exactly 729 because we used a decimal approximation for *b*, and not *b*'s exact value.

(2) Normally we would have chosen a value for *b* here (as opposed to *a*), but in this case choosing a value for *a* is much simpler. If we were to choose a value for *b*, then we would have to solve the equation $a^{2/5} = b$, which is precisely what we were trying to avoid.

* **Algebraic solution:** Since $a^{2/5} = b$, $a = b^{5/2}$, and $a^6 = (b^{5/2})^6 = b^{(5/2)6} = b^{15}$, choice (D).

Remark: To eliminate an exponent we raise to the reciprocal power. The reciprocal of $\frac{2}{5}$ is $\frac{5}{2}$. So in this question we raise each side of the equation $a^{2/5} = b$ to the $\frac{5}{2}$ power. On the left we get $(a^{2/5})^{5/2} = a^1 = a$. And as we have seen, on the right we get $b^{5/2}$.

9.

* 64 can be rewritten as 2^6, 4^3. 8^2, or 64^1. Therefore $\frac{1}{64}$ can be written as 2^{-6}, 4^{-3}, 8^{-2} or 64^{-1}. Since $a < b$, $a = 2$ and $b = 6$. When we raise 6 to the 3rd power we get 216. Thus, $c = 3$, and $abc = (2)(6)(3) = $ **36**.

10.

Solution using strategy 4: Let's choose a value for *a*, say $a =$ **14**. Then $b^2 = \frac{196-169}{14-13} = \frac{196-169}{1} = 27$, and so $b = \sqrt{27}$. We now substitute $b = \sqrt{27}$ into each answer and eliminate any choice that does not come out to 14.

(A) $27 - 13 = 14$
(B) $27 + 13 = 40$
(C) $\sqrt{\sqrt{27}} - \sqrt{13} \sim -1.326$
(D) $\sqrt{27} - \sqrt{13} \sim 1.59$
(E) $\sqrt{27} + \sqrt{13} \sim 8.8$

Since (B), (C), (D) and (E) are incorrect we can eliminate them. Therefore the answer is choice (A).

Remark: Technically it is possible that $b = -\sqrt{27}$. This will lead to negative values in choices (D) and (E), and choice (C) will be undefined.

*** Algebraic solution:** Recall that $x^2 - y^2$ factors as $(x - y)(x + y)$. Therefore $\frac{a^2 - 169}{a - 13} = \frac{(a - 13)(a + 13)}{a - 13} = a + 13$. So $b^2 = a + 13$, and thus, $a = b^2 - 13$, choice (A).

Remark: The condition $a \neq 13$ guarantees that $a + 13$ is always equal to $\frac{(a - 13)(a + 13)}{a - 13}$. For if a was allowed to be 13, then we would have that $a + 13 = 26$, whereas $\frac{(a - 13)(a + 13)}{a - 13}$ would be undefined.

11.

Solution using strategy 4: Let's pick numbers for a and b, say $a = b = 1$. Then $(7a)^{5b} - (7a)^{2b} = 7^5 - 7^2 =$ **16,758**. Put a nice big, dark circle around this number. Let's substitute $a = b = 1$ into each answer choice.

(A) $7^3 = 343$
(B) $7(1 - 1) = 0$
(C) $7^2[7^3 - 1] = 16{,}758$
(D) $7^2[49 - 1] = 2352$
(E) $7^2[7^5 - 1] = 823{,}494$

Since (A), (B), (D), and (E) all came out incorrect, the answer is choice (C).

Algebraic solution: Let's consider $7a$ as a block, and rename it x. So $(7a)^{5b} - (7a)^{2b} = x^{5b} - x^{2b} = x^{2b}(x^{3b} - 1) = (7a)^{2b}[(7a)^{3b} - 1]$, choice (C).

For more information on this technique, see **Strategy 19** in ***"The 32 Most Effective SAT Math Strategies."***

Remarks: In going from step 2 to step 3 in the sequence of equations above, we factored, and used the following rule of exponents: $x^z x^w = x^{z+w}$

If you are having trouble seeing this, look at the equation in reverse:

$$x^{2b}(x^{3b} - 1) = x^{2b}x^{3b} - x^{2b} = x^{2b+3b} - x^{2b} = x^{5b} - x^{2b}$$

Also note that we do not actually need to perform a substitution here. We can solve this problem in one step: $(3a)^{5b} - (3a)^{2b} = (3a)^{2b}[(3a)^{3b} - 1]$.

12.

* We write out each sum formally, line them up so that the numbers match up, and subtract term by term.

$$\begin{array}{r} 61 + 62 + 63 + 64 + \ldots + 897 + 898 + 899 \\ 64 + \ldots + 897 \quad\quad\quad\quad \\ \hline 61 + 62 + 63 \;+\; 0 + \ldots + \quad 0 + 898 + 899 \end{array}$$

So the answer is 61 + 62 + + 63 + 898 + 899 = **1983**.

Remark: For alternate solutions to this type of problem see Lesson 13.

OPTIONAL MATERIAL

LEVEL 6: ALGEBRA AND FUNCTIONS

1. Let the function h be defined by $h(x) = x^3 + 12$. If c is a positive number such that $h(c^2) = h(3d)$and $d = \sqrt{c}$, what is the value of $c^{\frac{3}{2}}$?

Solution

1.

* $h(c^2) = (c^2)^3 + 12 = c^6 + 12$ and $h(3d) = (3d)^3 + 12 = 27d^3 + 12$. So we have $c^6 + 12 = 27d^3 + 12$, and so $\frac{c^6}{d^3} = 27$. Substituting $c^{1/2}$ for d, we have $\frac{c^6}{c^{\frac{3}{2}}} = 27$. Now $\frac{c^6}{c^{\frac{3}{2}}} = c^{6\,-\,3/2} = c^{9/2}$. So $c^{9/2} = 27$. Now let's raise each side of this equation to the $\frac{1}{3}$ power. So $(c^{9/2})^{1/3} = 27^{1/3}$, and finally $c^{3/2} =$ **3**.

Lesson 15
Geometry

Reminder: Before beginning this lesson remember to redo the problems from Lessons 3, 7 and 11 that you have marked off. Do not "unmark" a question unless you get it correct.

Strategy 22 – Move the Sides of a Figure Around

Try to answer the following question using this strategy. **Do not** check the solution until you have attempted this question yourself.

Level 4: Geometry

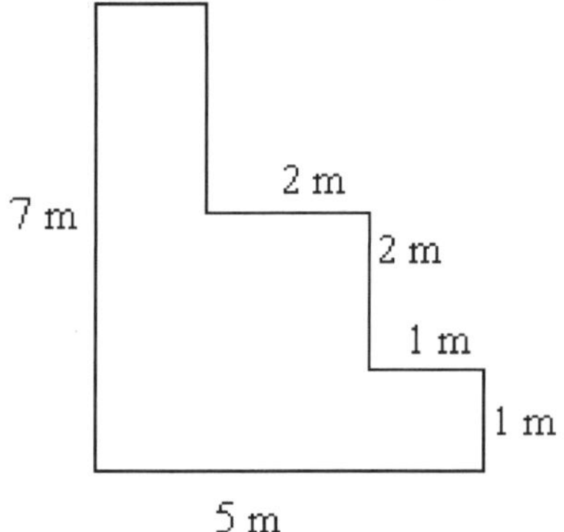

Note: Figure not drawn to scale.

1. Let P be the perimeter of the figure above in meters, and let A be the area of the figure above in square meters. What is the value of $P + A$?

Solution

* Recall that to compute the **perimeter** of the figure we need to add up the lengths of all 8 line segments in the figure. We "move" the two smaller horizontal segments up and the two smaller vertical segments to the right as shown below.

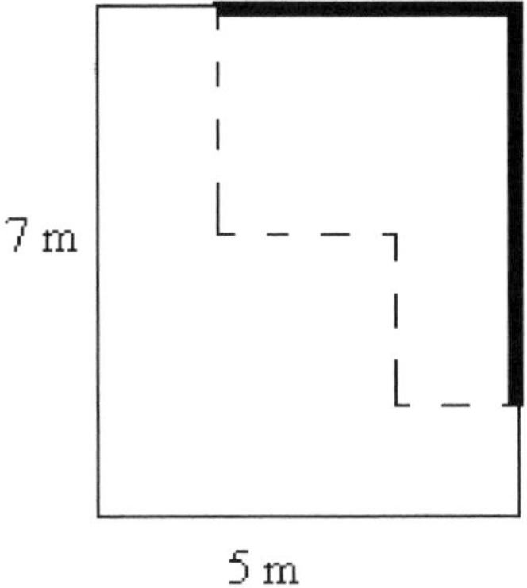

Note that the "bold" length is equal to the "dashed" length. Thus, the perimeter is

$$P = (2)(7) + (2)(5) = 14 + 10 = \mathbf{24} \text{ m.}$$

To compute the **area** of the figure we break the figure up into 3 rectangles and compute the length and width of each rectangle.

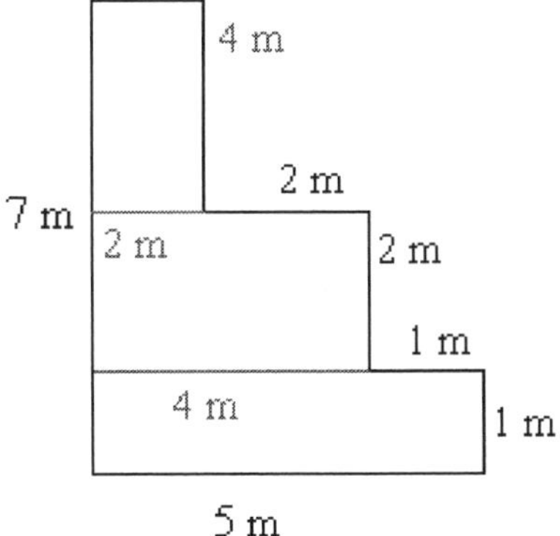

The length and width of the bottom rectangle are 5 and 1 making the area $5 \cdot 1 = 5$ m^2. The length of the middle rectangle is $5 - 1 = 4$, and the width is given as 2. So the area is $4 \cdot 2 = 8$ m^2. The length of the top rectangle is $4 - 2 = 2$, and the width of the top rectangle is $7 - 1 - 2 = 4$ Thus, the area is $2 \cdot 4 = 8$ m^2. We then get the total area by adding up the areas of the three rectangles: $A = 5 + 8 + 8 = \mathbf{21}$ m^2.

Finally, $P + A = 24 + 21 = \mathbf{45}$.

Remark: Notice that if we have the full length of a line segment, and one partial length of the same line segment, then we get the other partial length by subtracting the two given lengths.

Strategy 23 – Areas of Shaded Regions

Finding the area of a shaded region often involves subtracting two areas. The area formulas that you need are either formulas that are given to you in the front of the section or are given in the problem itself.

Try to answer the following question using this strategy. **Do not** check the solution until you have attempted this question yourself.

LEVEL 4: GEOMETRY

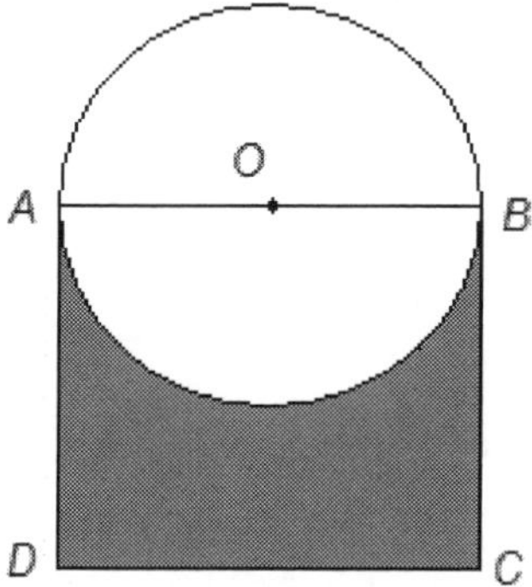

2. In the figure above, AB is a diameter of the circle with center O and $ABCD$ is a square. What is the area of the shaded region if the radius of the circle is 5?

   (A) $25(4-\frac{\pi}{2})$

   (B) $25(2-\frac{\pi}{2})$

   (C) $\pi(4-\pi)$

   (D) $\pi(2-\pi)$

   (E) $\pi(1-\pi)$

Solution

* A side of the square has length $s = 2r = 2\cdot 5 = 10$. The area of the square is then $s^2 = 10^2 = 100$.

The area of the circle is $\pi r^2 = \pi(5)^2 = 25\pi$. The area of the semicircle is then $\frac{25\pi}{2}$. The area of the shaded region is

$$\text{Area of Square} - \text{Area of Semicircle}$$
$$100 - \frac{25\pi}{2}$$
$$25(4 - \frac{\pi}{2})$$

Thus, the answer is choice (A).

Note: As an alternative to factoring in the last step we can do the computation $100 - \frac{25\pi}{2}$ in the calculator to get **60.73009183**. We then do the same with the answer choices until we get one that matches up. We would then see that choice (A) gives the same answer. Of course, this would be more time consuming, but it is better to be safe if you are not good at factoring, or you simply do not see that you need to factor.

Strategy 24 – Fitting Geometric Objects Inside Another Object

To see how many two-dimensional objects fit inside another two-dimensional object we divide areas. To see how many three-dimensional objects fit inside another three-dimensional object we divide volumes.

Try to answer the following question using this strategy. **Do not** check the solution until you have attempted this question yourself.

Level 4: Geometry

3. Rectangular bricks measuring $\frac{1}{2}$ meter by $\frac{1}{3}$ meter are sold in boxes containing 8 bricks each. What is the least number of boxes of bricks needed to cover a rectangular area that has dimensions 9 meters by 11 meters?

Solution

* The area of a face of one rectangular brick is $(\frac{1}{2})(\frac{1}{3}) = \frac{1}{6}$. The area of the rectangular region we want to cover is $(9)(11) = 99$. We can see how many bricks we need to cover this area by dividing the two areas.

$$99 \div (\frac{1}{6}) = 99 \cdot 6 = 594.$$

Now, $\frac{594}{8}$ = 74.25. So the number of boxes needed is **75**.

Remark: A common error would be to round 74.25 to 74. This is incorrect because 74 boxes will not contain enough bricks to cover the entire area. Indeed, 8(74) = 592 < 594.

Surface Area of a Rectangular Solid

The **surface area of a rectangular solid** is just the sum of the areas of all 6 faces. The formula is

$$A = 2lw + 2lh + 2wh$$

where l, w and h are the length, width and height of the rectangular solid, respectively.

In particular, the **surface area of a cube** is

$$A = 6s^2$$

where s is the length of a side of the cube.

Try to answer the following question about the surface area of a cube. **Do not** check the solution until you have attempted this question yourself.

LEVEL 4: GEOMETRY

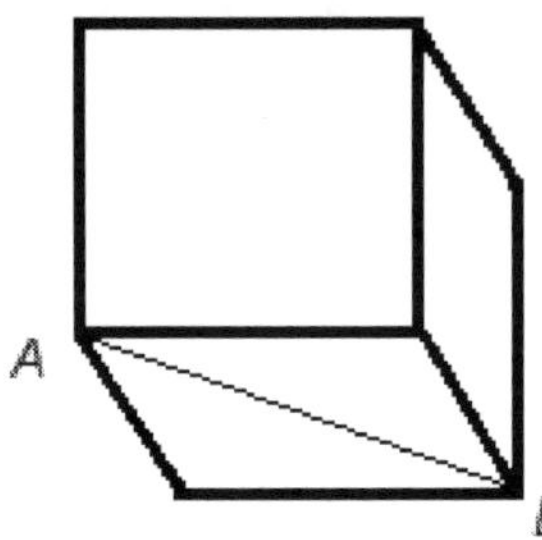

4. In the figure above, segment $\overline{AB}$ joins two vertices of the cube. If the length of $\overline{AB}$ is $3\sqrt{2}$, what is the surface area of the cube?

Solution

* The area of one of the faces is $s^2 = 9$ (see below for several methods of computing this). Thus, the surface area is $A = 6s^2 = 6\cdot 9 =$ **54**.

Methods for computing the area of a face:

(1) Since all sides of a square have equal length, an isosceles right triangle is formed. An isosceles right triangle is the same as a 45, 45, 90 triangle. So we can get the length of a side of the triangle just by looking at the formula for a 45, 45, 90 right triangle. Here s is 3. The area of the square is then (3)(3) = 9.

(2) If we let s be the length of a side of the square, then by the Pythagorean Theorem

$$s^2 + s^2 = (3\sqrt{2})^2$$
$$2s^2 = 18$$
$$s^2 = 9$$

(3) The area of a square is $\boldsymbol{A = \frac{d^2}{2}}$ where d is the length of the diagonal of the square. Therefore in this problem

$$A = \frac{d^2}{2} = \frac{(3\sqrt{2})^2}{2} = \frac{18}{2} = 9.$$

You're doing great! Let's just practice a bit more. Try to solve each of the following problems. The answers to these problems, followed by full solutions are at the end of this lesson. **Do not** look at the answers until you have attempted these problems yourself. Please remember to mark off any problems you get wrong.

LEVEL 3: GEOMETRY

5. How many spherical snowballs with a radius of 4 centimeters can be made with the amount of snow in a spherical snowball of radius 8 centimeters? (the volume V of a sphere with radius r is given by $\frac{4}{3}\pi r^3$.)

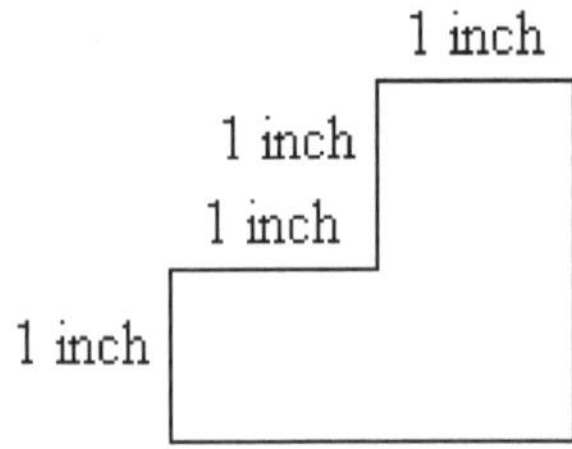

6. How many figures of the size and shape above are needed to completely cover a rectangle measuring 80 inches by 30 inches?

LEVEL 4: GEOMETRY

7. Cube X has surface area A. The edges of cube Y are 4 times as long as the edges of cube X. What is the surface area of cube Y in terms of A?

   (A) $2A$
   (B) $4A$
   (C) $8A$
   (D) $16A$
   (E) $64A$

8. If a 2-centimeter cube were cut in half in all three directions, then in square centimeters, the total surface area of the separated smaller cubes would be how much greater than the surface area of the original 2-centimeter cube?

LEVEL 5: GEOMETRY

9. For any cube, if the volume is V cubic centimeters and the surface area is S square centimeters, then S is directly proportional to V^n for $n =$

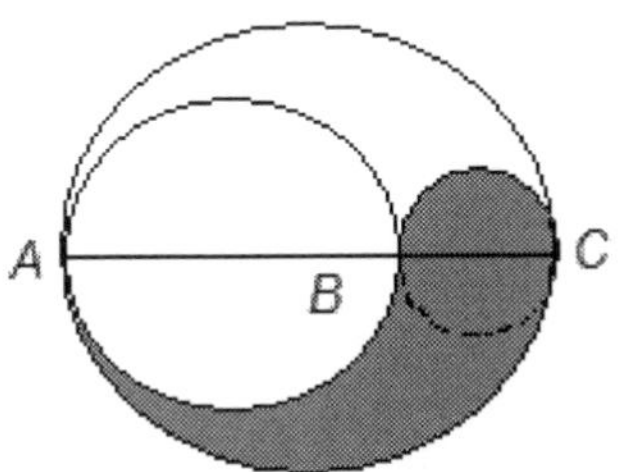

Note: Figure not drawn to scale

10. $\overline{AB}$, $\overline{BC}$, and $\overline{AC}$ are diameters of the three circles shown above. If $BC = 4$ and $AB = 5BC$, what is the area of the shaded region?

    (A) 48π
    (B) 24π
    (C) 12π
    (D) 6π
    (E) 3π

11. How many solid wood cubes, each with a total surface area of 294 square centimeters, can be cut from a solid wood cube with a total surface area of 2,646 square centimeters if no wood is lost in the cutting?

    (A) 3
    (B) 9
    (C) 27
    (D) 81
    (E) 243

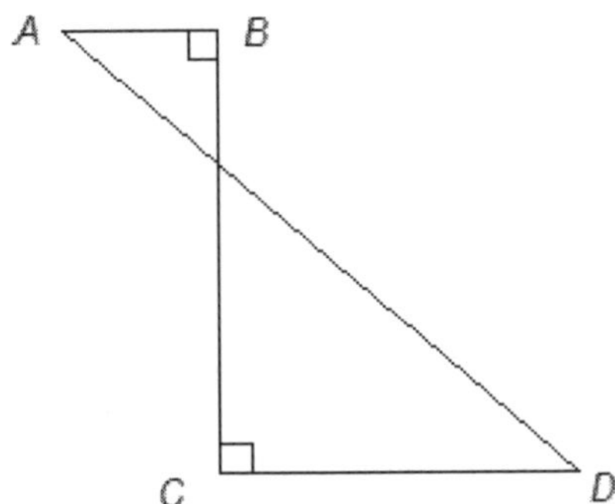

Note: Figure not drawn to scale.

12. In the figure above, $AB = 4$, $BC = 24$, and $AD = 26$. What is the length of line segment $\overline{CD}$?

Answers

1. 45	5. 8	9. 2/3, .666 or .667
2. A	6. 800	10. B
3. 75	7. D	11. C
4. 54.	8. 24	12. 6

Full Solutions

5.

*** Solution using strategy 24:** We divide the volumes.

$$\frac{\frac{4}{3}\pi\cdot 8^3}{\frac{4}{3}\pi\cdot 4^3} = \frac{8^3}{4^3} = \frac{512}{64} = \mathbf{8}.$$

6.

*** Solution using strategy 24:** The area of the given figure is 3 inches^2 and the area of the rectangle is $80\cdot 30 = 2400$ inches^2. We can see how many of the given figures cover the rectangle by dividing the two areas.

$$\frac{2400}{3} = \mathbf{800}.$$

Note: We can get the area of the given figure by splitting it into 3 squares each with area 1 inch^2 as shown below. Then 1 + 1 + 1 = 3

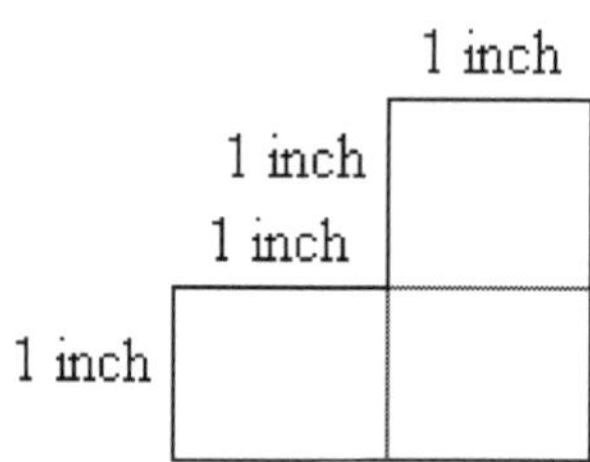

The area of the big square is $2\cdot 2 = 4$ inches^2, and the area of the little square is $1\cdot 1 = 1$ inch^2. So the area of the given figure is $4 - 1 = 3$ inches^2.

7.

Solution using strategy 4: Let's choose a value for the length of an edge of cube X, say $s = 1$. Then the surface area of X is $A = 6s^2 = 6(1)^2 = 6$. The length of an edge of cube Y is $4(1) = 4$, and so the surface area of Y is $6(4)^2 = 6\cdot 16 = \mathbf{96}$. Now we plug in $A = 6$ into each answer choice and eliminate any choice that does not come out to 96.

(A) 12
(B) 24
(C) 48
(D) 96
(E) 384

Since (A), (B), (C), and (E) all came out incorrect we can eliminate them. Therefore the answer is choice (D).

* **Algebraic solution:** Let s be the length of an edge of cube X. Then we have $A = 6s^2$. Since an edge of cube Y is 4 times the length of an edge of cube X, the length of an edge of cube Y is $4s$, so that the surface area of cube Y is $6(4s)^2 = 6 \cdot 16s^2 = 16(6s^2) = 16A$, choice (D).

8.

* The surface area of the 2-centimeter cube is $6(2)^2 = 6(4) = 24$. The surface area of each 1-centimeter cube is $6(1)^2 = 6(1) = 6$. Now, there are 8 of these smaller cubes so that the total surface area of the smaller cubes is $8(6) = 48$. So the answer is $48 - 24 =$ **24**.

9.

Solution using strategy 4: Let's choose a value for the length of a cube, say $s = 1$, Then $S = 6(1)^2 = 6$ and $V = 1^3 = 1$. Now let's try $s = 2$. Then we have $S = 6(2)^2 = 6(4) = 24$ and $V = 2^3 = 8$. We need

$$\frac{6}{1^n} = \frac{24}{8^n}$$

Cross multiplying gives us $6 \cdot 8^n = 24 \cdot 1^n = 24$, or equivalently $8^n = 4$. To solve this equation let's write $8 = 2^3$ and $4 = 2^2$. So we have $(2^3)^n = 2^2$, or equivalently $2^{3n} = 2^2$, Since the bases are the same we can set the exponents equal to each other. So $3n = 2$, and n = **2/3** (**.666** or **.667**)

* **Algebraic solution:** If s is the length of a side of the cube, then we have $S = 6s^2$ and $V = s^3$. Solving the second equation for s, we have $s = V^{1/3}$. Therefore $S = 6(V^{1/3})^2 = 6V^{2/3}$. So S is directly proportional to $V^{2/3}$ (with constant of proportionality 6). So $n =$ **2/3**.

10.

* **Solution using strategy 23:** We first find the radius of each of the three circles. The diameter of the small circle is 4, and so its radius is 2. The diameter of the medium-sized circle is $5 \cdot 4 = 20$, and so its radius is 10. The diameter of the largest circle is $20 + 4 = 24$, and so its radius is 12. We can now find the area of the shaded region as follows.

$$\begin{aligned} A &= \tfrac{1}{2}(\text{Area of big circle}) - \tfrac{1}{2}(\text{Area of medium circle}) + \tfrac{1}{2}(\text{Area of small circle}) \\ &= \tfrac{1}{2}(\pi\cdot 12^2) - \tfrac{1}{2}(\pi\cdot 10^2) + \tfrac{1}{2}(\pi\cdot 2^2) \\ &= \tfrac{1}{2}(\pi\cdot 144) - \tfrac{1}{2}(\pi\cdot 100) + \tfrac{1}{2}(\pi\cdot 4) \\ &= \tfrac{1}{2}\cdot 48\pi \\ &= 24\pi \end{aligned}$$

Thus, the answer is choice (B).

11.

*** Solution using strategy 24:** We first find the length of a side of each cube.

$$6s^2 = 294 \text{ and } 6s^2 = 2646$$
$$s^2 = 49 \qquad s^2 = 441$$
$$s = 7 \qquad s = 21$$

Thus the volume of each cube is $7^3 = 343$ and $21^3 = 9261$, respectively. We can see how many smaller cubes can be cut from the larger cube by dividing the two volumes: $\frac{9261}{343} = 27$, choice (C).

12.

*** Solution using strategy 22:** The problem becomes much simpler if we "move" $\overline{BC}$ to the left and $\overline{AB}$ to the bottom as shown below.

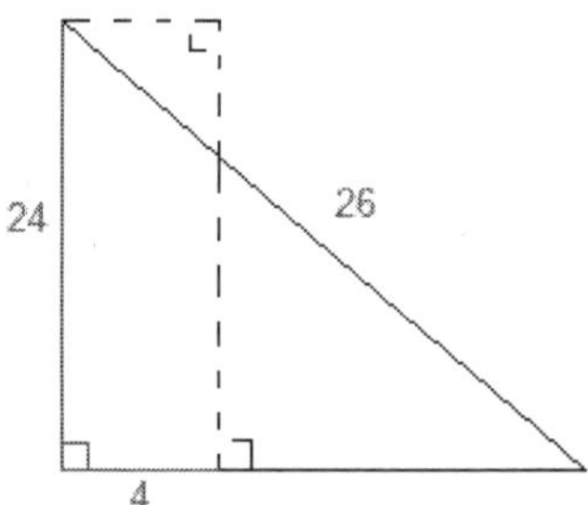

We now have a single right triangle and we can either use the Pythagorean Theorem, or better yet notice that 26 = (13)(2) and 24 = (12)(2). Thus the other leg of the triangle is (5)(2) = 10. So we see that $\overline{CD}$ must have length 10 – 4 = **6**.

Remark: If we didn't notice that this was a multiple of a 5-12-13 triangle, then we would use the Pythagorean Theorem as follows.

$$(x + 4)^2 + 24^2 = 26^2$$
$$(x + 4)^2 + 576 = 676$$
$$(x + 4)^2 = 100$$
$$x + 4 = 10$$
$$x = \mathbf{6}$$

LESSON 16
LOGIC AND SETS

Reminder: Before beginning this lesson remember to redo the problems from Lessons 4, 8 and 12 that you have marked off. Do not "unmark" a question unless you get it correct.

The Contrapositive

A statement of the form "if p, then q" is known as a **conditional** statement. An example of such a statement is "If you are a cat, then you have fur." Another common way to say this is "All cats have fur."

There are 3 other statements that often come up in association with a conditional statement. Let's use the example above to illustrate.

Conditional: If you are a cat, then you have fur.
Converse: If you have fur, then you are a cat.
Inverse: If you are not a cat, then you do not have fur.
Contrapositive: If you do not have fur, then you are not a cat.

The most important thing to know for the SAT is that the contrapositive is logically equivalent to the original conditional statement! The converse and inverse are not.

For example, suppose the conditional statement "All cats have fur" is true. You may want to rewrite this as "If you are a cat, then you have fur." It follows that "If you do not have fur, then you are not a cat" is also true.

In particular, if you are given the statement "Skittles does not have fur," you can infer "Skittles is not a cat."

Note that neither the converse nor the inverse is logically equivalent to the original conditional statement, but they are equivalent to each other.

Try to answer the following question using the contrapositive. **Do not** check the solution until you have attempted this question yourself.

Level 2: Logic

All of Jim's friends can ski.

1. If the statement above is true, which of the following statements must also be true?

   (A) If John cannot ski, then he is not Jim's friend
   (B) If Jeff can ski, then he is not Jim's friend.
   (C) If Joseph can ski, then he is Jim's friend.
   (D) If James is Jim's friend, then he cannot ski.
   (E) If Jordan is not Jim's friend, then he cannot ski.

Solution

* The given statement can be written in conditional form as "If you are Jim's friend, then you can ski." The contrapositive of this statement is "If you cannot ski, then you are not Jim's friend. Replacing "you" with "John" gives the correct answer as choice (A).

Quantifiers

There are two quantifiers.

The first one is "**For all**," or just "all." Another way to say this is "**Every**."

The second one is "**There exists**." Another way to say this is "**Some**."

The most important thing to know about these quantifiers is how to negate them. You can "pass a not through a quantifier by changing the quantifier." Let's look at an example.

The negation of the statement "All pigs have wings" is the statement "Not all pigs have wings." Now let's pass the "not" through the quantifier to get "Some pigs do not have wings." So the negation of "All pigs have wings" is "Some pigs do not have wings." Similarly, the negation of "Some pigs have wings" is "All pigs do not have wings," or equivalently "No pigs have wings."

The Principle of Double Negation

Note that the negation of the statement "Some pigs have wings" is "All pigs do not have wings." If we negate this statement again, we get "Not every pig does not have wings." So we see that "Some pigs have wings" is equivalent to "Not every pig does not have wings."

Similarly, the statement "All pigs have wings" is equivalent to "There does not exist a pig that does not have wings."

To summarize, if we apply negation before and after the quantifier, and change the quantifier, we get a statement equivalent to the original.

Sets and Venn diagrams

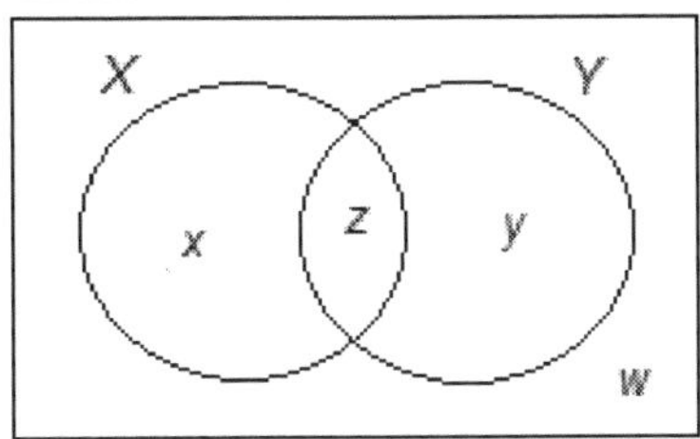

The figure above is a Venn diagram featuring two sets X and Y. Set X has $x + z$ elements, set Y has $y + z$ elements, there are z elements common to X and Y and there are w elements that are in neither X nor Y. Note that x is the number of elements in **only** X and y is the number of elements in **only** Y.

Besides using a Venn diagram, another option is to use the following formula:

Total = X + Y – Both + Neither

Example: There are 30 students in a music class. Of these students, 10 play the piano, 15 play the guitar, and 3 play both the piano and the guitar. How many students in the class do not play either of these two instruments?

Substituting these numbers into the formula, we have

$$30 = 10 + 15 - 3 + N.$$

So, $N = 30 - 22 = \mathbf{8}$.

Alternatively, the Venn diagram would look like this.

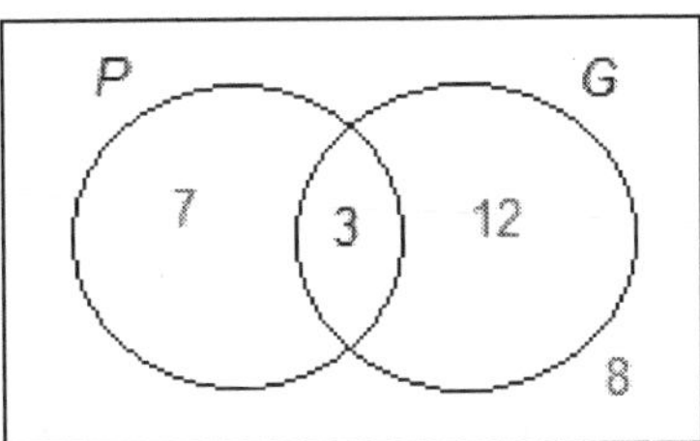

Note that we place the 3 first, then subtract 10 – 3 to get 7, and 15 – 3 to get 12. Finally, 30 – 7 – 3 – 12 = **8**.

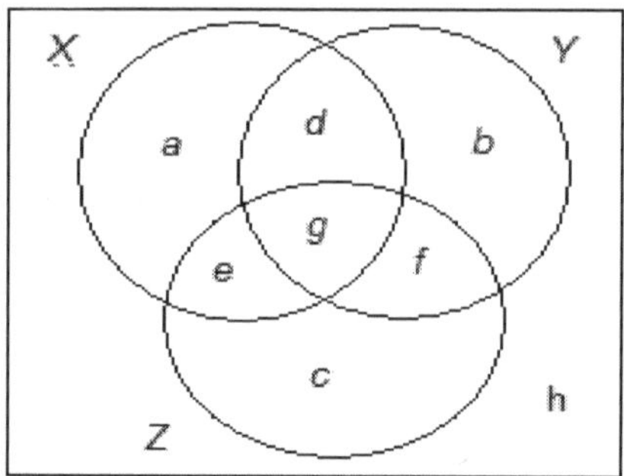

The figure above is a Venn diagram featuring three sets X, Y and Z. Set X has $a + d + e + g$ elements, set Y has $b + d + f + g$ elements, and set Z has $c + e + f + g$ elements. There are $d + g$ elements common to X and Y, there are $e + g$ elements common to X and Z, and there are $f + g$ elements common to Y and Z. Note that a is the number of elements in only X, b is the number of elements in only Y, c is the number of elements in only Z, and g is the number of elements common to X, Y and Z. Finally, h is the number of elements outside of X, Y and Z.

Try to answer the following question. **Do not** check the solution until you have attempted this question yourself.

Level 2: Sets

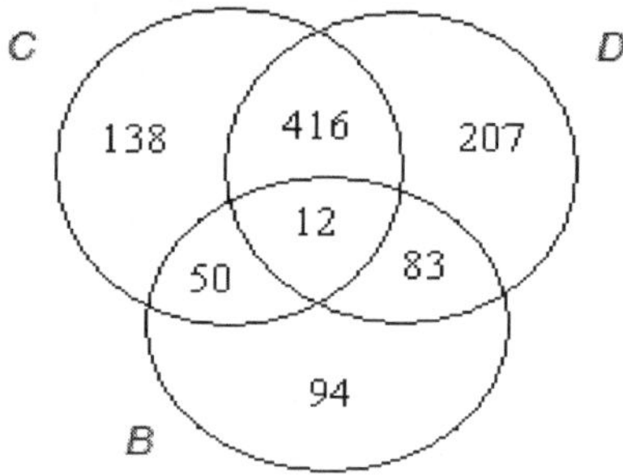

2. 1000 students were polled to determine which of the following animals they had as pets: cats (C), dogs (D), or birds (B). The Venn diagram above shows the results of the poll. How many students said they have exactly 2 of the 3 types of animals?

Solution

* 416 of the students have cats and dogs only.
50 of the students have cats and birds only.
83 of the students have dogs and birds only.

$$416 + 50 + 83 = \mathbf{549}.$$

Try to solve each of the following problems. The answers to these problems, followed by full solutions are at the end of this lesson. **Do not** look at the answers until you have attempted these problems yourself. Please remember to mark off any problems you get wrong.

LEVEL 3: LOGIC AND SETS

3. Let set A consist of the positive multiples of 15 that are less than 70, and let set B consist of the positive multiples of 9 that are less than 70. How many numbers do sets A and B have in common?

4. In a survey, 62 cat owners were asked about two brands of cat food, Brand X and Brand Y. Of the people surveyed, 26 used Brand X, 11 used Brand Y, and 4 used both brands. How many of the people surveyed didn't use either brand of cat food?

   (A) 15
   (B) 26
   (C) 27
   (D) 28
   (E) 29

5. Let A and B be two sets of numbers such that every number in B is also in A. Which of the following CANNOT be true?

   (A) If 1 is not in A, then 1 is not in B.
   (B) 2 is in A, but not in B.
   (C) 3 is in B, but not in A.
   (D) 4 is in neither A nor B.
   (E) 5 is in both A and B.

Fred sometimes eats vegetables.
Lisa never eats meat.

6. If the statements above are true, which of the following statements must also be true?

   I. Fred never eats meat.
   II. Lisa sometimes eats vegetables.
   III. Fred and Lisa never eat meat at the same time.

   (A) I only
   (B) II only
   (C) III only
   (D) I and III only
   (E) II, and III only

LEVEL 4: LOGIC AND SETS

If a beverage is listed in menu A, it is also listed in menu B.

7. If the statement above is true, which of the following statements must also be true?

   (A) If a beverage is listed in menu B, it is also in menu A.
   (B) If a beverage is not listed in menu A, it is not listed in menu B.
   (C) If a beverage is not listed in menu B, it is not listed in menu A.
   (D) If a beverage is not listed in menu B, it is in menu A.
   (E) If a beverage is listed in menu B, it is not listed in menu A.

Some birds in Bryer Park are ducks.

8. If the statement above is true, which of the following statements must also be true?

   (A) Every duck is in Bryer Park
   (B) If a bird is not a duck, it is in Bryer Park.
   (C) Every bird in Bryer Park is a duck.
   (D) All birds in Bryer Park are not ducks.
   (E) Not every bird in Bryer Park is not a duck.

9. Set A has a members, set B has b members, and set C consists of all members that are either in set A or set B with the exception of the d members that are common to both ($d > 0$). Which of the following represents the number of members in set C ?

   (A) $a + b + d$
   (B) $a + b - d$
   (C) $a + b + 2d$
   (D) $a + b - 2d$
   (E) $2a + 2b - 2d$

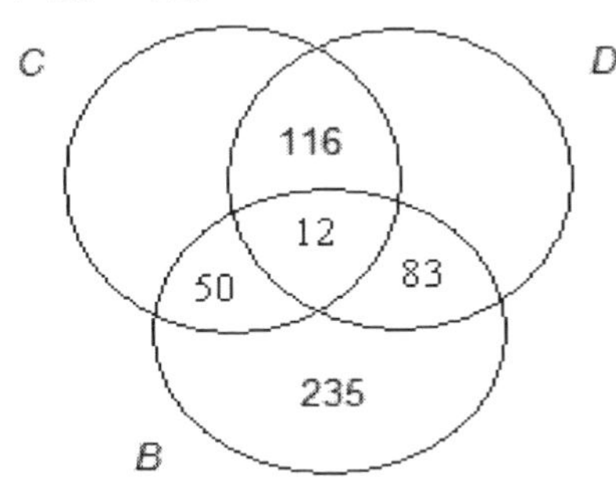

10. 1000 pet owners were polled to determine which of the following animals they had as pets: cats (C), dogs (D), or birds (B). The Venn diagram above shows the results of the poll except that two of the numbers are missing. If the total number of pet owners polled that said they had dogs as pets is equal to the total number of pet owners polled that said they had birds as pets, how many of the pet owners polled said they have cats as pets?

LEVEL 5: LOGIC AND SETS

11. In Dr. Steve's math class, 10 students have dogs and 15 students have cats. If a total of 19 students have only one of these animals, how many students have both dogs and cats?

12. At Brilliance University, the chess team has 16 members and the math team has 13 members. If a total of 7 students belong to only one of the two teams, how many students belong to both teams?

Answers

1. A	5. C	9. D
2. 549	6. C	10. 513
3. 1	7. C	11. 3
4. 29	8. E	12. 11

Full Solutions

3.

Solution by listing: $A = \{15, 30, 45, 60\}$ and $B = \{9, 18, 27, 36, 45, 54, 63\}$. The only number that sets A and B have in common is 45. Therefore the answer is **1**.

*** Solution using the least common multiple:** The least common multiple of 15 and 9 is 45. So the numbers that sets A and B have in common are the multiples of 45 less than 70. Well there is only one such number, 45 itself. So the answer is **1**.

Note: If you are having trouble finding the least common multiple of 15 and 9, go back and review Lesson 5.

4.

*** Solution using the formula "Total = X + Y – Both + Neither":**

$$\text{Total} = 62,\ X = 26,\ Y = 11, \text{ and Both} = 4.$$

$$62 = 26 + 11 - 4 + \text{Neither} = 33 + \text{Neither}.$$

Therefore, Neither = 62 – 33 = **29**.

Solution using a Venn diagram: We draw a Venn diagram

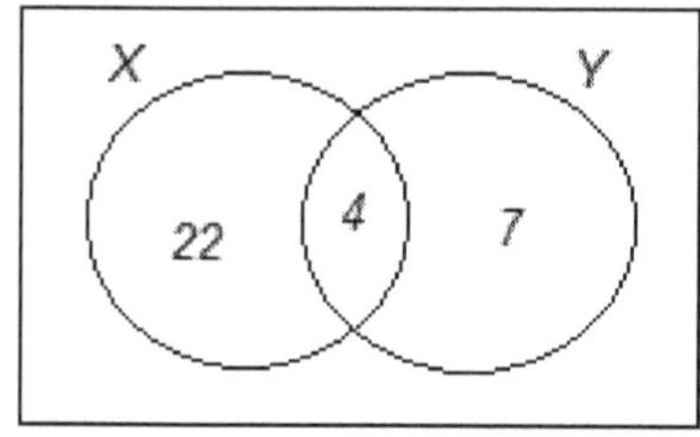

Note that when we draw the diagram we begin with the intersection. This is given to be 4. Now, 26 – 4 = 22, and 11 – 4 = 7. Finally,

$$62 - 22 - 4 - 7 = \mathbf{29}.$$

5.

* The given statement can be written in conditional form as "If you are a number in set B, then you are in set A." In particular, if 3 is in B, then 3 is in A. So the statement in choice (C) cannot be true.

6.

* Since nothing is mentioned relating Fred and meat, I does not have to be true. So we can eliminate choices (A) and (D). Since nothing is mentioned relating Lisa and vegetables, II does not have to be true. So we can eliminate choices (B) and (E). Therefore the answer is choice (C).

Remark: It is not necessary to look at III since we have already eliminated 4 of the answer choices. For completeness, to see that III is true, just observe that since Lisa never eats meat, she never eats meat at the same time as Fred.

7.

* Simply observe that the statement in choice (C) is the contrapositive of the given statement. So the answer is choice (C).

8.

* **Solution using the principle of double negation:** We negate the statement before and after the quantifier, and change the quantifier "some" to "every" to get choice (E).

9.

Solution using strategy 4: Let's let $A = \{1,2\}$ and $B = \{2,3,4\}$. Then it follows that $C = \{1,3,4\}$. We have $a = 2$, $b = 3$, and $d = 1$. The number of members in set C is **3**.

Now let's check each answer choice, and eliminate any choice that does not come out to 3.

(A) $2 + 3 + 1 = 6$
(B) $2 + 3 - 1 = 4$
(C) $2 + 3 + 2 = 7$
(D) $2 + 3 - 2 = 3$
(E) $4 + 6 - 2 = 8$

Since (A), (B), (C), and (E) came out incorrect we can eliminate them. Therefore the answer is choice (D).

*** Solution using the formula "Total = *X* + *Y* – Both + Neither":** The total number of members that are in either set *A* or set *B* is $a + b - d$. We need to subtract off the number of members common to both. We get $a + b - d - d = a + b - 2d$, choice (D).

Remark: It is easy to get tricked in this question. When you add $a + b$ you are counting the number of members common to *A* and *B* **twice** (one time for each set). So we've over counted by d elements. This is why we have to subtract *d* to get the total. Note that after we subtract *d* once, the common elements are still included in the total. We need to subtract *d* **again** to actually get rid of the common elements.

10.

* The total number of pet owners polled that said they had birds as pets is 235 + 50 + 83 + 12 = 380. Therefore the total number of pet owners polled that said they had dogs as pets is 380. So the missing number in the upper right circle is 380 – 116 – 83 – 12 = 169. So, the missing number in the upper left is 1000 – 169 – 235 – 116 – 50 – 83 – 12 = 335. Thus, the number of pet owners polled that said they have cats as pets is 335 + 50 + 116 + 12 = **513**.

11.

Solution using strategy 3: Let's take a guess. Maybe 4 students have both dogs and cats. It then follows that 10 – 4 = 6 students have just dogs, and 15 – 4 = 11 students have just cats. Therefore 6 + 11 = 17 students have only one of these animals. This is a bit too small, so let's **decrease** our guess a bit and say that 3 students have both dogs and cats. Then 10 – 3 = 7 students have just dogs, and 15 – 3 = 12 students have just cats. So, 7 + 12 = 19 students have only one of these animals. This is correct, and so the answer is **3**.

Note: If we accidently increased our guess from 4 it's not that big of a deal. For example, suppose we said that 5 students have both dogs and cats. Then 10 – 5 = 5 students have just dogs, and 15 – 5 = 10 students have just cats. So, 5 + 10 = 15 students have only one of these animals. Since this number is smaller than 17 we can see that we went in the wrong direction and the next natural guess would be 3.

Solution using the formula: We will use the formula Total = $C + D - B$, where C is the number of students that have cats, D is the number of students that have dogs, and B is the number of students that have both. We are given that $C = 10$, $D = 15$, and Total = $19 + B$ (see the **note** below). So, we have $19 + B = 10 + 15 - B$. Solving for B, we have the following:

$$19 + B = 10 + 15 - B$$
$$19 + B = 25 - B$$
$$2B = 25 - 19$$
$$2B = 6$$
$$B = \mathbf{3}$$

Note: We have used the fact here that the total number of students under consideration is equal to the number of students that have only one of the animals plus the number of students that have both animals.

*** Quick solution:** If we add the number of students that have dogs and the number of students that have cats we get 10 + 15 = 25. Note that in this total we have counted the students that have both dogs and cats twice. So if we subtract off the number of students that have only one of these animals we get that 2B = 25 – 19 = 6, where B is the number of students that have both dogs and cats. So B = **3**.

Remark: With a little bit of practice you can do this last computation very quickly in your head (or using your calculator). $\frac{25-19}{2} = \mathbf{3}$.

Algebraic solution: I include this solution for completeness. Let x be the number of students with only cats, z the number of students with only dogs, and y the number of students with both dogs and cats. We are given the following system of equations:

$$x + y = 10$$
$$y + z = 15$$
$$x + z = 19$$

There are several ways to solve this system of equations. One quick way is to add the first two equations, and then subtract the third equation.

$$x + 2y + z = 25$$
$$\underline{x + z = 19}$$
$$2y = 6$$
$$y = \mathbf{3}$$

Exercises: (1) For each of the methods above draw Venn diagrams illustrating each situation.

(2) Try to solve the system of equations given in the algebraic solution in other ways. For example, you can subtract the second equation from the first and then add the third equation. You can also do Gauss – Jordan reduction, etc.

12.

*** Quick solution:** $\frac{29-7}{2} = \mathbf{11}$.

Remark: This is just like problem 11. Each of the solutions to problem 11 will work here as well.

Lesson 17
Number Theory

Reminder: Before beginning this lesson remember to redo the problems from Lessons 1, 5, 9 and 13 that you have marked off. Do not "unmark" a question unless you get it correct.

"distance = rate · time charts"

When trying to solve difficult problems involving distance, rate, and time, it helps to set up a little chart, and use the formula when necessary.

Try to answer the following question using a chart. **Do not** check the solution until you have attempted this question yourself.

Level 4: Number Theory

1. Marco drove from home to work at an average speed of 50 miles per hour and returned home along the same route at an average speed of 46 miles per hour. If his total driving time for the trip was 4 hours, how many minutes did it take Marco to drive from work to home?

Solution

* Let's put the given information into the following chart.

	Distance	Rate	Time
home to work	d	50	$\frac{d}{50}$
work to home	d	46	$\frac{d}{46}$
total			4

Note that although we do not know either distance, we do know that they are the same, so we can call them both "*d*." Also, since

$$\text{distance} = \text{rate} \cdot \text{time},$$

we have that time = $\frac{\text{distance}}{\text{rate}}$. We use this to get the first two entries in column three. The total time is given in the question. So we have

$$\frac{d}{50} + \frac{d}{46} = 4$$
$$46d + 50d = 4 \cdot 50 \cdot 46$$
$$96d = 4 \cdot 50 \cdot 46$$
$$d = \frac{4 \cdot 50 \cdot 46}{96}$$

We want the time it takes Marco to drive from work to home, that is we want $\frac{d}{46}$.

This is equal to $\frac{d}{46} = \frac{4 \cdot 50}{96}$ in hours. To convert to minutes we multiply by 60.

$\frac{d}{46} = \frac{4 \cdot 50 \cdot 60}{96}$ = **125** minutes.

Xiggi's Formula

The following simple formula can be used to find an average speed when two individual speeds for the same distance are known.

$$\textbf{Average Speed} = \frac{\textbf{2(Speed 1)(Speed 2)}}{\textbf{Speed 1 + Speed 2}}$$

*Xiggi's formula is more widely known as the Harmonic Mean formula.

Try to answer the following question using Xiggi's formula. **Do not** check the solution until you have attempted this question yourself.

Level 5: Number Theory

2. An elephant traveled 7 miles at an average rate of 4 miles per hour and then traveled the next 7 miles at an average rate of 1 mile per hour. What was the average speed, in miles per hour, of the elephant for the 14 miles?

Solution

* We simply apply Xiggi's formula:

Average Speed = $\frac{2(4)(1)}{4+1}$ = **8/5** or **1.6**

Now try to answer this question using a chart.

Solution

Let's put the given information into the following chart.

	Distance	Rate	Time
1st part of trip	7	4	$\frac{7}{4}$
2nd part of trip	7	1	$\frac{7}{1} = 7$
total	14		8.75

Note that we computed the times by using "distance = rate · time" in the form "time = $\frac{\text{distance}}{\text{rate}}$." Finally, we use the formula in the form

$$\text{rate} = \frac{\text{distance}}{\text{time}} = \frac{14}{8.75} = \mathbf{1.6}.$$

Note: To get the total distance we add the two distances, and to get the total time we add the two times. Be careful – this doesn't work for rates!

Percent = "Out of 100"

Since the word percent means "out of 100," use the number 100 for totals in percent problems. This is just a specific example of Strategy 4 from Lesson 1.

Try to answer the following question using the number 100. **Do not** check the solution until you have attempted this question yourself.

LEVEL 5: NUMBER THEORY

3. If Ted's weight increased by 36 percent and Jessica's weight decreased by 22 percent during a certain year, the ratio of Ted's weight to Jessica's weight at the end of the year was how many times the ratio at the beginning of the year?

Solution

* **Solution using strategy 4:** Since this is a percent problem, let's choose 100 pounds for both Ted's weight and Jessica's weight at the beginning of the year. Ted's weight at the end of the year was then 100 + 36 = 136 pounds and Jessica's weight at the end of the year was 100 – 22 = 78 pounds. We then have that the ratio of Ted's weight to Jessica's weight at the beginning of the year was $\frac{100}{100}$ = 1, and the ratio of Ted's weight to Jessica's weight at the end of the year was $\frac{136}{78}$ ~ 1.7435897. We therefore grid in **1.74**.

Note: The computations are only this simple because we chose both numbers to be 100. Let's choose different numbers so that you can see how the computations become more difficult. Let's choose 150 pounds for Ted's weight at the beginning of the year and 75 pounds for Jessica's weight at the beginning of the year. 36% of 150 is 150(.36) = 54. So we have that Ted's weight was 150 + 54 = 204 at the end of the year. Also, 22% of 75 is 75(.22) = 16.5 pounds. It follows that Jessica's weight at the end of the year was 75 – 16.5 = 58.5 pounds. The ratio of Ted's weight to Jessica's weight at the beginning of the year was $\frac{150}{75}$ = 2, and the ratio of Ted's to Jessica's weight at the end of the year was $\frac{204}{58.5}$ ~ 3.487179. Finally, we have to solve the equation

$$2x \sim 3.487179$$
$$x \sim 3.487179/2 \sim 1.74$$

So we do get the same answer, but we put in a lot more effort.

Try to also solve this problem algebraically (without plugging in any numbers).

Solution

Let Ted's and Jessica's weights at the beginning of the year be x and y, respectively. Then at the end of the year their weights are $1.36x$ and $0.78y$. The ratio of Ted's weight to Jessica's weight at the beginning of the year was $\frac{x}{y}$, and the ratio of Ted's weight to Jessica's weight at the end of the year was $\frac{1.36x}{0.78y} = \frac{68}{39} \cdot \frac{x}{y}$ which is $\frac{68}{39}$ ~ 1.74359 times the ratio at the beginning of the year. We can therefore grid in **1.74**.

Now try to solve each of the following problems. The answers to these problems, followed by full solutions are at the end of this lesson. **Do not** look at the answers until you have attempted these problems yourself. Please remember to mark off any problems you get wrong.

Level 1: Number Theory

4. If Edna drove s miles in t hours, which of the following represents her average speed, in miles per hour?

   (A) $\frac{s}{t}$

   (B) $\frac{t}{s}$

   (C) $\frac{1}{st}$

   (D) st

   (E) s^2t

Level 2: Number Theory

5. Running at a constant speed, an antelope traveled 150 miles in 6 hours. At this rate, how many miles did the antelope travel in 5 hours?

Level 3: Number Theory

6. The ratio of the number of elephants to the number of zebras in a zoo is 3 to 5. What percent of the animals in the zoo are zebras?

   (A) 12.5%
   (B) 37.5%
   (C) 60%
   (D) 62.5%
   (E) 70%

7. What percent of 60 is 12? (Disregard the percent symbol when gridding in your answer.)

LEVEL 4: NUMBER THEORY

8. For nonzero numbers a, b, and c, if c is three times b and b is $\frac{1}{5}$ of a, what is the ratio of a^2 to c^2 ?

   (A) 9 to 25
   (B) 25 to 9
   (C) 5 to 9
   (D) 5 to 3
   (E) 3 to 5

9. If the ratio of two positive integers is 7 to 6, which of the following statements about these integers CANNOT be true?

   (A) Their sum is an even integer.
   (B) Their sum is an odd integer.
   (C) Their product is divisible by 11.
   (D) Their product is an even integer.
   (E) Their product is an odd integer.

10. If $x > 0$, then 4 percent of 7 percent of $5x$ equals what percent of x ? (Disregard the percent symbol when you grid your answer.)

LEVEL 5: NUMBER THEORY

11. There are m bricks that need to be stacked. After n of them have been stacked, then in terms of m and n, what percent of the bricks have not yet been stacked?

   (A) $\frac{m}{100(m-n)}\%$
   (B) $\frac{100(m-n)}{m}\%$
   (C) $\frac{100m}{n}\%$
   (D) $\frac{100n}{m}\%$
   (E) $\frac{m}{100n}\%$

12. Jason ran a race of 1600 meters in two laps of equal distance. His average speeds for the first and second laps were 11 meters per second and 7 meters per second, respectively. What was his average speed for the entire race, in meters per second?

Answers

1. 125	5. 125	9. E
2. 8/5 or 1.6	6. D	10. 1.4
3. 1.74	7. 20	11. B
4. A	8. B	12. 8.55 or 8.56

Full Solutions

6.

We can represent the number of elephants in the zoo by $3x$ and the number of zebras in the zoo by $5x$ for some number x. Then the total number of animals in the zoo is $8x$ which we set equal to 100. Now $8x = 100$ implies that $x = \frac{100}{8} = 12.5$. Since we want the percent of the animals in the park that are zebras, we need to find $5x = 5(12.5) = 62.5\%$, choice (D).

Important note: After you find x make sure you look at what the question is asking for. A common error is to give an answer of 12.5%. But the number of zebras is **not** equal to x. It is equal to $5x$.

* **Alternate solution:** We set up a ratio of the amount of zebras in the zoo to the total number of animals in the zoo.

zebras	5	x
animals	8	100

$$\frac{5}{8} = \frac{x}{100}$$

$$8x = 500$$

$$x = \frac{500}{8} = 62.5\text{, choice (D).}$$

For more information on this technique, see **Strategy 14** in ***"The 32 Most Effective SAT Math Strategies."***

7.

* The word "what" indicates an unknown, let's call it x. The word percent means "out of 100" or "divided by 100." The word "of" indicates multiplication, and the word "is" indicates an equal sign. So we translate the given sentence into an algebraic equation as follows.

$$\frac{x}{100} \cdot 60 = 12$$

So $x = \frac{12 \cdot 100}{60} = \mathbf{20}$.

8.

* **Solution using strategy 4:** Let's choose a value for a, say $a = 5$. Then $b = 1$, $c = 3$, and therefore the ratio of a^2 to c^2 is 25 to 9, choice (B).

Algebraic solution: $b = \left(\frac{1}{5}\right)a$, and so $c = 3b = 3\left(\frac{1}{5}\right)a = \frac{3a}{5}$. It follows that $\frac{a^2}{c^2} = \frac{a^2}{\left(\frac{3a}{5}\right)^2} = \frac{a^2 \cdot 25}{9a^2} = \frac{25}{9}$. Therefore the ratio of a^2 to c^2 is 25 to 9, choice (B).

9.

Solution using Strategy 4: Let's choose two positive integers that are in the ratio of 7 to 6, say 7 and 6. Then we have 7 + 6 = 13 and (7)(6) = 42. Since 13 is odd we can eliminate choice (B). Since 42 is even we can eliminate choice (D). The answer is therefore (A), (C) or (E).

We will now choose two new numbers that are in the same ratio. A simple way to do this is to multiply our original numbers by an integer, say 2. So our new numbers are 14 and 12. Then we have 14 + 12 = 26 and (14)(12) = 168. Since 26 is even we can eliminate choice (A). So we're down to either (C) or (E).

Looking at choice (C) seems to indicate that perhaps we should multiply our original numbers by 11. So our new numbers are (7)(11) = 77 and (6)(11) = 66. The product of these numbers is (77)(66) = 5082. This is divisible by 11. We can therefore eliminate choice (C), and the answer is choice (E).

Notes: (1) Choice (E) is correct because we eliminated the other 4 choices. The reality of the situation is that we have not actually answered this question. Using the previous method there is no reason to believe that there is no choice of integers that will produce an odd product. In this sense the more advanced method below is more enlightening.

(2) To see that 5082 is divisible by 11 we can simply divide 5082 by 11 in our calculator. The result is 462. Since this is an integer, 5082 is divisible by 11. In fact, 5082 = (11)(462).

* **Advanced Method:** If the ratio of two positive integers is 7 to 6, then the integers can be written as $7x$ and $6x$ for some number x. It follows that the sum is $7x + 6x = 13x$, and the product is $(7x)(6x) = 42x^2 = 2(21x^2)$. Since the product has a factor of 2 it is always even. Thus the product can never be odd, and the answer is choice (E).

Remarks: (1) If x is an odd integer, then $13x$ is the product of two odd integers. Therefore the sum will be odd. If x is an even integer, then $13x$ is the product of an odd integer and an even integer. Therefore the sum will be even.

(2) If x is any multiple of 11, then $42x^2$ will be divisible by 11.

(3) Note that in order for $7x$ and $6x$ to both be integers, x must also be an integer because 7 and 6 have no common factors (contrast this with $2x$ and $4x$ where x can be any multiple of 1/2). This shows that when we substitute an acceptable value for x in the expression $2(21x^2)$ we will not inadvertently cancel the 2.

10.

Solution using strategy 4: Since this is a percent problem let's choose $x = 100$. Then 7 percent of $5x$ is 7 percent of 500 which is (.07)(500) = 35. 4 percent of 7 percent of $5x$ is 4 percent of 35 which is (.04)(35) = 1.4. Since we began with $x = 100$, the answer is **1.4**.

* **Direct solution:** 4 percent of 7 percent of $5x$ is $(.04)(.07)(5x) = .014x$ which is 1.4 percent of x. So we grid in **1.4**.

11.

Solution using strategy 4: Since this is a percent problem we choose 100 for the total number of bricks. So $m = 100$. For n, let's choose 25, so that 25 bricks have been stacked, and 100 – 25 = 75 have not been stacked. Since we started with 100 as our total, **75%** of the bricks have not been stacked. **Remember to put a big, dark circle around 75%.** We make the substitutions m = 100 and n = 25 into each answer choice.

(A) 100/7500 ~ 0.0133%
(B) 7500/100 = 75%
(C) 10,000/25 = 400%
(D) 2500/100 = 25%
(E) 25/10,000 = 0.0025%

We now compare each of these percents to the percent that we put a nice big, dark circle around. Since (A), (C), (D) and (E) are incorrect we can eliminate them. Therefore the answer is choice (B).

Important note: (B) is **not** the correct answer simply because it is equal to 75%. It is correct because all 4 of the other choices are **not** 75%. **You absolutely must check all five choices!**

* **Algebraic solution:** The total number of bricks is m. Since n bricks have been stacked, it follows that $m - n$ have not been stacked. To get the **fraction** of bricks that have not been stacked we divide the **number** that have not been stacked by the total. This is $\frac{m-n}{m}$. To change this to a **percent** we multiply by 100, to get $\frac{100(m-n)}{m}$ %, choice (B).

Note: The last step in the algebraic solution is equivalent to the usual ratio computation where we are changing the denominator to 100.

bricks not stacked	$m - n$	x
total bricks	m	100

$$\frac{m-n}{m} = \frac{x}{100}$$

$$100(m-n) = mx$$

$$\frac{100(m-n)}{m} = x$$

12.

* **Solution using Xiggi's formula:**

Average Speed $= \frac{2(11)(7)}{11+7} = \frac{154}{18}$ ~ 8.555555. So grid in **8.55** or **8.56**.

Solution using a chart:

	Distance	Rate	Time
lap 1	800	11	$\frac{800}{11} \sim 72.727$
lap 2	800	7	$\frac{800}{7} \sim 114.286$
total	1600	x	187.01

$$x = \text{average rate} = \frac{\text{distance}}{\text{time}} \sim \frac{1600}{187.01} \sim 8.5555$$

So we grid in **8.55** or **8.56**.

OPTIONAL MATERIAL

CHALLENGE QUESTION

1. Use the formula $d = rt$ to derive Xiggi's formula.

Solution

* Recall that Xiggi's formula is used when we are given two rates for the **same** distance. So let d be the common distance, and r_1 and r_2 the two rates. Let's use a chart.

Distance	Rate	Time
d	r_1	$\frac{d}{r_1}$
d	r_2	$\frac{d}{r_2}$
$2d$		$\frac{d}{r_1} + \frac{d}{r_2}$

Note that we get the first two entries in the last column by using the formula $d = rt$, and we get the last row by addition (note that the this cannot be done in the middle column). We now apply the formula $d = rt$ to the middle column to get $2d = r(\frac{d}{r_1} + \frac{d}{r_2})$. Multiply each side of this equation by r_1r_2 to get $2dr_1r_2 = r(dr_2 + dr_1) = rd(r_1 + r_2)$. Finally, we divide each side of this equation by $d(r_1 + r_2)$ to get $r = \frac{2r_1r_2}{r_1 + r_2}$.

LESSON 18
FUNCTIONS

Reminder: Before beginning this lesson remember to redo the problems from Lessons 2, 6, 10 and 14 that you have marked off. Do not "unmark" a question unless you get it correct.

Graphs of Functions

If f is a function, then

$f(a) = b$ is equivalent to "the point (a, b) lies on the graph of f."

Example 1:

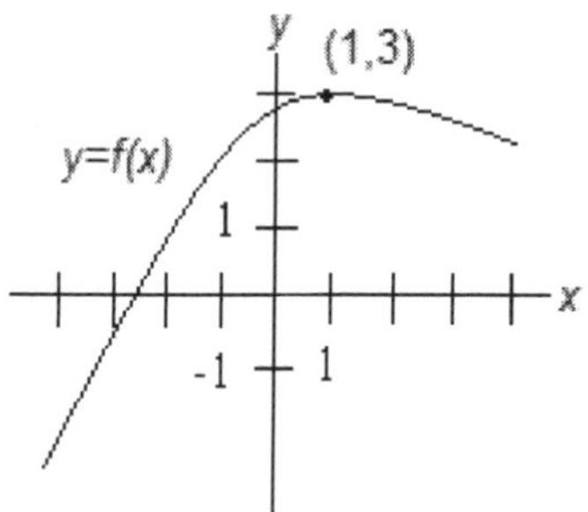

In the figure above we see that the point (1,3) lies on the graph of the function f. Therefore $f(1) = 3$.

Try to answer the following question using this fact. **Do not** check the solution until you have attempted this question yourself.

LEVEL 4: FUNCTIONS

1. In the xy-plane, the graph of the function h, with equation $h(x) = ax^2 - 16$, passes through the point (-2,4). What is the value of a?

Solution

* Since the graph of h passes through the point (-2,4), $h(-2) = 4$. But by direct computation $h(-2) = a(-2)^2 - 16 = 4a - 16$. So $4a - 16 = 4$. Therefore $4a = 20$, and so $a = \mathbf{5}$.

Function Facts

Fact 1: The ***y*-intercept** of the graph of a function $y = f(x)$ is the point on the graph where $x = 0$ (if it exists). There can be at most one y-intercept for the graph of a function. A y-intercept has the form $(0, b)$ for some real number b. Equivalently, $f(0) = b$.

Fact 2: An ***x*-intercept** of the graph of a function is a point on the graph where $y = 0$. There can be more than one x-intercept for the graph of a function or none at all. An x-intercept has the form $(a, 0)$for some real number a. Equivalently, $f(a) = 0$.

Example 2:

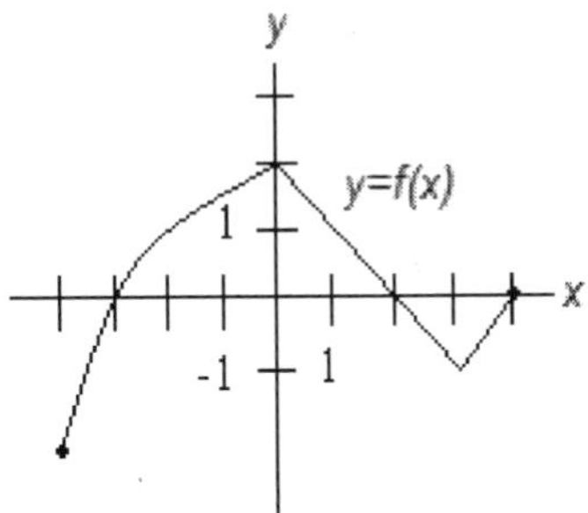

In the figure above we see that the graph of f has y-intercept (0,2) and x-intercepts (-3,0), (2,0) and (4,0).

Fact 3: If the graph of $f(x)$ is above the x-axis, then $f(x) > 0$. If the graph of f is below the x-axis, then $f(x) < 0$. If the graph of f is higher than the graph of g, then $f(x) > g(x)$

Example 3: In the figure for example 2 above, observe that $f(x) < 0$ for $-4 \leq x < -3$ and $2 < x < 4$. Also observe that $f(x) > 0$ for $-3 < x < 2$.

Fact 4: As x gets very large, $\frac{1}{x}$ gets very small.

Example 4: Let $f(x) = \frac{3x^2 + \frac{1}{x}}{x^2}$. Then for large x, $f(x) \sim \frac{3x^2}{x^2} = 3$. So, for example $f(10^{100}) \sim 3$.

Even and Odd Functions

A function f with the property that $f(-x) = f(x)$ for all x is called an **even** function. For example, $f(x) = |x|$ is an even function because

$$f(-x) = |-x| = |x| = f(x).$$

A function f with the property that $f(-x) = -f(x)$ for all x is called an **odd** function. For example, $g(x) = \frac{1}{x}$ is odd because

$$g(-x) = \frac{1}{-x} = -\frac{1}{x} = -g(x).$$

A **polynomial function** is a function for which each **term** has the form ax^n where a is a real number and n is a positive integer.

Polynomial functions with only even powers of x are even functions. Keep in mind that a constant c is the same as cx^0, and so c is an even power of x. Here are some examples of polynomial functions that are even.

$$f(x) = x^2 \qquad g(x) = 4 \qquad h(x) = 3x^8 - 2x^6 + 9$$

Polynomial functions with only odd powers of x are odd functions. Keep in mind that x is the same as x^1, and so x is an odd power of x. Here are some examples of polynomial functions that are odd.

$$f(x) = x^3 \qquad g(x) = x \qquad h(x) = 3x^{11} - 2x^5 + 9x$$

A quick graphical analysis of even and odd functions: The graph of an even function is **symmetrical with respect to the y-axis**. This means that the y-axis acts like a "mirror," and the graph "reflects" across this mirror.

The graph of an odd function is **symmetrical with respect to the origin**. This means that if you rotate the graph 180 degrees (or equivalently, turn it upside down) it will look the same as it did right side up.

So another way to determine if $f(-x) = f(x)$ is to graph f in your graphing calculator, and see if the y-axis acts like a mirror. Another way to determine if $f(-x) = -f(x)$ is to graph f in your graphing calculator, and see if it looks the same upside down. This technique will work for **all** functions (not just polynomials).

Try to answer the following question about even functions. **Do not** check the solution until you have attempted this question yourself.

LEVEL 5: FUNCTIONS

2. For which of the following functions is it true that $f(-x) = f(x)$ for all values of x?

   (A) $f(x) = x^2 + 5$
   (B) $f(x) = x^2 + 5x$
   (C) $f(x) = x^3 + 5x$
   (D) $f(x) = x^3 + 5$
   (E) $f(x) = x + 5$

Solutions

Solution using strategy 4: Let's choose a value for *x*, say *x* = 2. We compute *f*(-2) and *f*(2) for each answer choice.

	f(-2)	*f*(2)
(A)	9	9
(B)	-6	14
(C)	-18	18
(D)	-3	13
(E)	3	7

Since choices (B), (C), (D) and (E) do not match up, we can eliminate them. The answer is therefore choice (A).

Important note: (A) is **not** the correct answer simply because both computations gave the same answer. It is correct because all 4 of the other choices did **not** work. **You absolutely must check all five choices!**

* **Quick solution:** We are looking for an even function. Each answer choice is a polynomial. Therefore the answer is the one with only even powers of *x*. This is choice (A) (remember that $5 = 5x^0$).

Graphical solution: Begin putting each of the five answer choices into your graphing calculator (starting with choice (C) of course), and choose the one that is symmetrical with respect to the *y*-axis. This is choice (A).

Now try to solve each of the following problems. The answers to these problems, followed by full solutions are at the end of this lesson. **Do not** look at the answers until you have attempted these problems yourself. Please remember to mark off any problems you get wrong.

Level 3: Functions

3. The function h is defined by $h(x) = 5x^2 - cx + 3$, where c is a constant. In the xy-plane, the graph of $y = h(x)$ crosses the x-axis where $x = 1$. What is the value of c?

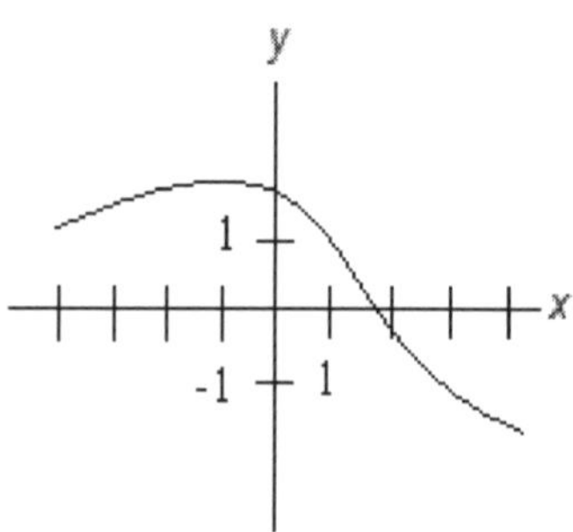

4. The figure above shows the graph of the function f. Which of the following is less than $f(1)$?

   (A) $f(-3)$
   (B) $f(-2)$
   (C) $f(-1)$
   (D) $f(0)$
   (E) $f(3)$

Level 4: Functions

5. If $r^2s > 10^{200}$, then the value of $\frac{rs+\frac{1}{r}}{7rs}$ is closest to which of the following?

   (A) 0.1
   (B) 0.15
   (C) 0.2
   (D) 0.25
   (E) 0.3

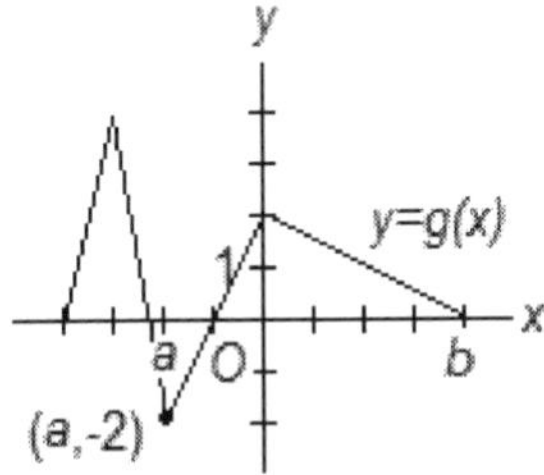

6. The figure above shows the graph of the function g in the xy-plane. Which of the following are true?

I. $g(b) = 0$
II. $g(a) + g(b) + g(0) = 0$
III. $g(a) > g(b)$

(A) None
(B) I only
(C) II only
(D) I and II only
(E) I, II, and III

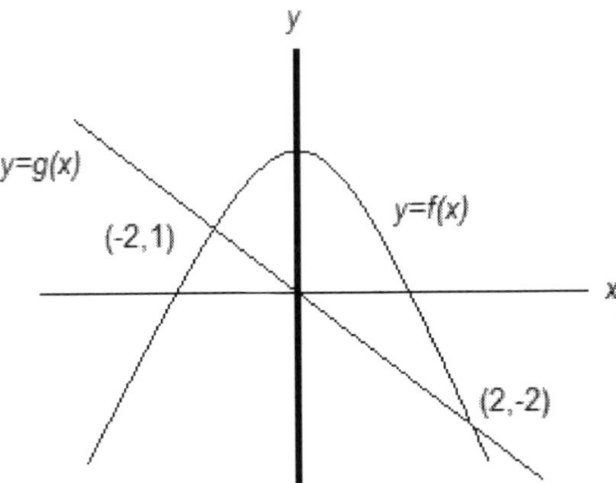

7. In the xy-plane above, the graph of the function f is a parabola, and the graph of the function g is a line. The graphs of f and g intersect at (-2,1) and (2,-2). For which of the following values of x is $f(x) - g(x) < 0$?

(A) -3
(B) -1
(C) 0
(D) 1
(E) 2

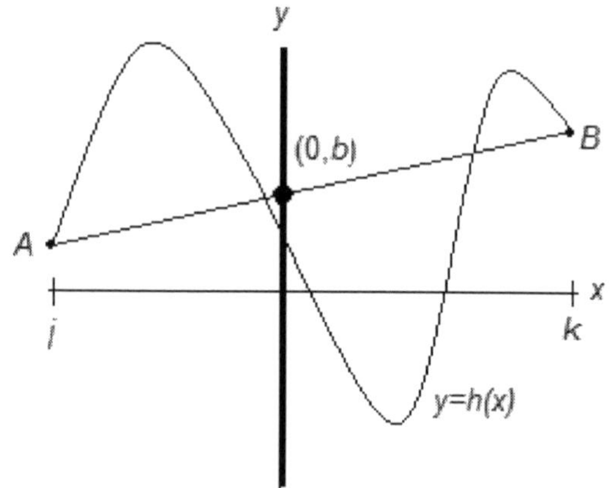

8. The figure above shows the graph of the function h and line segment $\overline{AB}$, which has a y-intercept of $(0, b)$. For how many values of x between j and k does $h(x) = b$?

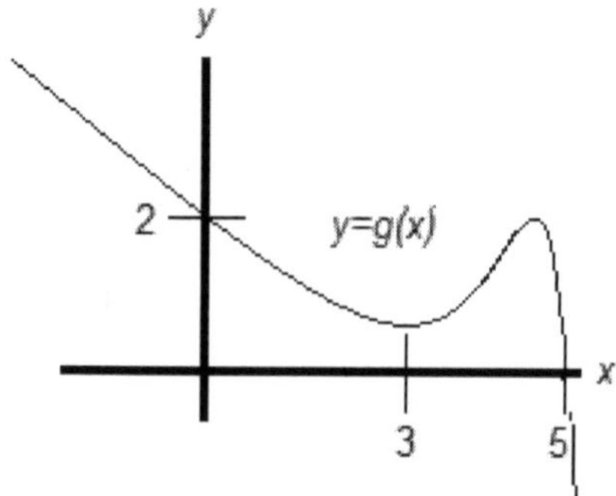

9. A portion of the graph of the function g is shown in the xy-plane above. What is the x-intercept of the graph of the function h defined by $h(x) = g(x - 1)$?

   (A) (1,0)
   (B) (2,0)
   (C) (3,0)
   (D) (4,0)
   (E) (6,0)

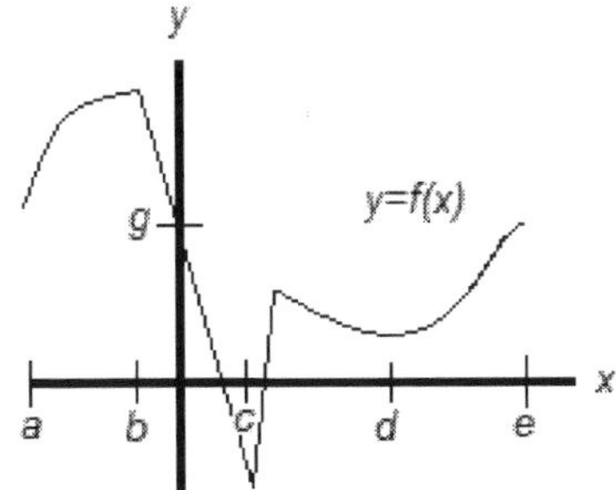

10. The figure above shows the graph of the function f on the interval $a < x < e$. Which of the following expressions represents the difference between the maximum and minimum values of $f(x)$ on this interval?

    (A) $f(b - e)$
    (B) $f(b - c)$
    (C) $f(a) - f(e)$
    (D) $f(b) - f(c)$
    (E) $f(b) - f(e)$

LEVEL 5: FUNCTIONS

x	3	6	9
$f(x)$	5	a	11

x	6	12	24
$g(x)$	1	b	13

11. The tables above show some values for the functions f and g. If f and g are linear functions, what is the value of $7a - 3b$?

12. For all positive integers x, the function f is defined by $f(x) = (\frac{1}{b^5})^x$, where b is a constant greater than 1. Which of the following is equivalent to $f(3x)$?

    (A) $\sqrt[3]{f(x)}$
    (B) $(f(x))^3$
    (C) $3f(x)$
    (D) $\frac{1}{3}f(x)$
    (E) $\frac{1}{9}f(x)$

Answers

1. 5	5. B	9. E
2. A	6. D	10. D
3. 8	7. A	11. 41
4. E	8. 3	12. B

Full Solutions

3.

* A graph crosses the x-axis at a point where $y = 0$. Thus, the point (1, 0) is on the graph of $y = h(x)$. So, $0 = h(1) = 5(1)^2 - c + 3 = 5 - c + 3 = 8 - c$. Therefore $8 - c = 0$, and therefore $c = \mathbf{8}$.

4.

* Let's draw a horizontal line through the point $(1, f(1))$. To do this start on the x-axis at 1 and go straight up until you hit the curve. This height is $f(1)$. Now draw a horizontal line through this point.

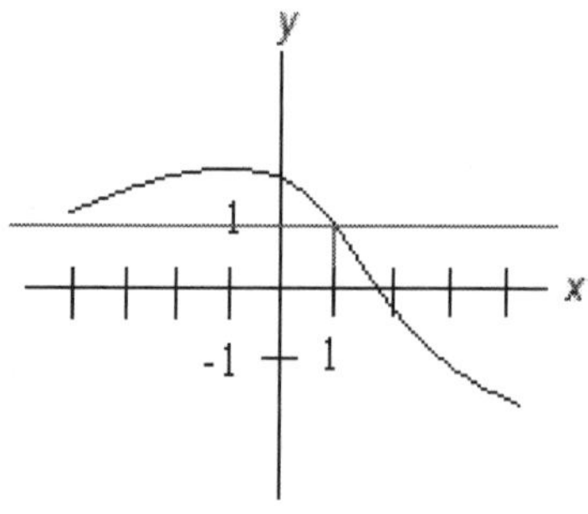

Now, notice that the graph is below this line when $x = 3$. So $f(3)$ is less than $f(1)$. Therefore the answer is choice (E).

5.

Solution using strategy 4: Let's let $s = 1$. Then r must be very large. We cannot make r as large as the problem would like (our calculators will give an error), but we can still plug in a large value for r, say $r = 100{,}000$. So we get $\frac{(100{,}000)(1)+\frac{1}{100{,}000}}{7(100{,}000)(1)} \sim .14286$. The closest number in the answer choices to this value is 0.15, choice (B).

Algebraic solution: Let's simplify the complex fraction by multiplying the numerator and denominator by *r*. Then the expression becomes $\frac{r\left(rs+\frac{1}{r}\right)}{r(7rs)} = \frac{(r^2s+1)}{7r^2s} = \frac{r^2s}{7r^2s} + \frac{1}{7r^2s} = \frac{1}{7} + \frac{1}{7r^2s}$. Since r^2s is very large, $\frac{1}{r^2s}$ is very small, and $\frac{1}{7r^2s}$ is even smaller. So $\frac{1}{7} + 0 = \frac{1}{7} \sim .14286$ is a very close approximation to the answer. The closest number in the answer choices to this value is 0.15, choice (B).

* **A combination of the two methods:** We can begin by plugging in a 1 for *s*. It follows that r^2 is extremely large. Although *r* is much smaller than r^2 it is still extremely large so that $\frac{1}{r}$ is extremely small. So we can approximate the value of the expression by setting $\frac{1}{r} = 0$. So, after setting $s = 1$ and $\frac{1}{r} = 0$ we get $\frac{r}{7r} = \frac{1}{7} \sim .14286$. The closest number in the answer choices to this value is 0.15, choice (B).

6.

* Note that $(a,-2)$, $(0,2)$, and $(b,0)$ are on the graph. Equivalently, we have $g(a) = -2$, $g(0) = 2$, and $g(b) = 0$.

Since $g(b) = 0$, I is true. Also $g(a) + g(b) + g(0) = -2 + 0 + 2 = 0$. So II is true. Since $-2 < 0$, we see that III is false. Thus, the answer is choice (D).

7.

Solution using strategy 1: Let's add some information to the picture.

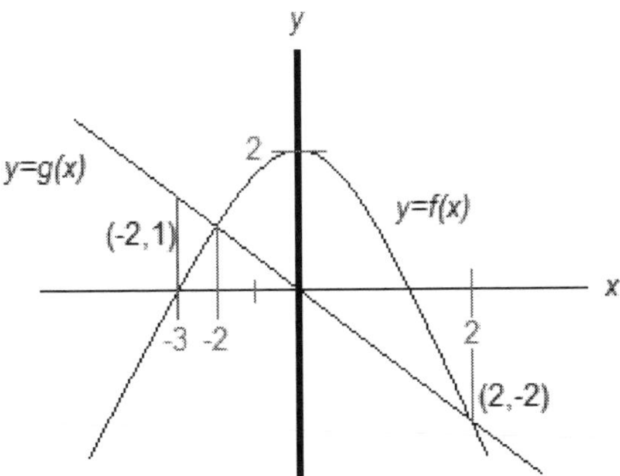

Now let's start with choice (C). Since the point (0,2) is on the graph of *f*, we have that $f(0) = 2$. Since the point (0,0) is on the graph of *g*, we have $g(0) = 0$. So $f(0) - g(0) = 2 - 0 = 2 > 0$. So we can eliminate choice (C).

A moment's thought should lead you to suspect that choice (A) might be the answer (if you do not see this it is okay – just keep trying answer choices until you get there). Since the point (-3,0) is on the graph of f, we have $f(-3) = 0$. It looks like (-3,1.5) is on the graph of g, so that $g(-3) = 1.5$. So $f(-3) - g(-3) = 0 - 1.5 = -1.5 < 0$. Thus, the answer is choice (A).

* **Geometric solution:** $f(x) - g(x) < 0$ is equivalent to $f(x) < g(x)$. Graphically this means that $f(x)$ is lower than $g(x)$. This happens at $x = -3$, choice (A).

Remark: If $-2 < x < 2$, then the graph of f is higher than the graph of g. This means that $f(x) > g(x)$, or equivalently $f(x) - g(x) > 0$. If $x < -2$ or $x > 2$, then the graph of f is lower than the graph of g. This means $f(x) < g(x)$, or equivalently $f(x) - g(x) < 0$.

8.

* Let's draw a horizontal line through the point (0, b).

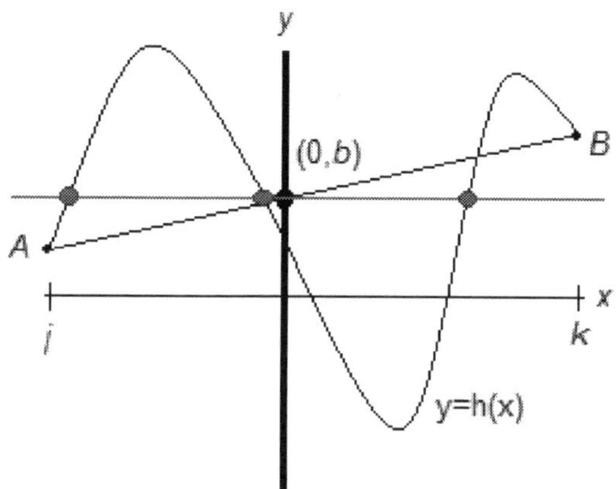

Now, notice that this line hits the graph of h **3** times.

9.

Geometric solution: Since the point (5,0) is on the graph, $g(5) = 0$. It follows that $h(6) = g(6 - 1) = g(5) = 0$. So the point (6,0) is on the graph of h, choice (E).

Remark: Formally, we can solve the equation $x - 1 = 5$ to get $x = 6$.

* **Solution using a basic transformation:** If we replace x by $x - 1$ in the function g, then the graph of g is shifted to the right 1 unit. So the "new" x-intercept is at (6,0), choice (E).

See Lesson 22 for a review of the basic transformations.

10.

* Let's just point out the maximum and minimum values of *f(x)* in the figure.

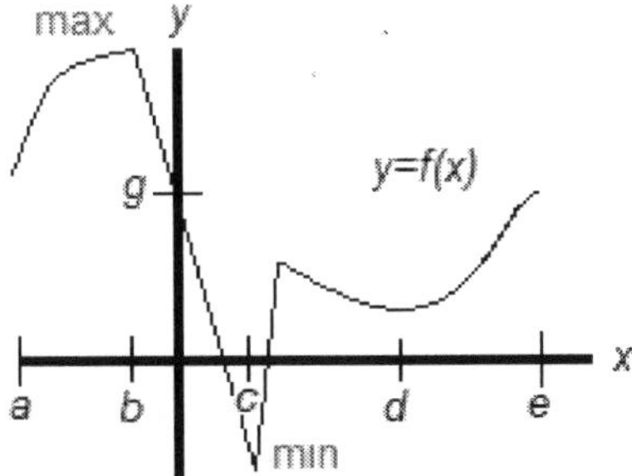

Simply note that the maximum is *f*(b) and the minimum is *f*(c). Thus, the difference between the maximum and minimum is *f*(b) – *f*(c), choice (D).

Note: The maximum and minimum values of a function *f* are always the *y*-coordinates of the points. Equivalently, they have the form *f(x).* We say that the maximum or minimum **occurs** at *x*.

11.

Clever solution: Since the function *f* is linear, "**equal jumps in *x* lead to equal jumps in *f(x)*.**" Note that in the table the jumps in *x* are equal: *x* keeps increasing by 3 units. Therefore the jumps in *f(x)* must be equal. So *a* must be equal to 8.

Similarly, since the function *g* is linear, "**equal jumps in *x* lead to equal jumps in *g(x)*.**" But the jumps in *x* are **not** equal. We can make them equal however if we just slip in the number 18. The "new" table looks like this.

x	6	12	18	24
$g(x)$	1	b		13

Now the jumps in *x* are equal: *x* keeps increasing by 6 units. Therefore the jumps in *g(x)* must be equal. With just a little trial and error it is not hard to see that the jumps in *g(x)* need to be 4, so that *b* = 5.

Finally, we have 7*a* – 3*b* = 7(8) – 3(5) = 56 – 15 = **41**.

Note: By a **jump** in *x* we mean the difference between two *x*-values. For example, in the first table, the jump in *x* when *x* goes from 3 to 6 is 3. Let us abbreviate this as an "*x*-jump." For example, in the first table, the *x*-jump from *x* = 6 to *x* = 9 is 9 – 6 = 3.

* **Quickest solution:** We have that $a = \frac{5+11}{2} = \frac{16}{2} = 8$, and we also have $b = \frac{13-1}{3} + 1 = \frac{12}{3} + 1 = 4 + 1 = 5$. So $7a - 3b = 7(8) - 3(5) = 56 - 15 =$ **41.**

Note about intervals and subintervals: If $a < c$, the length of the interval from a to c is $c - a$. If there are n subintervals between a and c, the length of each subinterval is $\frac{c-a}{n}$. We used this in the quickest solution to find b ($a = 1$, $c = 13$, $n = 3$, and we add the "starting point" 1).

Solution using the slope formula: Let's first compute the slope of the line which is the graph of f. We first need two points. We will use (3, 5) and (9, 11). The slope of the line is then $\frac{11-5}{9-3} = \frac{6}{6} = 1$. We can also use the points (3, 5) and (6, a) to compute the slope. So the slope of the line is $m = \frac{a-5}{6-3} = \frac{a-5}{3}$. So we have $\frac{a-5}{3} = 1$. Therefore $a - 5 = 3$, and so $a = 8$.

Now let's compute the slope of the line which is the graph of g. We will use the points (6, 1) and (24, 13). It then follows that the slope of the line is $\frac{13-1}{24-6} = \frac{12}{18} = \frac{2}{3}$. We can also use the points (6, 1) and (12, b) so that the slope of the line is $m = \frac{b-1}{12-6} = \frac{b-1}{6}$. So we have that $\frac{b-1}{6} = \frac{2}{3}$. Therefore $3(b - 1) = 12$, and so $b - 1 = 4$. Therefore $b = 4 + 1 = 5$.

Finally, we have $7a - 3b = 7(8) - 3(5) = 56 - 15 =$ **41**.

12.

Solution using strategy 4: Let's let $b = 2$. Then $f(x) = \left(\frac{1}{32}\right)^x$. Now let's plug in a value for x, say $x = 1$. Then $f(3x) = f(3) = \left(\frac{1}{32}\right)^3 \sim$ **.00003**. Put a nice, big, dark circle around this number, and now plug $x = 1$ into each answer choice.

(A) $\sqrt[3]{f(1)} = \sqrt[3]{\frac{1}{32}} \sim .315$

(B) $(f(1))^3 = \left(\frac{1}{32}\right)^3 \sim .00003$

(C) $3f(1) = 3\left(\frac{1}{32}\right) = .09375$

(D) $\frac{1}{3}\big(f(1)\big) = \frac{1}{3}\left(\frac{1}{32}\right) \sim .0104.$

(E) $\frac{1}{9}\big(f(1)\big) = \frac{1}{9}\left(\frac{1}{32}\right) \sim .0035$

We can eliminate choices (A), (C), (D), and (E), and therefore the answer is choice (B).

* **Algebraic solution:** $f(3x) = \left(\frac{1}{b^5}\right)^{3x} = \left(\left(\frac{1}{b^5}\right)^{x}\right)^{3} = (f(x))^3$, choice (B).

OPTIONAL MATERIAL

LEVEL 6: FUNCTIONS

1. The graphs of $y = bx^2$ and $y = k - bx^2$ intersect at points A and B. If the length of $\overline{AB}$ is equal to d, what is the value of $\frac{bd^2}{k}$?

Solution

* Let's begin by drawing a picture.

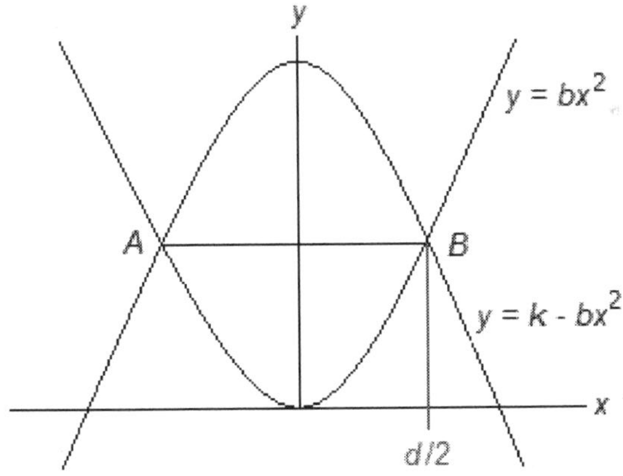

First note that the x-coordinate of point B is $\frac{d}{2}$. Since the two graphs intersect at B, we have $b(\frac{d}{2})^2 = k - b(\frac{d}{2})^2$. So $2b(\frac{d}{2})^2 = k$. Thus, $\frac{2bd^2}{2^2} = k$, so $bd^2=2k$, and therefore $\frac{bd^2}{k}$ = **2**.

Lesson 19
Geometry

Reminder: Before beginning this lesson remember to redo the problems from Lessons 3, 7, 11 and 15 that you have marked off. Do not "unmark" a question unless you get it correct.

Advanced Relationships in Circles

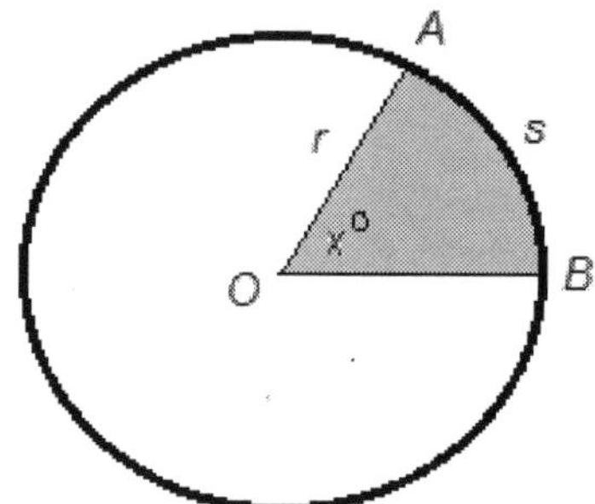

Consider the circle in the figure above. Notice that $\overline{OA}$ and $\overline{OB}$ are both radii of the circle. Therefore $OA = OB = r$. If we know the radius r, then we can find the diameter d of the circle, the circumference C of the circle, and the area A of the circle. Indeed, $d = 2r$, $C = 2\pi r$, and $A = \pi r^2$. In fact, if we know any one of the four quantities we can find the other three. For example, if we know that the area of a circle is $A = 9\pi$, then it follows that $r = 3$, $d = 6$, and $C = 6\pi$.

Now, suppose that in addition to the radius r, we know the angle x. We can then use the following ratio to find the length s of arc AB.

$$\frac{x}{360} = \frac{s}{C}$$

For example, if we are given that $r = 5$ and $x = 45$, then we have

$$\frac{45}{360} = \frac{s}{10\pi}$$

So $360s = 450\pi$, and therefore $s = \frac{450\pi}{360} = \frac{5\pi}{4}$.

In this particular example we can use a little shortcut. Just note that a 45 degree angle gives $\frac{1}{8}$ of the total degree measure of the circle, and therefore the arc length is $\frac{1}{8}$ of the circumference. So $s = \frac{10\pi}{8} = \frac{5\pi}{4}$.

We can also use the following ratio to find the area a of sector AOB.

$$\frac{x}{360} = \frac{a}{A}$$

For example, if again we are given that $r = 5$ and $x = 45$, then we have

$$\frac{45}{360} = \frac{a}{25\pi}$$

So $360a = 1125\pi$, and therefore $a = \frac{1125\pi}{360} = \frac{25\pi}{8}$.

Again, we can take a shortcut in this example and just divide the area of the circle by 8 to get $a = \frac{25\pi}{8}$.

A very difficult problem might give you the angle x and the area of sector AOB and ask you to find the length of arc AB, or vice versa.

Example: Suppose that A and B are points on a circle with center O, the measure of angle AOB is 35 degrees and minor arc AB has length π. What is the area of sector AOB?

We begin by setting up a ratio to find the circumference of the circle.

$$\frac{35}{360} = \frac{\pi}{C}$$

We cross multiply to get $35C = 360\pi$. So $C = \frac{360\pi}{35} = \frac{72\pi}{7}$.

Next we find the radius of the circle using the formula $C = 2\pi r$. So we have $2\pi r = \frac{72\pi}{7}$, and so $r = \frac{36}{7}$.

Now, the area of the circle is $\pi(\frac{36}{7})^2 = \frac{1296\pi}{49}$.

Finally, we set up another ratio to find the area a of the sector.

$$\frac{35}{360} = \frac{a}{(\frac{1296\pi}{49})}$$

We cross multiply to get $\frac{6480\pi}{7} = 360a$. Therefore $a = \frac{6480\pi}{7 \cdot 360} = \boldsymbol{\frac{18\pi}{7}}$.

Now try to solve each of the following problems. The answers to these problems, followed by full solutions are at the end of this lesson. **Do not** look at the answers until you have attempted these problems yourself. Please remember to mark off any problems you get wrong.

LEVEL 2: GEOMETRY

1. In the xy-plane, the point (0, 2) is the center of a circle that has radius 2. Which of the following is NOT a point on the circle?

   (A) (0, 4)
   (B) (-2, 4)
   (C) (2, 2)
   (D) (-2, 2)
   (E) (0, 0)

LEVEL 3: GEOMETRY

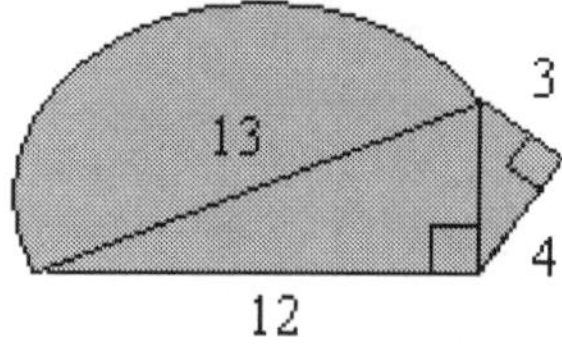

2. What is the total area of the shaded region above to the nearest integer?

LEVEL 4: GEOMETRY

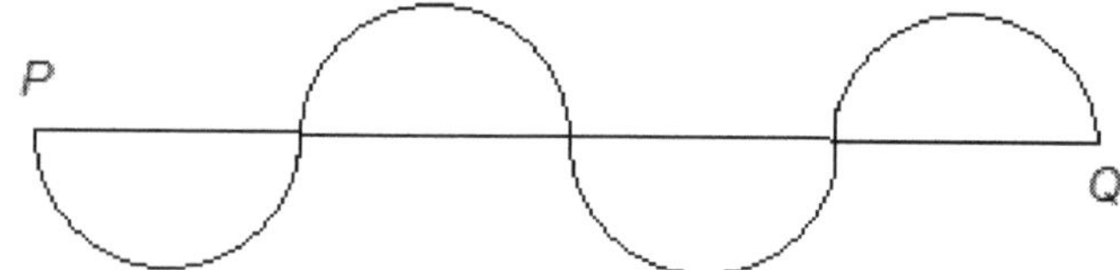

3. In the figure above, the diameters of the four semicircles are equal and lie on line segment $\overline{PQ}$. If the length of line segment $\overline{PQ}$ is $\frac{96}{\pi}$, what is the length of the curve from P to Q?

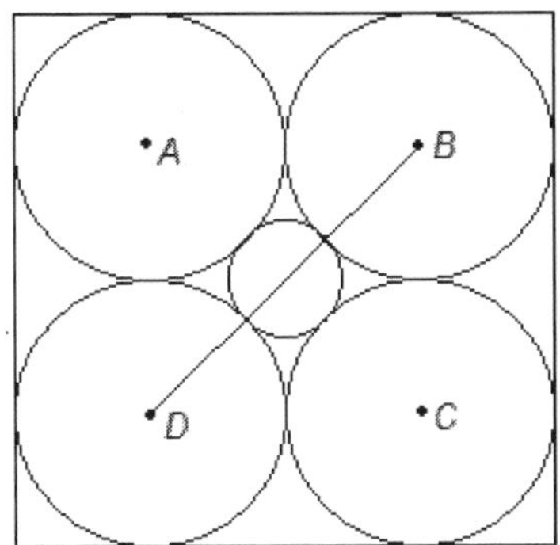

4. In the figure above, each of the points A, B, C, and D is the center of a circle of diameter 6. Each of the four large circles is tangent to two of the other large circles, the small circle, and two sides of the square. What is the length of segment $\overline{BD}$?

(A) $6\sqrt{3}$
(B) $6\sqrt{2}$
(C) $3\sqrt{2}$
(D) 9
(E) 6

LEVEL 5: GEOMETRY

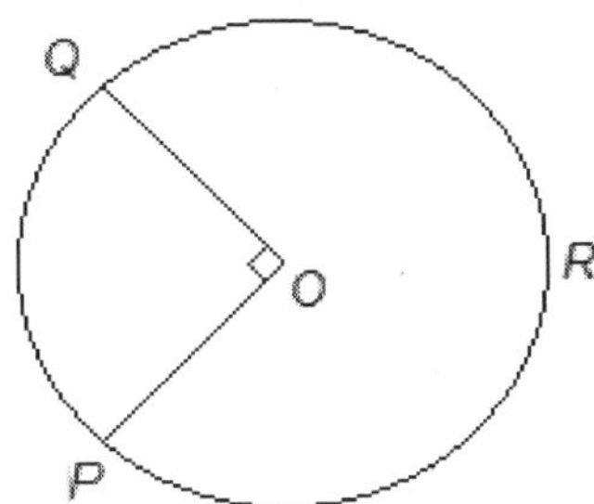

5. In the figure above, the circle has center O and radius 8. What is the length of arc PRQ?

(A) 12π
(B) $24\sqrt{2}$
(C) 6π
(D) $12\sqrt{2}$
(E) $3\pi\sqrt{2}$

6. When the area of a certain circle is divided by 4π, the result is the cube of an integer. Which of the following could be the circumference of the circle?

   (A) 2π
   (B) 8π
   (C) 16π
   (D) 32π
   (E) 64π

7. If the diameter of a circle is doubled, by what percent is the area of the circle increased? (Disregard the percent symbol when you grid your answer.)

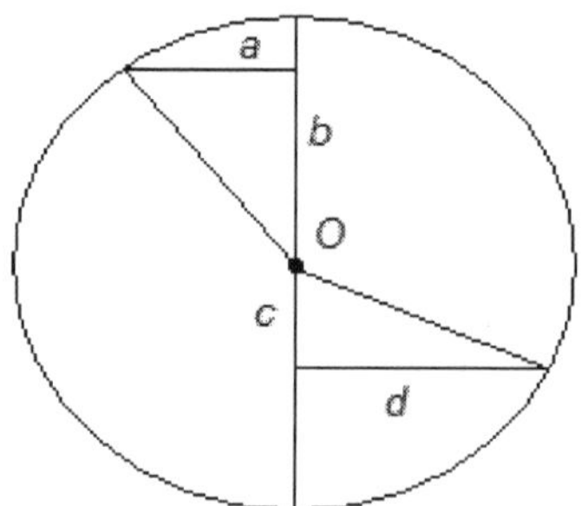

8. In the figure above, O is the center of the circle, the two triangles have legs of lengths a, b, c, and d, as shown, $a^2 + b^2 + c^2 + d^2 = 15$, and the area of the circle is $k\pi$. What is the value of k ?

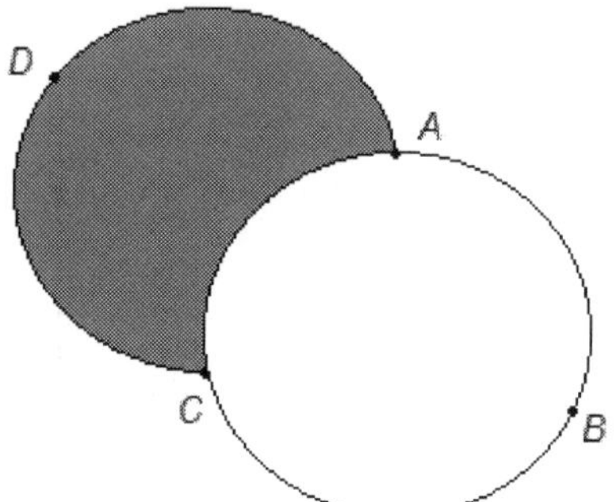

Note: Figure not drawn to scale.

9. In the above figure, arcs ABC and ADC each measure 270 degrees and each of these arcs is part of a circle of radius 8 inches. What is the area of the shaded region to the nearest inch?

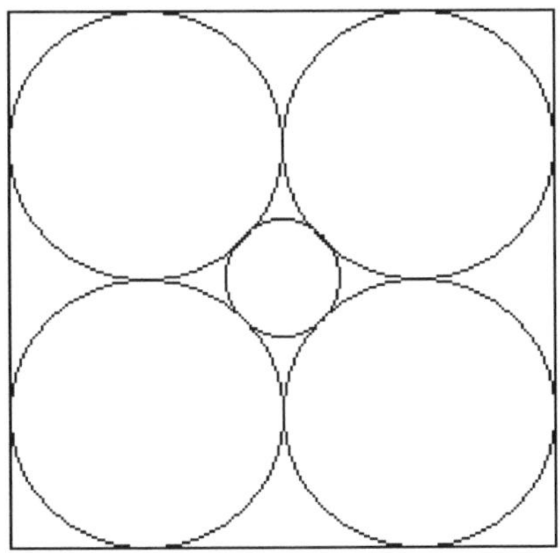

10. In the figure above, each of the four large circles is tangent to two of the other large circles, the small circle, and two sides of the square. If the radius of each of the large circles is 4, what is the diameter of the small circle?

    (A) $\sqrt{2}$ (approximately 1.414)
    (B) 1
    (C) $8\sqrt{2} - 8$ (approximately 3.314)
    (D) $4\sqrt{2} - 4$ (approximately 1.657)
    (E) $\sqrt{2} - 1$ (approximately 0.414)

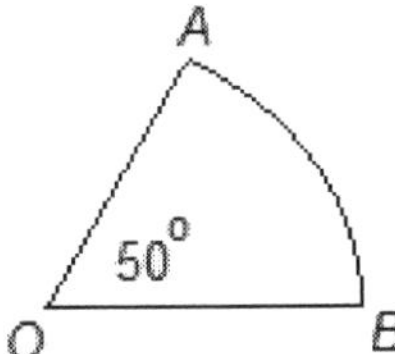

11. In the figure above, AB is the arc of a circle with center O. If the length of arc AB is 4π, what is the area of region OAB to the nearest tenth?

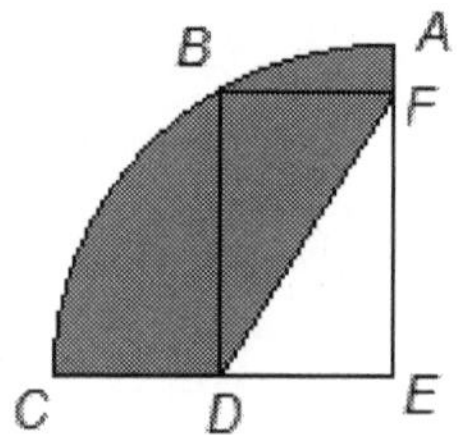

12. In the figure above, arc ABC is one quarter of a circle with center E, and radius 12. If the length plus the width of rectangle $BDEF$ is 16, then what is the perimeter of the shaded region?

    (A) $16 + 16\pi$
    (B) $20 + 6\pi$
    (C) $28 + 6\pi$
    (D) $2 + 12\pi$
    (E) $24 + 12\pi$

Answers

1. B	5. A	9. 165
2. 102	6. D	10. C
3. 48	7. 300	11. 90.5
4. B	8. 15/2 or 7.5	12. B

Full Solutions

2.

* Note that the side not labeled in the picture has length 5. To see this you can use either of the Pythagorean triples 3, 4, 5, or 5, 12, 13. If you do not remember these triples you can use the Pythagorean Theorem:

$$c^2 = 3^2 + 4^2 = 9 + 16 = 25. \text{ So } c = 5.$$

or

$$13^2 = 12^2 + b^2. \text{ So } 169 = 144 + b^2, \text{ and } b^2 = 25. \text{ Thus, } b = 5.$$

Recall that the area of a triangle is $A = \frac{1}{2}bh$. The area of the smaller triangle is $(\frac{1}{2})3 \cdot 4 = 6$. The area of the larger triangle is $(\frac{1}{2})12 \cdot 5 = 30$.

Recall also that the area of a circle is πr^2. Thus, the area of the given semicircle is $(\frac{1}{2})\pi(\frac{13}{2})^2 = (\frac{169}{8})\pi \sim 66.36614481 = 66$ to the nearest integer.

Therefore the total area to the nearest integer is 6 + 30 + 66 = **102**.

3.

* The diameter of each semicircle is $\frac{96}{\pi} \div 4 = 24/\pi$. Thus the circumference of each semicircle is $\frac{1}{2}(\pi)(\frac{24}{\pi}) = 12$. Since we are adding up the lengths of four such semicircles, the answer is (4)(12) = **48**.

Remark: Since a semicircle is half of a circle, the circumference of a semicircle with radius r is $C = \pi r$ (or $C = \frac{\pi d}{2}$).

4.

* We form a right triangle and observe that segments BC and CD each have length 6.

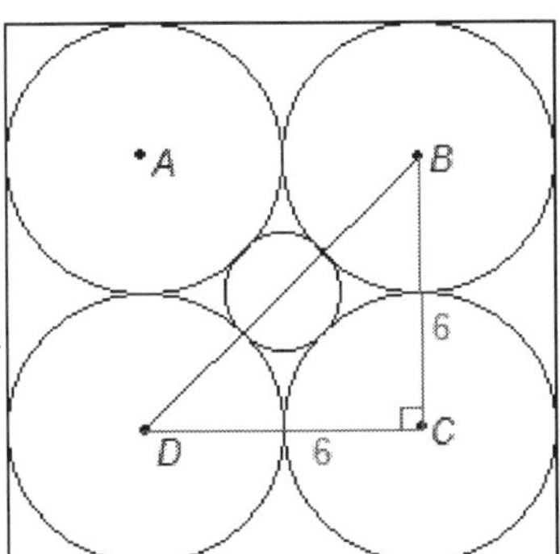

Note that a 45, 45, 90 triangle is formed (or use the Pythagorean Theorem) to get that $BD = 6\sqrt{2}$, choice (B).

5.

Solution using a ratio: Note that there are 270 degrees in arc PRQ and the circumference of the circle is $C = 2\pi r = 16\pi$. So we solve for s in the following ratio.

$$\frac{270}{360} = \frac{s}{16\pi}$$

Cross multiplying gives $360s = 4320\pi$, and so $s = \frac{4320\pi}{360} = 12\pi$, choice (A).

* **Quick solution:** Note that arc PQR is $\frac{3}{4}$ of the circumference of the circle and therefore PQR has length $s = (\frac{3}{4})(16\pi) = 12\pi$, choice (A).

6.
* **Solution using strategy 1:** Let's begin with choice (C) and suppose that the circumference is $C = 2\pi r = 16\pi$. Then $r = 8$ and $A = 64\pi$. When we divide 64π by 4π we get 16 which is **not** the cube of an integer.

Let's try choice (D) next. Then $C = 2\pi r = 32\pi$, so that $r = 16$ and $A = 256\pi$. When we divide 256π by 4π we get 64. Since $64 = 4^3$, the answer is choice (D).

7.
Solution using strategy 4: Let's start with $d = 2$. Then $r = 1$ and $A = \pi$. Now let's double the diameter to $d = 4$. Then $r = 2$ and $A = 4\pi$. We now use the percent change formula.

$$Percent\ Change = \frac{Change}{Original} \times 100$$

The **original** value is π and the **change** is $4\pi - \pi = 3\pi$. So the area of the circle is increased by $(\frac{3\pi}{\pi})\cdot 100 =$ **300** percent.

* **Algebraic solution:** Note that if the diameter is doubled, then so is the radius. So, if the area of the original circle is πr^2, then the area of the new circle is $\pi(2r)^2 = 4\pi r^2$. Thus, the **change** is $4\pi r^2 - \pi r^2 = 3\pi r^2$. Therefore the area of the circle is increased by $(\frac{3\pi r^2}{\pi r^2})\cdot 100 =$ **300** percent.

8.
* Notice that the hypotenuse of each triangle is a radius of the circle. By the Pythagorean Theorem, $a^2 + b^2 = r^2$ and $c^2 + d^2 = r^2$. So,

$$a^2 + b^2 + c^2 + d^2 = 2r^2$$

Since the left hand side of the above equation is also equal to 15, we have that $2r^2 = 15$, and therefore $r^2 = \frac{15}{2}$.

Since the area of a circle is $A = \pi r^2$, we see that $k =$ **15/2** or **7.5**.

9.
* Let's draw some pictures.

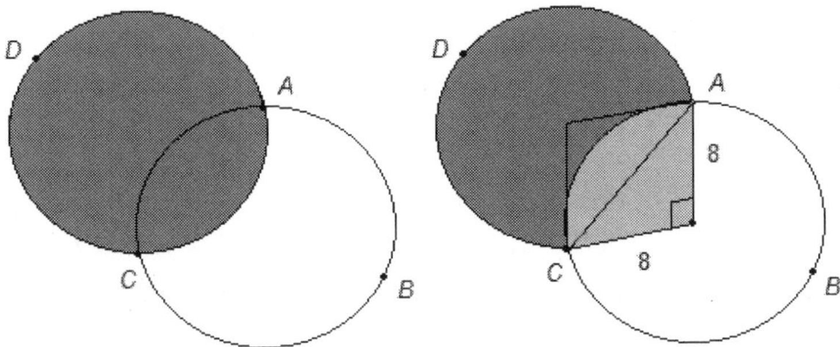

First note that the area we are looking for is the area of the whole circle (the shaded region in the figure on the left) minus the smaller shaded area in the figure on the left. The area of the whole circle is $\pi r^2 = 64\pi$.

We can find half of that smaller area by taking the light grey area on the left minus the light gray triangle on the left in the rightmost figure.

The light grey area is the area of a sector of the circle that is $\frac{1}{4}$ the area of the whole circle. So it is 16π. The area of the triangle is $(\frac{1}{2})(8)(8) = 32$. So half the area we are looking for is $16\pi - 32$.

The final area is $A = 64\pi - 2(16\pi - 32) = 64\pi - 32\pi + 64 = 32\pi + 64$ which to the nearest inch is **165**.

10.

* We draw an isosceles right triangle.

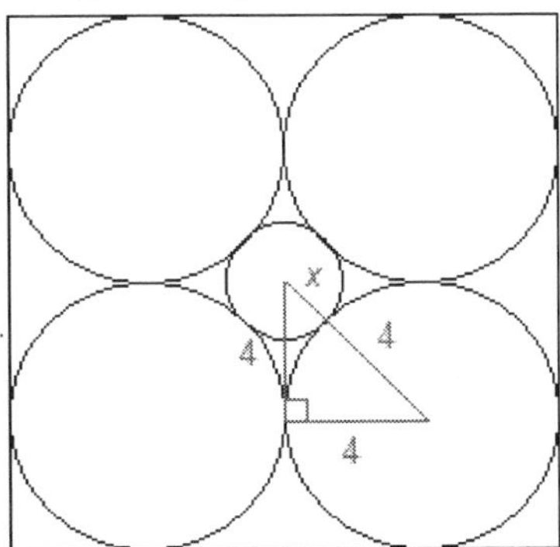

Note that each length labeled with a 4 is equal to the radius of one of the larger circles (the radius is half the diameter). The length labeled x is the radius of the smaller circle. An isosceles right triangle is the same as a 45, 45, 90 right triangle. By looking at the formula for a 45, 45, 90 triangle we see that $x + 4 = 4\sqrt{2}$ and so $x = 4\sqrt{2} - 4$, choice (C).

Remark: We can also use the Pythagorean Theorem to find x. We have $(x + 4)^2 = 4^2 + 4^2 = 16 + 16 = 32$. So $x + 4 = \sqrt{32} = 4\sqrt{2}$ and so $x = 4\sqrt{2} - 4$, choice (C).

Also, if you are uncomfortable simplifying square roots, you can simply perform the computations in your calculator and compare with the numbers next to "approximately" in the answer choices.

11.

* We first find the circumference of the circle using the ratio $\frac{50}{360} = \frac{4\pi}{C}$.

Cross multiplying gives $50C = 1440\pi$, so $C = \frac{1440\pi}{50} = \frac{144\pi}{5}$. Since $C = 2\pi r$, we have $2\pi r = \frac{144\pi}{5}$, so $r = \frac{72}{5}$. The area of the circle is $A = \pi r^2 = \frac{5184\pi}{25}$. Now we find the area of the sector using the ratio $\frac{50}{360} = \frac{a}{(5184\pi)/25}$.

Cross multiplying gives us $360a = 10{,}368\pi$. So $a = \frac{10{,}368\pi}{360} \sim 90.478$. To the nearest tenth this is **90.5**.

12.

* It does not say "Figure not drawn to scale." So let's assume it is. Then $CD = 6$ because it looks like half the radius. Similarly $DE = 6$, and therefore $EF = 16 - 6 = 10$ (because the length plus the width of the rectangle is 16). Now $\overline{EA}$ is a radius, so $FA = 12 - 10 = 2$. $\overline{EB}$ (not drawn) is also a radius. So $EB = 12$. Since both diagonals of a rectangle are congruent, $DF = 12$. The circumference of a circle with radius 12 is

$$C = 2\pi r = 2\pi(12) = 24\pi.$$

Arc AC is a quarter circle, and thus has length $AC = \frac{24\pi}{4} = 6\pi$.

Finally, we just add to get the perimeter.

$$CD + DF + FA + ABC = 6 + 12 + 2 + 6\pi = 20 + 6\pi, \text{ choice (B).}$$

Remark: Although the above method gives us the correct answer, the method of solution is actually **not** correct. Note that triangle DEF is a right triangle, and therefore should satisfy the Pythagorean Theorem. But $DE^2 + EF^2 = 6^2 + 10^2 = 136$. So DF should be approximately 11.66, and **not** 12. The error that we made was in assuming that $CD = DE$. Note that this error does not matter as far as getting the solution is concerned, but the more advanced student should try to solve this problem the correct way (not on the SAT, but at home for practice).

A correct solution for the advanced student: This is quite difficult, and is only included for completeness. Since the length plus the width of the rectangle is 16, if we let $DE = x$, then $EF = 16 - x$. Recall that $\overline{DF}$ is congruent to $\overline{BE}$, and so $DF = 12$, the radius of the circle. By the Pythagorean Theorem, $x^2 + (16 - x)^2 = 12^2$. So $x^2 + 256 - 32x + x^2 = 144$. Simplifying this gives us $2x^2 - 32x + 112 = 0$. We divide through by 2 to get $x^2 - 16x + 56 = 0$. We can use the quadratic formula to solve for x.

$$x = \frac{16 \pm \sqrt{(-16)^2 - (4)(1)(56)}}{2} = \frac{16 \pm \sqrt{32}}{2} = \frac{16 \pm 4\sqrt{2}}{2} = 8 \pm 2\sqrt{2}$$

We let $DE = x = 8 - 2\sqrt{2}$ so that $EF = 16 - x = 16 - (8 - 2\sqrt{2}) = 8 + 2\sqrt{2}$. So $CD = 12 - (8 - 2\sqrt{2}) = 4 + 2\sqrt{2}$ and $FA = 12 - (8 + 2\sqrt{2}) = 4 - 2\sqrt{2}$.

Finally $CD + DF + FA + AC = (4 + 2\sqrt{2}) + 12 + (4 - 2\sqrt{2}) + 6\pi = 20 + 6\pi$, choice (B). (See the original solution above to see where 6π comes from.)

Remark: We could have chosen x to be $8 + 2\sqrt{2}$. The solution would come out the same. The value of x that we chose matches the picture a little better.

OPTIONAL MATERIAL

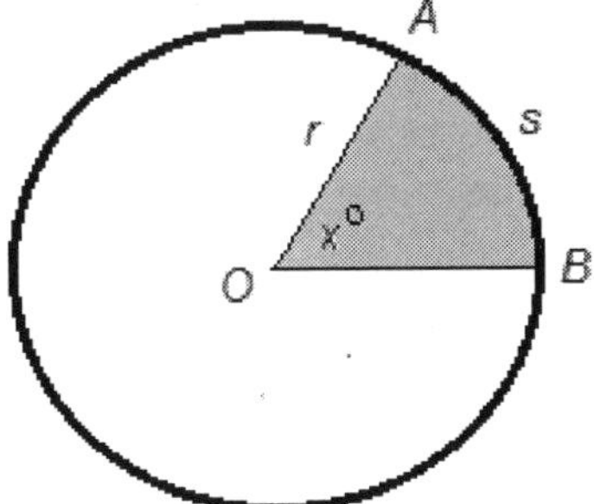

If we solve for s and a in the ratios $\frac{x}{360} = \frac{s}{C}$ and $\frac{x}{360} = \frac{a}{A}$, we get

$$\boldsymbol{s = \frac{\pi r x}{180}} \qquad \text{and} \qquad \boldsymbol{a = \frac{\pi r^2 x}{360}}$$

If you like you can memorize these formulas. I prefer to just set up the ratios.

LESSON 20
STATISTICS

Reminder: Before beginning this lesson remember to redo the problems from Lessons 4, 8, 12 and 16 that you have marked off. Do not "unmark" a question unless you get it correct.

The Median of a Set of Consecutive Integers

If x is the least integer in a list of $n+1$ consecutive integers, then the median of the set is $x+\frac{n}{2}$.

Example: Compute the median of 5, 6, 7,..., 127.

By the fence-post formula there are 127 – 5 + 1 = 123 integers in this list. Therefore the median is 5 + 122/2 = **66**.

Remarks: (1) See Lesson 13 for a review of the fence-post formula.

(2) Note that if the number of integers in the list is odd, the median will be an integer. If the number of integers in the list is even, the median will not be an integer.

(3) If the number of integers in the list is even, then there are two middle numbers, and the median is the average of these two numbers.

Try to solve each of the following problems. The answers to these problems, followed by full solutions are at the end of this lesson. **Do not** look at the answers until you have attempted these problems yourself. Please remember to mark off any problems you get wrong.

LEVEL 1: STATISTICS

1. For which of the following lists of 5 numbers is the average (arithmetic mean) greater than the median?

   (A) 3, 3, 5, 8, 8
   (B) 2, 3, 5, 6, 7
   (C) 3, 3, 5, 7, 7
   (D) 3, 4, 5, 6, 7
   (E) 1, 4, 5, 6, 7

LEVEL 3: STATISTICS

2. Set X contains only the integers 0 through 180 inclusive. If a number is selected at random from X, what is the probability that the number selected will be greater than the median of the numbers in X?

TEST GRADES OF STUDENTS IN MATH CLASS

Test Grade	60	65	75	95	100
Number of students with that grade	3	12	4	5	1

3. The test grades of the 25 students in a math class are shown in the chart above. What is the median test grade for the class?

4. Daniel and eight other students took two exams, and each exam yielded an integer grade for each student. The two grades for each student were added together. The sum of these two grades for each of the nine students was 150, 183, 100, 126, 151, 171, 106, 164, and Daniel's sum, which was the median of the nine sums. If Daniel's first test grade was 70, what is one possible grade Daniel could have received on the second test?

LEVEL 4: STATISTICS

5. On a certain exam, the median grade for a group of 25 students is 67. If the highest grade on the exam is 90, which of the following could be the number of students that scored 67 on the exam?

   I. 5
   II. 20
   III. 24

   (A) I only
   (B) III only
   (C) I and II only
   (D) I and III only
   (E) I, II, and III

6. If the average (arithmetic mean) of a, b, and 37 is 42, what is the average of a and b?

7. A farmer purchased several animals from a neighboring farmer: 6 animals costing \$100 each, 10 animals costing \$200 each, and k animals costing \$400 each, where k is a positive odd integer. If the median price for all the animals was \$200, what is the greatest possible value of k?

8. If the average (arithmetic mean) of k and $k + 7$ is b and if the average of k and $k - 11$ is c, what is the sum of b and c?

   (A) $2k - 2$
   (B) $2k - 1$
   (C) $2k$
   (D) $2k + \frac{1}{2}$
   (E) $4k$

9. Twenty six people were playing a game. 1 person scored 50 points, 3 people scored 60 points, 4 people scored 70 points, 5 people scored 80 points, 6 people scored 90 points, and 7 people scored 100 points. Which of the following correctly shows the order of the median, mode and average (arithmetic mean) of the 26 scores?

   (A) average < median< mode
   (B) average < mode < median
   (C) median < mode < average
   (D) median < average < mode
   (E) mode < median < average

10. If the average (arithmetic mean) of the measures of two noncongruent angles of an isosceles triangle is 75°, which of the following is the measure of one of the angles of the triangle?

   (A) 110°
   (B) 120°
   (C) 130°
   (D) 140°
   (E) 150°

LEVEL 5: STATISTICS

11. Let a, b and c be numbers with $a < b < c$ such that the average of a and b is 7, the average of b and c is 11, and the average of a and c is 10. What is the average of a, b and c?

$$\frac{1}{x^3}, \frac{1}{x^2}, \frac{1}{x}, x^2, x^3$$

12. If $-1 < x < 0$, what is the median of the five numbers in the list above?

    (A) $\frac{1}{x^3}$
    (B) $\frac{1}{x^2}$
    (C) $\frac{1}{x}$
    (D) x^2
    (E) x^3

Answers

1. A	5. E	9. A
2. .497	6. 89/2 or 44.5	10. B
3. 65	7. 15	11. 28/3 or 9.33
4. 80 or 81	8. A	12. E

Full Solutions

2.

* There are a total of 181 integers and 90 of them are greater than the median. So the desired probability is $\frac{90}{181}$ ~ .4972375691. So we grid in **.497**.

Remark: By the fence-post formula there are 180 – 0 + 1 = 181 integers in the list. Thus, the median of the numbers in set *X* is 0 + $\frac{180}{2}$ = 90.

Again, by the fence-post formula, there are 180 – 91 + 1 = 90 integers greater than the median.

3.

Solution by listing: Let's list the test grades in increasing order, including repetitions.

60, 60 ,60, 65, 65, 65, 65, 65, 65, 65, 65, 65, 65, 65, 65, 75, 75, 75, 75, 95, 95, 95, 95, 95, 100

Now strike off two numbers at a time simultaneously, one from each end until just one number is left.

~~60~~, ~~60~~ ,~~60~~, ~~65~~, ~~65~~, ~~65~~, ~~65~~, ~~65~~, ~~65~~, ~~65~~, ~~65~~, ~~65~~, 65, ~~65~~, ~~65~~, ~~75~~, ~~75~~, ~~75~~, ~~75~~, ~~95~~, ~~95~~, ~~95~~, ~~95~~, ~~95~~, ~~100~~

We see that the answer is **65**.

* **Doing it in your head:** You can do this problem very quickly without writing anything down. If we "strike off" the 100, the 5 95's and the 4 75's (for a total of 10 numbers), then we should "strike off" the 3 60's, and 7 of the 65's. Since there are more 65s, the median is **65**.

Remark: If *n* numbers are listed in increasing (or decreasing) order, with *n* odd, then the median of these numbers is the *k*th number where $k = \frac{n+1}{2}$. In this example, $n = 25$. So $k = \frac{26}{2} = 13$, and the 13th test grade is 65.

4.

* Let's begin by writing the sums in increasing order.

100, 106, 126, 150, 151, 164, 171, 183

Since Daniel's sum is the median, it is 150 or 151. Let's pick one, say 150. Since Daniel's first test grade was 70, it follows that his second test grade was 150 – 70 = **80**.

Remark: The other choice yields the answer 151 – 70 = **81**.

5.

* The highest exam grade must be 90. If the other 24 exam grades are 67, then the median will be 67. So III is possible.

If 5 of the exam grades are 90 and the remaining 20 are 67, then the median will be 67. So II is possible.

Finally, if 10 of the exam grades are 90, 10 are 60 and 5 are 67, then the median will be 67. So I is possible.

Therefore the answer is choice (E).

6.

*** Solution using Strategy 20:** The Sum of the 3 numbers is $42 \cdot 3 = 126$. Thus, $a + b + 37 = 126$, and it follows that $a + b = 89$. So the Average of a and b is **89/2** = **44.5**.

Solution using Strategy 4: Let's let $a = 42$ and $b = 47$. We make this choice because 37 and 47 are both 5 units from 42. Then the average of a and b is $\frac{a+b}{2} = \frac{42+47}{2}$ = **89/2** = **44.5**.

7.

*** Solution by listing:** Let's list the prices in increasing order, including repetitions.

100, 100, 100, 100, 100, 100, 200, 200, 200, 200, 200, 200, 200, 200, 200, **200**, 400,...

In order for k to be as large as possible we need the 200 in bold to be the median. Since there are 15 numbers **before** the bold 200, we need 15 numbers **after** the bold 200 as well. So k = **15**.

8.

*** Solution using Strategy 20:** Note that the sum of k and $k + 7$ is $k + (k + 7) = 2k + 7$, so that $2k + 7 = 2b$. Similarly, the sum of k and $k - 11$ is $k + (k - 11) = 2k - 11$ so that $2k - 11 = 2c$. So,

$$2b + 2c = 4k - 4$$
$$2(b + c) = 4k - 4$$
$$b + c = \frac{4k-4}{2} = \frac{4k}{2} - \frac{4}{2} = 2k - 2$$

Thus, the answer is choice (A).

Solution using Strategy 4: Let us choose a value for k, say $k = 5$. It follows that $k + 7 = 5 + 7 = 12$ and $k - 11 = 5 - 11 = -6$. So,

$$b = \frac{5+12}{2} = \frac{17}{2} = 8.5$$
$$c = \frac{5-6}{2} = -\frac{1}{2} = -0.5$$

and the sum of b and c is $b + c = 8.5 - 0.5$ = **8**. **Put a nice big, dark circle around this number so that you can find it easily later.** We now substitute $k = 5$ into each answer choice.

(A) 8
(B) 9
(C) 10
(D) 10.5
(E) 20

Compare each of these numbers to the number that we put a nice big, dark circle around. Since (B), (C), (D) and (E) are incorrect we can eliminate them. Therefore the answer is choice (A).

Important note: (A) is **not** the correct answer simply because it is equal to 8. It is correct because all 4 of the other choices are **not** 8. **You** absolutely must check all five choices!

9.

* The median of 26 numbers is the average of the 13th and 14th numbers when the numbers are listed in increasing order (see remark below).

50, 60, 60, 60, 70, 70, 70, 70, 80, 80, 80, 80, **80**, **90**

So we see that the median is $\frac{80 + 90}{2}$ = 85.

The mode is the number that appears most frequently. This is **100**.

Finally, we compute the average.

$$\frac{1\cdot 50 + 3\cdot 60 + 4\cdot 70 + 5\cdot 80 + 6\cdot 90 + 7\cdot 100}{26} = \frac{2150}{26} \sim 82.69.$$

Thus, we see that average < median < mode. This is choice (A).

Remark: If n numbers are listed in increasing (or decreasing) order, with n even, then the median of these numbers is the average of the kth and (k + 1)st numbers where $k = \frac{n}{2}$. In this example, n = 26. So k = 13, and the 13th and 14th numbers are 80 and 90. (Compare this with the remark at the end of the solution to problem 5.)

10.

* **Solution using strategy 20:** The Sum of the measures of the two noncongruent angles of the isosceles triangle is (75)(2) = 150°.

Thus, the third angle is 180 – 150 = 30°. Since the triangle is isosceles, one of the original angles must also be 30°. It follows that the other original angle was 180 – 30 – 30 = 120°, choice (B).

11.

*** Solution using strategy 20:** We change the averages to sums.

$$a + b = 14$$

$$b + c = 22$$

$$a + c = 20$$

Adding these 3 equations gives us $2a + 2b + 2c = 56$. So $a + b + c = 28$. Finally, we divide by 3 to get that the average of a, b and c is **28/3**.

Remark: We can also grid in the decimal **9.33**.

12.

*** Solution using strategy 4:** Let's choose $x = -0.5$.

We use our calculator to compute the given expressions.

$$\frac{1}{x^3} = -8 \quad \frac{1}{x^2} = 4 \quad \frac{1}{x} = -2 \quad x^2 = 0.25 \quad x^3 = -0.125$$

Now let's place them in increasing order.

-8, -2, -0.125, 0.25, 4

The median is -0.125 which is x^3, choice (E).

OPTIONAL MATERIAL

CHALLENGE QUESTIONS: STATISTICS

1. Show that if x is the least integer in a set of $n + 1$ consecutive integers, then the median of the set is $x + \frac{n}{2}$.

2. Show that in a set of consecutive integers, the average (arithmetic mean) and median are equal.

Solutions

1.

Assume that the integers are written in increasing order. If n is even, then $n + 1$ is odd, and the median is in position $\frac{n+2}{2} = \frac{n}{2} + 1$. Note that $x = x + 0$ is in the 1st position, $x + 1$ is in the 2nd position, etc. Thus, $x + \frac{n}{2}$ is in position $\frac{n}{2} + 1$.

If n is odd, then $n + 1$ is even, and the median is the average of the integers in positions $\frac{n+1}{2}$ and $\frac{n+1}{2} + 1$. These integers are $x + \frac{n+1}{2} - 1$ and $x + \frac{n+1}{2}$. So their average is $(\frac{1}{2})(2x + (n + 1) - 1) = (\frac{1}{2})(2x + n) = x + \frac{n}{2}$.

2.

Let $\{x, x + 1, x + 2, \ldots, x + n\}$ be a set of $n + 1$ consecutive integers. The average is equal to

$$\frac{(n+1)x + (1 + 2 + \cdots + n)}{n+1} = \frac{(n+1)x}{n+1} + \frac{n(n+1)}{2(n+1)} = x + \frac{n}{2}.$$

Remark: See Lesson 13 for methods of showing that $1 + 2 + \ldots + n = \frac{n(n+1)}{2}$.

LESSON 21
NUMBER THEORY

Reminder: Before beginning this lesson remember to redo the problems from Lessons 1, 5, 9, 13 and 17 that you have marked off. Do not "unmark" a question unless you get it correct.

Search for a Pattern

If a question is asking about large numbers, it may be helpful to start with smaller numbers and search for a pattern.

Try to answer the following question by searching for a pattern. **Do not** check the solution until you have attempted this question yourself.

LEVEL 5: NUMBER THEORY

1. In an empty square field, m rows of m trees are planted so that the whole field is filled with trees. If k of these trees lie along the boundary of the field, which of the following is a possible value for k ?

   (A) 14
   (B) 49
   (C) 86
   (D) 125
   (E) 276

Solution

* We will systematically try values for *m*, and draw a picture of the situation to determine the corresponding value for *k*.

Here is the picture for $m = 3$.

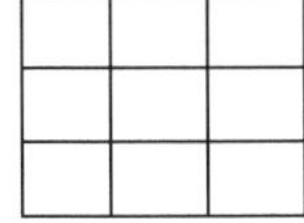

Note that $k = 9 - 1 = 8$.

Here is the picture for $m = 4$.

Note that $k = 16 - 4 = 12$.

So the pattern appears to be 8, 12, 16, 20, 24, 28,... Make sure that you keep drawing pictures until this is clear to you. So we see that the answer must be divisible by 4.

Beginning with choice (C) we have $\frac{86}{4} = 21.5$. So choice (C) is not the answer. We can eliminate choices (B) and (D) because they end in an odd digit. Trying choice (E) we have $\frac{276}{4} = 69$. Thus 276 is divisible by 4, and choice (E) is the answer.

Some rigorous mathematics: Let's prove that for each m, the corresponding k is divisible by 4. For fixed m, the total number of trees is m^2, and the total number of trees that are **not** on the boundary is $(m-2)^2 = m^2 - 4m + 4$. Thus, the number of trees on the boundary is

$$k = m^2 - (m^2 - 4m + 4) = m^2 - m^2 + 4m - 4 = 4m - 4 = 4(m - 1)$$

which is divisible by 4.

Sums and Products of Odd and Even Integers

The following describes what happens when you add and multiply various combinations of even and odd integers.

$$\begin{array}{ll} e + e = e & ee = e \\ e + o = o & eo = e \\ o + e = o & oe = e \\ o + o = e & oo = o \end{array}$$

For example, the sum of an even and an odd integer is odd ($e + o = o$).

Try to answer the following question. **Do not** check the solution until you have attempted this question yourself.

Level 5: Number Theory

2. If x and y are integers and $x^2y + xy^2 + x^2y^2$ is odd, which of the following statements must be true?

I. x is odd
II. xy is odd
III. $x + y$ is odd

(A) I only
(B) II only
(C) III only
(D) I and II only
(E) I, II, and III

Solution

* Note that $x^2y + xy^2 + x^2y^2 = xy(x + y + xy)$. The only way a product can be odd is if each factor is odd. Therefore x, y and $x + y + xy$ all must be odd. Since the product of two odd integers is odd, xy must also be odd. If $x + y$ were odd, then $x + y + xy$ would be the sum of two odds, thus even. Thus, $x + y$ cannot be odd. Therefore the answer is choice (D).

Sequences and Products of Consecutive Integers

In a sequence of two consecutive integers, one of the integers is always divisible by 2 (even). In a sequence of three consecutive integers, one of the integers is always divisible by 3. In general, in a sequence of n consecutive integers, one of the integers is always divisible by n.

It follows that the product of n consecutive integers is divisible by $n!$. For example, the product of two consecutive integers is divisible by 2! = 2, the product of three consecutive integers is divisible by 3! = 6, and the product of four consecutive integers is divisible by 4! = 24, etc.

Try to answer the following question. **Do not** check the solution until you have attempted this question yourself.

Level 5: Number Theory

3. If n is a positive integer and $k = n^3 - n$, which of the following statements about k must be true for all values of n?

I. k is a multiple of 3
II. k is a multiple of 4
III. k is a multiple of 6

(A) I only
(B) II only
(C) III only
(D) I and III only
(E) I, II, and III

Solution

$$n^3 - n = n(n^2 - 1) = n(n - 1)(n + 1) = (n - 1)n(n + 1).$$

Thus $n^3 - n$ is a product of 3 consecutive integers. The product of 3 consecutive integers is divisible by $3! = 6$, and therefore also by 3. If we let $n = 2$, then $k = 6$. So k does **not** have to be a multiple of 4. Thus, the answer is choice (D).

Before we go on, try to also answer this question using strategy 4.

Solution

Let's try some values for n.

$n = 2$. Then $k = 6$. This shows that II can be false. So we can eliminate choices (B) and (E).

$n = 3$. Then $k = 24$. This is divisible by both 3 and 6.

$n = 4$. Then $k = 60$. This is again divisible by both 3 and 6.

The evidence seems to suggest that the answer is choice (D).

Remark: This method is a bit risky. Since this is a Level 5 problem, there is a chance that some large value of n might provide a counterexample. In this case, it turns out not to be the case, and the answer is in fact choice (D).

Now try to solve each of the following problems. The answers to these problems, followed by full solutions are at the end of this lesson. **Do not** look at the answers until you have attempted these problems yourself. Please remember to mark off any problems you get wrong.

LEVEL 5: NUMBER THEORY

4. The first two numbers of a sequence are 5 and 7, respectively. The third number is 12, and, in general, every number after the second is the sum of the two numbers immediately preceding it. How many of the first 400 numbers in the sequence are odd?

   (A) 268
   (B) 267
   (C) 266
   (D) 134
   (E) 133

5. If $\frac{jk}{v}$ is an integer which of the following must also be an integer?

   (A) jkv
   (B) $\frac{3j^2k^2}{v^2}$
   (C) $\frac{jv}{k}$
   (D) $\frac{kv}{j}$
   (E) $\frac{j}{kv}$

6. In how many of the integers from 1 to 150 does the digit 7 appear at least once?

7. If n is a positive integer such that the units (ones) digit of $n^2 + 4n$ is 7 and the units digit of n is <u>not</u> 7, what is the units digit of $n + 3$?

8. A list consists of 20 consecutive positive integers. Which of the following could be the number of integers in the list that are divisible by 19?

I. None
II. One
III. Two

(A) I only
(B) II only
(C) III only
(D) II and III only
(E) I, II, and III

9. If k, m, and n are distinct positive integers such that n is divisible by m, and m is divisible by k, which of the following statements must be true?

I. n is divisible by k.
II. $n = mk$.
III. n has more than 2 positive factors.

(A) I only
(B) III only
(C) I and II only
(D) I and III only
(E) I, II, and III

10. If $a_k = 5 + 5^2 + 5^3 + 5^4 + \cdots + 5^k$, for which of the following values of k will a_k be divisible by 10?

(A) 5
(B) 17
(C) 66
(D) 81
(E) 99

11. The sum of c and $2d$ is equal to k, and the product of c and $2d$ is equal to j. If j and k are positive numbers, what is $\frac{10}{c}+\frac{5}{d}$ in terms of j and k?

    (A) $\frac{j}{10k}$
    (B) $\frac{10k}{j}$
    (C) $10jk$
    (D) $\frac{10}{j}+\frac{5}{k}$
    (E) $\frac{10}{2j+k}$

12. The integer k is equal to m^2 for some integer m. If k is divisible by 20 and 24, what is the smallest possible positive value of k?

Answers

1. E	5. B	9. D
2. D	6. 24	10. C
3. D	7. 2	11. B
4. B	8. D	12. 3600

Full Solutions

4.

* Start writing out the terms of the sequence.

5, 7, 12, 19, 31, 50, 81, 131, 212, ...

Notice that the pattern is odd, odd, even, odd, odd, even, ...

The greatest number less than 400 that is divisible by 3 is 399. So of the first 399 numbers in the sequence $\frac{2}{3}\cdot 399 = 266$ are odd. The 400th term is odd, and therefore the answer is $266 + 1 = 267$, choice (B).

Remark: Notice that this is also a "remainders in disguise" problem. We checked divisibility by 3 because the pattern repeats every third term. Any term which is divisible by 3 behaves like the third term of the sequence. Any term which has a remainder of 1 when divided by 3 behaves like the first term of the sequence. And any term which has a remainder of 2 when divided by 3 behaves like the second term of the sequence. Here is the sequence listed while keeping track of which remainder it goes with.

remainder 1 (odd)	remainder 2 (odd)	No remainder (even)
5	7	12
19	31	50
81	131	212
343	...	...

5.

Solution using strategy 4: Let's choose values for *j*, *k*, and *v*, say $j = 3$, $k = 4$, and $v = 2$. Then $\frac{jk}{v} = \frac{3 \cdot 4}{2} = 6$, an integer. So the given condition is satisfied. Now let's check the answer choices.

(A) 3*4*2 = 24

(B) 3(9)(16)/4 = 108

(C) 3*2/4 = 1.5

(D) 4*2/3 ~ 2.67

(E) 3/(4*2) = .375

So we can eliminate choices (C), (D), and (E). Let's try another set of numbers, say $j = .5$, $k = 1$, and $v = .5$. Then $\frac{jk}{v} = \frac{.5 \cdot 1}{.5} = 1$. Let's check the remaining answer choices.

(A) .5*1*.5 = .25

(B) 3(.25)(1)/.25 = 3

So we can eliminate choice (A), and the answer is choice (B).

* **Advanced method:** Let $\frac{jk}{v}$ be an integer. Then $\frac{3j^2k^2}{v^2} = 3(\frac{jk}{v})^2$ is an integer because the product of integers is an integer.

Remark: If you are having trouble seeing that the expression in the advanced method is an integer, the following might help. Since $\frac{jk}{v}$ is an integer, we can write $\frac{jk}{v} = n$ for some integer *n*. It then follows that $\frac{3j^2k^2}{v^2} = 3(\frac{jk}{v})^2 = 3n^2$ is an integer because when we multiply integers together we get an integer.

6.

* Let's list these integers **carefully**.

7, 17, 27, 37, 47, 57, 67, **70, 71, 72, 73, 74, 75, 76, 77, 78, 79**, 87, 97, 107, 117, 127, 137, 147

We see that there are **24** such integers.

7.

* By plugging in values of n, we find that for $n = 9$,

$$n^2 + 4n = 9^2 + 4 \cdot 9 = 81 + 36 = 117.$$

So $n = 9$ works, and $n + 3 = 9 + 3 = 12$. So the units digit of $n + 3$ is **2**.

Advanced solution showing the independence of *n*: $n^2 + 4n = n(n + 4)$. So we are looking at positive integers 4 units apart whose product ends in 7. Since 7 is odd, n must be odd. So n must end in 1, 3, 5, or 9. Note that we skip $n = 7$ since the problem forbids us from using it.

If n ends in 1, then $n + 4$ ends in 5, and $n(n + 4)$ ends in 5.
If n ends in 3, then $n + 4$ ends in 7, and $n(n + 4)$ ends in 1.
If n ends in 5, then $n + 4$ ends in 9, and $n(n + 4)$ ends in 5.
If n ends in 9, then $n + 4$ ends in 13, and $n(n + 4)$ ends in **7**.

So n ends in a 9, and $n + 3$ ends in a **2**.

8.

* **Solution using strategy 4:** Consider the following two lists.

1, 2, 3, ..., 19, 20
19, 20, 21, .., 37, 38

The first list consists of twenty consecutive integers with one integer divisible by 19, and the second list consists of twenty consecutive integers with two integers divisible by 19. Thus, the answer is either choice (D) or (E).

Now recall that remainders are cyclical. If we start with a positive integer not divisible by 19, then within 19 integers we will arrive at one that is divisible by 19. Therefore the answer is choice (D).

As an example, if we begin with a positive integer that has a remainder of 1 when divided by 19, then the sequence of remainders is as follows.

1, 2, 3, 4, ..., 17, 18, 0, 1

Recall: In a sequence of n consecutive integers, one of the integers is always divisible by n. In this example we have 20 consecutive integers. So if we take the first 19, then one of these is divisible by 19.

9.
* Let's pick some numbers. Let $k = 3$, $m = 15$, and $n = 30$. Then n is divisible by m, and m is divisible by k. Let's look at each roman numeral now.

I. 30 is divisible by 3. True.
II. 30 = 15·3. False.
III. The factors of 30 are 1, 2, 3, 5, 6, 10, 15, and 30. True.

Since II is false we can eliminate choices (C) and (E). Answer choice (D) would be a good guess at this point. There are now 2 ways to complete this problem:

Method 1: Pick another set of numbers and verify that I and III are still true. This will give more evidence that choice (D) is correct, thus making choice (D) the best guess.

Method 2 (advanced): Let's show that I and III always hold under the given conditions.

Let's start with I. Since n is divisible by m, there is an integer b such that $n = mb$. Since m is divisible by k, there is an integer c such that $m = kc$. Thus, $n = mb = (kc)b = k(cb)$. Since cb is an integer it follows that n is divisible by k.

And now III. Since n is divisible by m, m is a factor of n. We also just showed that n is divisible by k. So k is a factor of n. Also, every integer is a factor of itself. Thus n is a factor of n. So k, m, and n are 3 factors of n. The problem tells us they are distinct.

Therefore the answer is choice (D).

10.
* **Solution by searching for a pattern:** $a_1 = 5$ which is **not** divisible by 10.
$a_2 = 5 + 5^2 = 30$ which is divisible by 10.
$a_3 = 5 + 5^2 + 5^3 = 155$ which is **not** divisible by 10.
$a_4 = 5 + 5^2 + 5^3 + 5^4 = 780$ which is divisible by 10.

Note that a_k is divisible by 10 precisely when k is even. Thus, the answer is choice (C).

Remarks: (1) Make sure to write out as many values of a_k as you need to convince yourself that a_k is divisible by 10 precisely when k is even.

(2) Note that $5 + 5^2 + 5^3 + \ldots + 5^k = 5(1 + 5 + 5^2 + \ldots + 5^{k-1})$. This expression is 5 times an integer so that it is divisible by 5. It will therefore be divisible by 10 if and only if $1 + 5 + 5^2 + \ldots + 5^{k-1}$ is even (divisible by 2). Since each term here is odd, this sum will be even if and only if there is an even number of terms, i.e. k is even.

11.

Solution using Strategy 4: Let's choose values for c and d, say $c = 10$ and $d = 5$. Then $k = c + 2d = 10 + 2(5) = 20$, and $j = c(2d) = 10(2\cdot5) = 100$. Now, $\frac{10}{c}+\frac{5}{d}=\frac{10}{10}+\frac{5}{5}=$ **2. Put a nice big, dark circle around this number so that you can find it easily later.** We now substitute $k = 20$ and $j = 100$ into each answer choice and use our calculator.

(A) 100/(10*20) = .5
(B) 10*20/100 = 2
(C) 10*100*20 = 20,000
(D) 10/100 + 5/20 = .35
(E) 10/(2*100 + 20) ~ .045

Compare each of these numbers to the number that we put a nice big, dark circle around. Since (A), (C), (D) and (E) are incorrect we can eliminate them. Therefore the answer is choice (B).

* **Algebraic solution:** We get a common denominator of $2cd$ by multiplying the numerator and denominator of the left term by $2d$, and the right term by $2c$.

$$\frac{10}{c}+\frac{5}{d}=\frac{10(2d)}{c(2d)}+\frac{5(2c)}{d(2c)}=\frac{20d}{2cd}+\frac{10c}{2cd}=\frac{10(2d+c)}{2cd}=\frac{10k}{j}.$$

This is answer choice (B).

12.

* We are looking for the smallest perfect square that is divisible by the least common multiple of 20 and 24. Now $20 = 2^2\cdot5$, and $24 = 2^3\cdot3$. So $\text{lcm}(20,24) = 2^3\cdot3\cdot5$. The least perfect square divisible by this number is $2^4\cdot3^2\cdot5^2 =$ **3600**.

LESSON 22
ALGEBRA AND FUNCTIONS

Reminder: Before beginning this lesson remember to redo the problems from Lessons 2, 6, 10, 14 and 18 that you have marked off. Do not "unmark" a question unless you get it correct.

Standard Form for a Quadratic Function

The standard form for a quadratic function is

$$\boldsymbol{y - k = a(x - h)^2}.$$

The graph is a parabola with **vertex** at (h, k). The parabola opens upwards if $a > 0$ and downwards if $a < 0$.

Example 1: Let the function f be defined by $f(x) = 7(x - 3)^2 + 5$. For what value of x will the function f have its minimum value?

The graph of this function is an upward facing parabola with vertex (3,5). Therefore the answer is *x* = **3**.

Remark: Note that in this example *k* = 2 and *k* is on the right hand side of the equation instead of on the left.

General Form for a Quadratic Function

The general form for a quadratic function is

$$\boldsymbol{y = ax^2 + bx + c}.$$

The graph of this function is a parabola whose vertex has *x*-coordinate

$$-\frac{\boldsymbol{b}}{\boldsymbol{2a}}$$

The parabola opens upwards if $a > 0$ and downwards if $a < 0$.

Example 2: Let the function f be defined by $f(x) = -3x^2 - 8x + 1$. For what value of x will the function f have its maximum value?

The graph of this function is a downward facing parabola, and we see that a = -3, and b = -8. Therefore the x-coordinate of the vertex is $x = \frac{8}{-6}$ = **-4/3** .

Sum and Product of Roots of a Quadratic Function

Let $\boldsymbol{r}$ and $\boldsymbol{s}$ be the roots of the quadratic equation $\boldsymbol{x^2 + bx + c = 0}$. Then

$$\boldsymbol{b = -(r + s)} \quad \text{and} \qquad \boldsymbol{c = rs}.$$

Try to answer the following question using these formulas. **Do not** check the solution until you have attempted this question yourself.

LEVEL 4: ALGEBRA AND FUNCTIONS

$$(x - 6)(x - 2n) = x^2 - 8nx + k$$

1. In the equation above, n and k are constants. If the equation is true for all values of x, what is the value of k?

Solution

* The left hand side is 0 when x = 6 and x = $2n$. The coefficient of x is the negative of the sum of these roots, so $8n = 2n + 6$, or $6n = 6$. So $n = 1$. The constant term is the product of these roots, so that $k = 6\cdot 2$ = **12**.

Before we go on, try to solve this problem in two other ways.

(1) By plugging in specific values for x (Strategy 4 from Lesson 1).
(2) By multiplying out the left hand side and equating coefficients.

Solutions

(1) Let's plug in some simple values for x.

x = 0: $12n = k$
x = 6: $0 = 36 - 48n + k$

Substituting $12n$ for k in the second equation yields $0 = 36 - 36n$, so that $36n = 36$, and $n = 1$. Finally, $k = 12n = 12\cdot 1$ = **12**.

(2) Multiply out the left hand side (FOIL) to get

$$x^2 - 2nx - 6x + 12n = x^2 - (2n + 6)x + 12n$$

Setting the coefficient of x on the left equal to the coefficient of x on the right yields $-(2n + 6) = -8n$, or $2n + 6 = 8n$, or $6n = 6$. So $n = 1$. Equating the constant terms on left and right yields $12n = k$. Substituting 1 in for n gives $k = 12\cdot 1 =$ **12**.

Special Factoring

Students that are trying for an 800 may want to memorize the following three special factoring formulas.

$$(x + y)^2 = x^2 + y^2 + 2xy$$
$$(x - y)^2 = x^2 + y^2 - 2xy$$
$$(x + y)(x - y) = x^2 - y^2$$

Try to answer the following question using the appropriate formula. **Do not** check the solution until you have attempted this question yourself.

LEVEL 4: ALGEBRA AND FUNCTIONS

2. If $c > 0$, $s^2 + t^2 = c$, and $st = c + 5$, what is$(s + t)^2$ in terms of c ?

   (A) $c + 5$
   (B) $c + 10$
   (C) $2c + 5$
   (D) $2c + 10$
   (E) $3c + 10$

Solution

* $(s + t)^2 = s^2 + t^2 + 2st = c + 2(c + 5) = c + 2c + 10 = 3c + 10$, choice (E).

Basic Transformations

Let $y = f(x)$, and $k > 0$. We can move the graph of f around by applying the following basic transformations.

$y = f(x) + k$	shift up k units
$y = f(x) - k$	shift down k units
$y = f(x - k)$	shift right k units
$y = f(x + k)$	shift left k units
$y = -f(x)$	reflect in x-axis
$y = f(-x)$	reflect in y-axis.

Example: Let $f(x) = x^2$. If you move the graph of f right 3 units and down 2 units you get the graph of the function g. What is the definition of g?

We have $g(x) = (x - 3)^2 - 2$. Here is a picture.

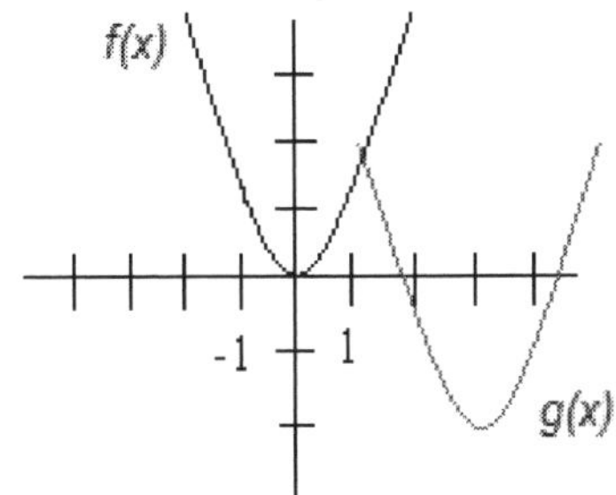

Now try to solve each of the following problems. The answers to these problems, followed by full solutions are at the end of this lesson. **Do not** look at the answers until you have attempted these problems yourself. Please remember to mark off any problems you get wrong.

LEVEL 4: FUNCTIONS

$$y = -5(x - 3)^2 + 2$$

3. In the xy-plane, line ℓ passes through the point (-1,5) and the vertex of the parabola with the equation above. What is the slope of line ℓ?

   (A) $-\frac{4}{3}$
   (B) $-\frac{3}{4}$
   (C) 0
   (D) $\frac{3}{4}$
   (E) $\frac{4}{3}$

4. The function g is defined by $g(x) = 4x^2 - 7$. What are all possible values of $g(x)$ where $-3 < x < 3$?

   (A) $4 < g(x) < 36$
   (B) $0 < g(x) < 36$
   (C) $0 < g(x) < 29$
   (D) $-7 \leq g(x) < 29$
   (E) $-7 \leq g(x) < 0$

$$-2x^2 + bx + 5$$

5. In the xy-plane, the graph of the equation above assumes its maximum value at $x = 2$. What is the value of b?

   (A) -8
   (B) -4
   (C) 4
   (D) 8
   (E) 10

6. For all real numbers x, let the function g be defined by $g(x) = p(x - h)^2 + k$, where p, h, and k are constants with $p, k > 0$. Which of the following CANNOT be true?

   (A) $g(7) = -h$
   (B) $g(7) = 2$
   (C) $g(0) = -2$
   (D) $g(0) = 2$
   (E) $g(-3) = h$

LEVEL 5: ALGEBRA

7. If $x + y = 2k - 1$, and $x^2 + y^2 = 9 - 4k + 2k^2$, what is xy in terms of k?

   (A) $k - 2$
   (B) $(k - 2)^2$
   (C) $k + 2$
   (D) $(k + 2)^2$
   (E) $k^2 - 4$

8. If $x^2 = 9$ and $y^2 = 5$, then $(2x + y)^2$ could equal which of the following?

   (A) 41
   (B) 61
   (C) 121
   (D) $61 - 12\sqrt{5}$
   (E) $41 + 12\sqrt{5}$

9. Let the function g be defined by $g(x) = a(x - h)^2$, where h is a positive constant, and a is a negative constant. For what value of x will the function g have its maximum value?

(A) $-h$
(B) $-a$
(C) 0
(D) a
(E) h

10. For how many integers n is $(4n - 11)(5n + 3)$ a negative number?

(A) None
(B) One
(C) Two
(D) Three
(E) Four

11. If $x^2 - y^2 = 10 - k - 3k^2$, $x - y = 5 - 3k$, and $k \neq \frac{5}{3}$, what is $x + y$ in terms of k?

(A) $k - 2$
(B) $(k - 2)^2$
(C) $k + 2$
(D) $(k + 2)^2$
(E) $k^2 - 4$

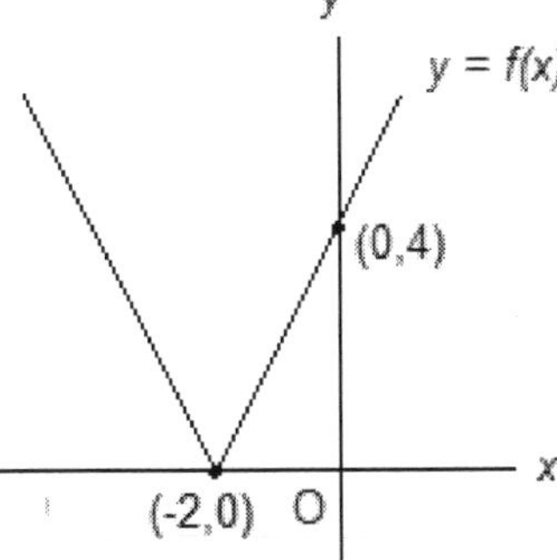

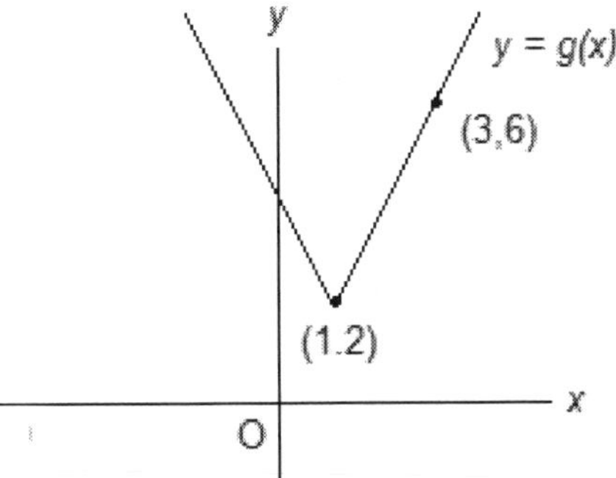

12. The figures above show the graphs of the functions f and g. The function f is defined by $f(x) = 2|x + 2|$ and the function g is defined by $g(x) = f(x + h) + k$, where h and k are constants. What is the value of $|h - k|$?

Answers

1. 12	5. 8	9. E
2. E	6. C	10. D
3. B	7. E	11. C
4. D	8. E	12. 5

Full Solutions

3.

*** Solution using the standard form of a quadratic equation:** The vertex of the parabola is (3,2). Therefore the slope of the line is

$$\frac{5-2}{-1-3} = \frac{3}{-4} = -\frac{3}{4}$$

This is answer choice (B).

4.

Solution using strategy 4: Let's try a value for x in the given range, say $x = 0$. Then $g(x) = -7$. So we can eliminate choices (A), (B), and (C). Let's try $x = 2$ next. Then $g(x) = 4(2)^2 - 7 = 4 \cdot 4 - 7 = 16 - 7 = 9$. So we can eliminate choice (E). Thus, the answer is choice (D).

* **Quick solution:** g is an **even** function. So we need only check the possible values of $g(x)$ for which $0 \leq x < 3$. We have $g(0) = -7$ and $g(3) = 4(3)^2 - 7 = 4(9) - 7 = 36 - 7 = 29$. So the answer is choice (D).

Solution using the general form for a quadratic function: Using the formula $x = -\frac{b}{2a}$ we see that the x-coordinate of the vertex of the parabola is $x = 0$ (since $b = 0$). The parabola opens upwards ($a = 4 > 0$). So the minimum value of $g(x)$ is $g(0) = -7$. We substitute $x = 3$ (or x -= - 3) to find the upper bound: $g(3) = 4(3)^2 - 7 = 4 \cdot 9 - 7 = 36 - 7 = 29$. So we must have $-7 \leq g(x) < 29$, choice (D).

Graphical solution: In your graphing calculator press Y=, and under Y1=, type 4X^2 – 7. Press WINDOW and set Xmin = -3, Xmax = 3, Ymin = -7, and Ymax = 29. Then press GRAPH. The graph is a perfect fit, so the answer is choice (D).

Remark: We chose the window in the last solution by using the smallest and largest values that appear in the answer choices.

5.

Solution using the general form for a quadratic function: Using the formula $x = -\frac{b}{2a}$ we have $-\frac{b}{2(-2)} = 2$. So $b =$ **8**.

Solution using differential calculus: The derivative of $y = -2x^2 + bx + 5$ is $y' = -4x + b$. We set the derivative equal to 0 and plug in $x = 2$ to get $-4(2) + b = 0$, or $b =$ **8**.

6.

Solution using strategy 1: Let's start with choice (C) and suppose that $g(0) = -2$. Then we have $-2 = p(0 - h)^2 + k = ph^2 + k$. Since p and k are greater than 0, $ph^2 + k > 0$. Therefore $ph^2 + k$ CANNOT be -2, and the answer is choice (C).

Eliminating the other answer choices: This isn't necessary to solve the problem, but for completeness let's show that each of the other answer choices CAN be true.

(A) If $g(7) = -h$, then $-h = p(7 - h)^2 + k$. Let $h = -1$. Then $1 = 64p + k$, and so $k = 1 - 64p$. Now let $p = \frac{1}{128}$. Then $k = 1 - \frac{1}{2} = \frac{1}{2}$.

(B) If $g(7) = 2$, then $2 = p(7 - h)^2 + k$. Let $h = 0$. Then $2 = 49p + k$, and so $k = 2 - 49p$. Now let $p = \frac{1}{49}$. Then $k = 2 - 1 = 1$.

(D) If $g(0) = 2$, then $2 = p(0 - h)^2 + k$. Let $h = 0$ and $p = 1$. Then $k = 2$.

(E) If $g(-3) = h$, then $h = p(-3 - h)^2 + k$. Let $h = 1$. Then $1 = 16p + k$, and so $k = 1 - 16p$. Now let $p = \frac{1}{32}$. Then $k = 1 - \frac{1}{2} = \frac{1}{2}$.

7.

Solution by picking numbers: Let $k = 0$. Then $x + y = -1$, and $x^2 + y^2 = 9$.

$$(x + y)^2 = (x + y)(x + y) = x^2 + 2xy + y^2 = x^2 + y^2 + 2xy.$$
$$(-1)^2 = 9 + 2xy$$
$$1 = 9 + 2xy$$
$$-8 = 2xy$$
$$-4 = xy$$

Put a nice big dark circle around the number **-4**. Now substitute $k = 0$ into each answer choice.

(A) -2
(B) 4
(C) 2
(D) 4
(E) -4

Since (A), (B), (C), and (D) came out incorrect we can eliminate them, and the answer is choice (E).

* **Algebraic solution:** We use the first special factoring formula.

$$(x + y)^2 = x^2 + y^2 + 2xy.$$
$$(2k - 1)^2 = 9 - 4k + 2k^2 + 2xy$$
$$4k^2 - 4k + 1 = 9 - 4k + 2k^2 + 2xy$$
$$2k^2 - 8 = 2xy$$
$$2(k^2 - 4) = 2xy$$
$$k^2 - 4 = xy$$

So $xy = k^2 - 4$, choice (E).

8.
* Taking positive square roots in our calculator gives $x = 3$ and $y \sim 2.236$. Substituting into the given expression we get $(2 \cdot 3 + 2.236)^2 \sim 67.832$. Let's see if choice (E) matches with this. We put the number in choice (E) in our calculator to get approximately 67.832. Thus the answer is choice (E).

Remark for the advanced student: There is no reason that choice (E) has to be the answer. The values we got for x and y are not the only solutions to the given equations. x can also be -3, and y can also be approximately -2.236. If the answer we got didn't agree with any of the answer choices we would have to try other values for x and y (there are four possibilities all together).

A complete algebraic solution for the advanced student: I do **not** recommend solving the problem this way on the SAT.

There are two possibilities for x: $x = 3$ and $x = -3$
There are two possibilities for y: $y = \sqrt{5}$ and $y = -\sqrt{5}$
So, there are 4 possibilities for $(2x + y)^2$.

$$(2 \cdot 3 + \sqrt{5})^2 = (6 + \sqrt{5})(6 + \sqrt{5}) = 36 + 6\sqrt{5} + 6\sqrt{5} + 5 = 41 + 12\sqrt{5}$$

Since this is answer choice (E) we can stop. We do not need to do the other three computations. The answer is choice (E).

9.
* **Solution using the standard form of a quadratic equation:** The function $g(x) = a(x - h)^2$ is in standard form and thus has a graph that is a parabola with $(h, 0)$ for its vertex. Since $a < 0$ the parabola opens downwards. Thus the maximum occurs at $x = h$, choice (E).

Graphical solution: Let's choose values for h and a, say $h = 2$ and $a = -1$. So $g(x) = -(x - 2)^2$. If we put this in our graphing calculator we see that the maximum occurs when $x =$ **2**. Substituting our chosen values for h and a into each answer choice yields

(A) -2
(B) 1
(C) 0
(D) -1
(E) 2

We can therefore eliminate choices (A), (B), (C) and (D). Thus, the answer is choice (E).

10.
* We first figure out the **real** numbers where the expression is 0. To do this just set each factor to 0:

$$4n - 11 = 0 \qquad 5n + 3 = 0$$
$$4n = 11 \qquad 5n = -3$$
$$n = \frac{11}{4} = 2.75 \qquad n = -\frac{3}{5} = -.6$$

We want to find all integer solutions of the inequality

$$(4n - 11)(5n + 3) < 0.$$

A good guess is to just count all the integers between -.6 and 2.75. We have 0, 1, and 2. Thus, it seems that there are **three** (more explanation below the remark). The answer to this question is in fact choice (D).

Remark: We choose the "inside" of the two numbers because the answer choices indicate that there must be finitely many solutions - the "outsides" give infinitely many solutions.

Deeper understanding of the mathematics: The given expression is a polynomial (in particular, it is quadratic, so that its graph is a parabola). Polynomials are "continuous everywhere," that is you never lift your pencil from your paper when drawing them. Thus, the only way they can change from positive to negative (or vice versa) is by passing through zero. So once you find the zeros, you need only test one value in each of the intervals determined by these zeros (in this case there are three) to determine if you get negative or positive results in the **whole** interval.

Thus, we need only test 3 values to be certain of our answer - one value less than -.6, one value between -.6 and 2.75, and one value greater than 2.75. Let us choose the numbers -1, 0, and 3.

$n = -1$: $(4n - 11)(5n + 3) = (4(-1) - 11)(5(-1) + 3) = (-15)(-2) > 0$.
$n = 0$: $(4n - 11)(5n + 3) = (4(0) - 11)(5(0) + 3) = (-11)(3) < 0$.
$n = 3$: $(4n - 11)(5n + 3) = (4(3) - 11)(5(3) + 3) = (1)(18) > 0$.

Notice that we didn't need to finish these computations to determine if the result was positive or negative. We just used the fact that the product of two negatives is positive, the product of a negative and a positive is negative, and the product of two positives is positive.

Since 0 gave a negative answer, any number in the interval from -.6 to 2.75 will give a negative answer. Similarly, any number less than -.6 will give a positive answer, as will any number greater than 2.75.

We have now verified that choice (D) is the answer.

Graphical Analysis: The graph of $f(n) = (4n - 11)(5n + 3)$ is an upward facing parabola. To see this we can FOIL the expression to get

$$f(n) = 20n^2 - 43n - 33.$$

All we actually need here is that the first term is $20n^2$. Since 20 is positive, the parabola faces upwards. This analysis shows that it is the middle portion which is negative. So we need only count the integers between -.6 and 2.75. This can be verified by graphing the function in your graphing calculator.

Alternatively, if either of the external intervals were negative, then there would be an infinite number of integer solutions. Since there is no answer choice that allows for this possibility, the only reasonable place to look is between the given roots.

11.

Solution by picking numbers: Let $k = 0$. Then $x^2 - y^2 = 10$ and $x - y = 5$. We have

$$x^2 - y^2 = (x - y)(x + y)$$
$$10 = 5(x + y)$$
$$x + y = \frac{10}{5} = \mathbf{2}.$$

Put a nice big dark circle around the number **2**. Now let's substitute $k = 0$ into each answer choice.

(A) -2
(B) 4
(C) 2
(D) 4
(E) -4

Since (A), (B), (D), and (E) came out incorrect we can eliminate them, and the answer is choice (C).

* **Algebraic solution:** We use the third special factoring formula.

$$(x + y)(x - y) = x^2 - y^2.$$
$$(x + y)(5 - 3k) = 10 - k - 3k^2.$$
$$(x + y)(5 - 3k) = (5 - 3k)(2 + k)$$
$$(x + y) = 2 + k.$$

So $x + y = k + 2$, choice (C).

Remark: The question excludes $k = \frac{5}{3}$ because in this case we cannot divide each side of the equation by $5 - 3k$ (we would be dividing by zero).

12.

* Notice that to get the graph of g we shift the graph of f 3 units to the right, and 2 units up. Therefore $g(x) = f(x - 3) + 2$. So $h = -3$ and $k = 2$. Therefore $|h - k| = |-3 - 2| = |-5| = \mathbf{5}$.

OPTIONAL MATERIAL

LEVEL 6: ALGEBRA AND FUNCTIONS

1. Let f and g be functions such that $f(x) = ax^2 + bx + c$ and $g(x) = ax + b$. If $g(1) = 2b - a + 25$ and $g(2) = 2a - 24$, then for what value of x does $f(x) = f(8)$, where $x \neq 8$?

CHALLENGE QUESTION

2. Show that $x^2 + y^2 + z^2 \geq xy + yz + zx$ for positive numbers x, y, and z.

Solutions

1.

* $g(1) = a(1) + b = a + b$. So $a + b = 2b - a + 25$, and therefore $2a = b + 25$. $g(2) = a(2) + b = 2a + b$, and so $2a + b = 2a - 24$. Thus, $b = -24$. We also have $2a = b + 25 = -24 + 25 = 1$. Thus $a = \frac{1}{2}$.

It follows that $f(x) = \frac{x^2}{2} - 24x + c$, and $f(8) = \frac{8^2}{2} - 24(8) + c = -160 + c$. If $f(x) = f(8)$, then $\frac{x^2}{2} - 24x + c = -160 + c$, and so $\frac{x^2}{2} - 24x + 160 = 0$. Let's multiply each side of this equation by 2 to eliminate the denominator. We get $x^2 - 48x + 320 = 0$. There are several ways to solve this equation.

Factoring: $(x - 8)(x - 40) = 0$. So $x =$ **40**.

Completing the square: We take half of -48, which is -24, and square this number to get 576. We then add 576 to each side of the equation to get $x^2 - 48x + 576 + 320 = 576$. This is equivalent to $(x - 24)^2 = 256$. We now apply the square root property to get $x - 24 = \pm 16$. So $x = 24 \pm 16$. This yields the two solutions $24 - 16 = 8$, and $24 + 16 =$ **40**.

The quadratic formula:

$$x = \frac{-b \pm \sqrt{b^2 - 4ac}}{2a} = \frac{48 \pm \sqrt{2304 - 1280}}{2} = \frac{48 \pm \sqrt{1024}}{2} = \frac{48 \pm 32}{2} = 24 \pm 16.$$

As in the previous solution we get $x = 8$ or $x =$ **40**.

Graphically: In your graphing calculator press the Y= button, and enter the following.

Y1 = X^2 – 48X + 320

Now press ZOOM 6 to graph the parabola in a standard window. It needs to be zoomed out, so we will need to extend the viewing window. Press the WINDOW button, and change Xmax to 100, Ymin to -50, and Ymax to 50. Then press 2nd TRACE (which is CALC) 2 (or select ZERO). Then move the cursor just to the left of the second *x*-intercept and press ENTER. Now move the cursor just to the right of the second *x*-intercept and press ENTER again. Press ENTER once more, and you will see that the x-coordinate of the second *x*-intercept is **40**.

Remark: The choices made for Xmax, Ymin and Ymax were just to try to ensure that the second *x*-intercept would appear in the viewing window. Many other windows would work just as well.

2.

The following inequalities are equivalent.

$$x^2 + y^2 + z^2 \geq xy + yz + zx$$
$$2x^2 + 2y^2 + 2z^2 \geq 2xy + 2yz + 2zx$$
$$(x^2 - 2xy + y^2) + (y^2 - 2yz + z^2) + (z^2 - 2zx + x^2) \geq 0$$
$$(x - y)^2 + (y - z)^2 + (z - x)^2 \geq 0$$

Since the last inequality is obviously true, so is the original inequality.

Lesson 23
Geometry

Reminder: Before beginning this lesson remember to redo the problems from Lessons 3, 7, 11, 15 and 19 that you have marked off. Do not "unmark" a question unless you get it correct.

The Generalized Pythagorean Theorem

The length d of the long diagonal of a rectangular solid is given by

$$d^2 = a^2 + b^2 + c^2$$

where a, b and c are the length, width and height of the rectangular solid.

Example: Find the length of the longest line segment with endpoints on a cube with side length 11.

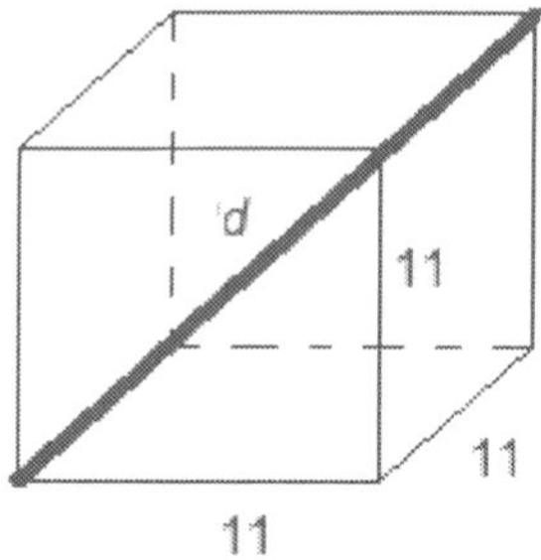

* In this example, our rectangular solid is a cube with a, b and c all equal to 11. So $d^2 = a^2 + b^2 + c^2 = 11^2 + 11^2 + 11^2 = 11^2 \cdot 3$. So $d = \mathbf{11\sqrt{3}}$.

Strategy 31 – Open Up a Cylinder to Get a Rectangle

When we cut a cylinder down the height and open it up we get a rectangle. One side of the rectangle has the height of the cylinder as its length. The other side has the circumference of a base of the cylinder as its length.

You may want to take a flat rectangular object such as a piece of paper or paper towel and put two sides together to form a cylinder. Open and close your cylinder and note how one of the sides of the rectangle corresponds to the circumference of the cylinder.

Try to answer the following question using this strategy. **Do not** check the solution until you have attempted this question yourself.

LEVEL 5: GEOMETRY

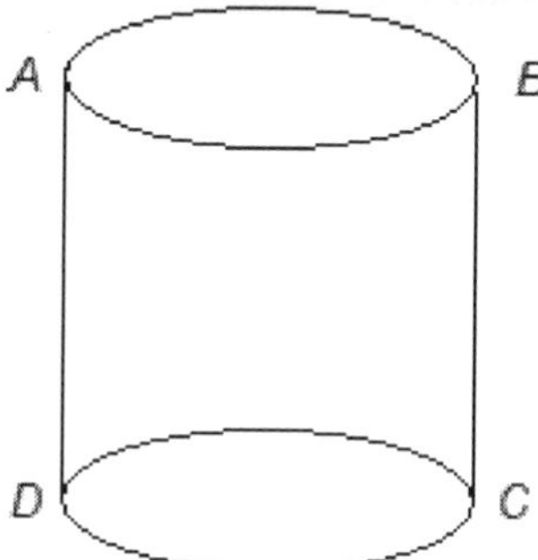

1. The figure shown above is a right circular cylinder. The circumference of each circular base is 20, the length of AD is 14, and AB and CD are diameters of each base respectively. If the cylinder is cut along AD, opened, and flattened, what is the length of AC to the nearest tenth?

Solution

* When we cut and unfold the cylinder as described we get the following rectangle.

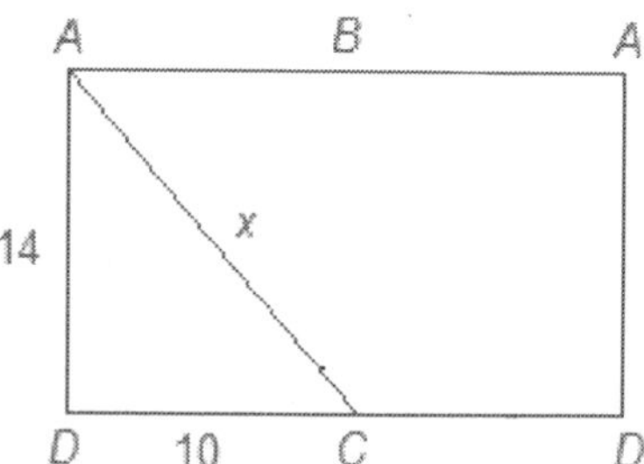

Notice that *C* is right in the middle of the rectangle. A common error would be to put *C* as one of the vertices. Note also that the length of the rectangle is 20 so that *DC* is 10. We can now use the Pythagorean Theorem to find *AC*.

$$x^2 = 10^2 + 14^2 = 100 + 196 = 296$$
$$x = \sqrt{296} \sim 17.20465$$

Since the question asks for the answer to the nearest tenth, we grid in **17.2**.

Equations of Lines in General Form

The **general form of an equation of a line** is $\boldsymbol{ax + by = c}$ where a, b and c are real numbers. If $b \neq 0$, then the slope of this line is $m = -\frac{a}{b}$. If $b = 0$, then the line is vertical and has no slope.

Let us consider 2 such equations.

$$\boldsymbol{ax + by = c}$$
$$\boldsymbol{dx + ey = f}$$

(1) If there is a number r such that $ra = d$, $rb = e$, and $rc = f$, then the two equations represent the **same line**. Equivalently, the two equations represent the same line if $\frac{a}{d} = \frac{b}{e} = \frac{c}{f}$. In this case the system of equations has **infinitely many solutions**.

(2) If there is a number r such that $ra = d$, $rb = e$, but $rc \neq f$, then the two equations represent **parallel** but distinct lines. Equivalently, the two equations represent parallel but distinct lines if $\frac{a}{d} = \frac{b}{e} \neq \frac{c}{f}$. In this case the system of equations has **no solution**.

(3) Otherwise the two lines intersect in a single point. In this case $\frac{a}{d} \neq \frac{b}{e}$, and the system of equations has a **unique solution**.

These three cases are illustrated in the figure below.

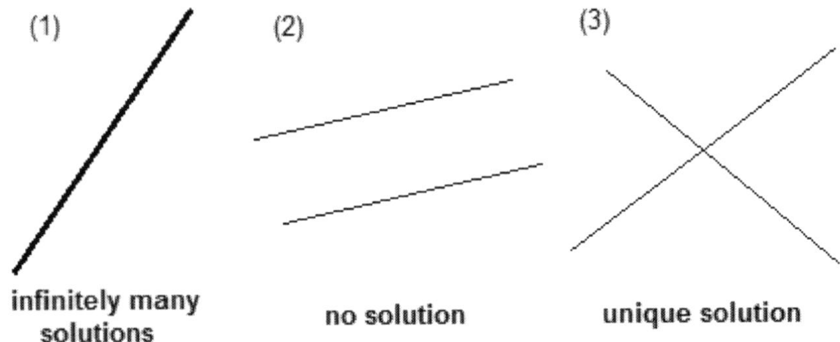

Example: The following two equations represent the same line.

$$\boldsymbol{2x + 8y = 6}$$
$$\boldsymbol{3x + 12y = 9}$$

To see this note that $\frac{2}{3}=\frac{8}{12}=\frac{6}{9}$.(or equivalently, let $r=\frac{3}{2}$ and note that $\left(\frac{3}{2}\right)(2)=3$, $\left(\frac{3}{2}\right)(8)=12$, and $\left(\frac{3}{2}\right)(6)=9$.

The following two equations represent parallel but distinct lines.

$$\mathbf{2x+8y=6}$$
$$\mathbf{3x+12y=10}$$

This time $\frac{2}{3}=\frac{8}{12}\neq\frac{6}{10}$.

The following two equations represent a pair of intersecting lines.

$$\mathbf{2x+8y=6}$$
$$\mathbf{3x+10y=9}$$

This time $\frac{2}{3}\neq\frac{8}{10}$.

Try to answer the following question. **Do not** check the solution until you have attempted this question yourself.

Level 4: Geometry

$$3x-7y=12$$
$$kx+21y=-35$$

2. For which of the following values of k will the system of equations above have no solution?

   (A) 9
   (B) 3
   (C) 0
   (D) -3
   (E) -9

As mentioned above, the system of equations

$$ax+by=c$$
$$dx+ey=f$$

has no solution if $\frac{a}{d}=\frac{b}{e}\neq\frac{c}{f}$. So we solve the equation $\frac{3}{k}=\frac{-7}{21}$. Cross multiplying yields 63 = -7k so that k = 63/(-7) = -9, choice (E).

Note: In this problem $\frac{b}{e}\neq\frac{c}{f}$. Indeed, $\frac{-7}{21}\neq\frac{12}{-35}$. This guarantees that the system of equations has no solution instead of infinitely many solutions.

* **Quick solution:** We multiply -7 by -3 to get 21. So k = (3)(-3) = -9, choice (E).

Now try to solve each of the following problems. The answers to these problems, followed by full solutions are at the end of this lesson. **Do not** look at the answers until you have attempted these problems yourself. Please remember to mark off any problems you get wrong.

LEVEL 3: GEOMETRY

3. The volume of a right circular cylinder is 2662π cubic centimeters. If the height is twice the base radius of the cylinder, what is the base radius of the cylinder?

4. In the xy-coordinate plane, line n passes through the points (0,2) and (1,0). If line m is perpendicular to line n, what is the slope of line m?

5. Point O lies in plane P. How many circles are there in plane P that have center O and an area of 100π centimeters?

   (A) None
   (B) One
   (C) Two
   (D) Three
   (E) More than three

LEVEL 4: GEOMETRY

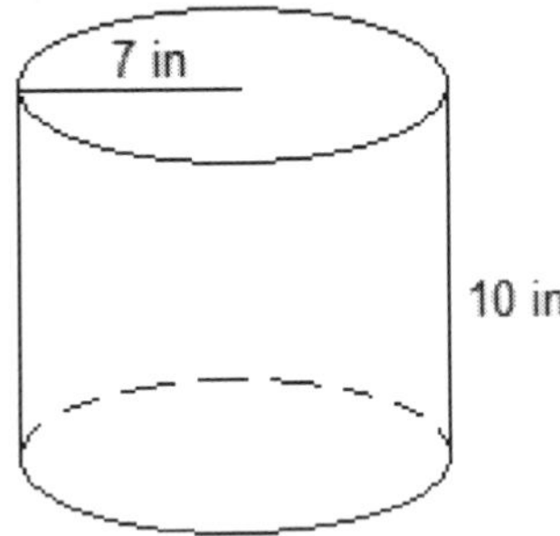

6. The figure above is a right circular cylinder with a height of 10 inches and a base radius of 7 inches. What is the surface area, in square inches, of the cylinder to the nearest integer?

7. A container in the shape of a right circular cylinder has an inside base diameter of 10 centimeters and an inside height of 6 centimeters. This cylinder is completely filled with fluid. All of the fluid is then poured into a second right circular cylinder with a larger inside base diameter of 14 centimeters. What must be the minimum inside height, in centimeters, of the second container?

   (A) $\frac{5}{\sqrt{7}}$
   (B) $\frac{7}{5}$
   (C) 5
   (D) $\frac{150}{49}$
   (E) $2\sqrt{78}$

8. Points P and Q are on the surface of a sphere that has a volume of 972π cubic meters. What is the greatest possible length, in meters, of line segment $\overline{PQ}$? (The volume of a sphere with radius r is $V = \frac{4}{3}\pi r^3$.)

9. In the xy-plane, line ℓ is the graph of $5x + ky = 8$, where k is a constant. The graph of $10x + 22y = 17$ is parallel to line ℓ. What is the value of k?

LEVEL 5: GEOMETRY

10. A cube with volume 343 cubic inches is inscribed in a sphere so that each vertex of the cube touches the sphere. What is the length of the radius, in inches, of the sphere?

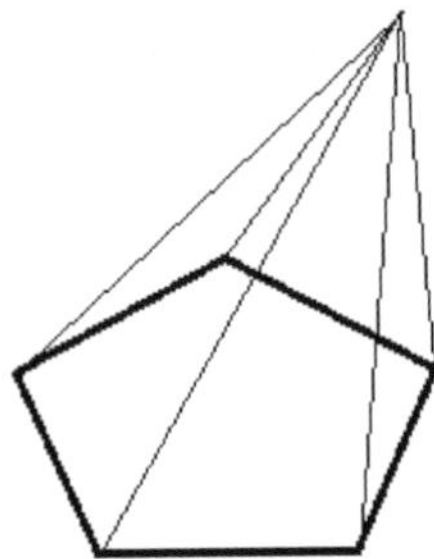

11. The figure above is a pyramid with four isosceles triangular faces and a base that is a regular pentagon. Points A, B, C, D and E (not shown) are the midpoints of the edges that are not in the plane of the base. Line segments are to be drawn on the triangular faces such that each segment connects two of these points. Which of the following is a representation of how these line segments could appear if viewed through the pentagonal base?

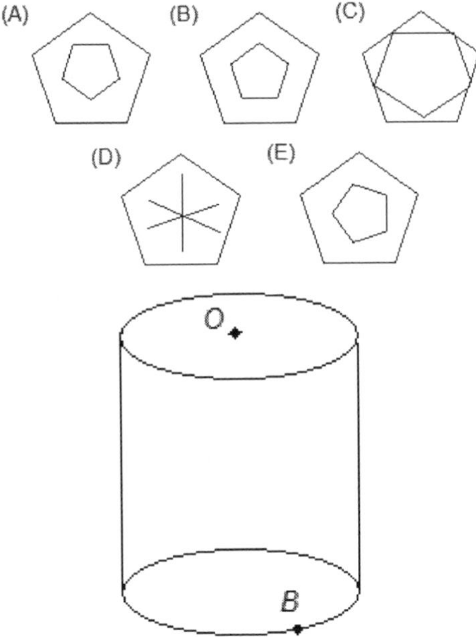

12. The figure above shows a right circular cylinder with diameter 6 and height 9. If point O is the center of the top of the cylinder and B lies on the circumference of the bottom of the cylinder, what is the straight-line distance between O and B?

Answers

1. 17.2	5. B	9. 11
2. E	6. 748	10. 6.06
3. 11	7. D	11. B
4. 1/2 or .5	8. 18	12. 9.48 or 9.49

Full Solutions

3.

*** Algebraic solution:**

$$V = \pi r^2 h$$
$$2662\pi = \pi r^2(2r)$$
$$1331 = r^3$$
$$11 = r.$$

Therefore the answer is **11**.

4.

*** Solution using strategy 28:** We first compute the slope of line *n*. We can do this by plotting the two points, and computing $\frac{\text{rise}}{\text{run}} = -\frac{2}{1}$ (to get from (0,2) to (1,0) we go down 2 and right 1). Since line *m* is perpendicular to line *n*, the slope of line m is the negative reciprocal of the slope of line *n*. So the answer is **1/2** or **.5**.

Remark: We can also find the slope of line n by using the slope formula $m = \frac{y_2 - y_1}{x_2 - x_1} = \frac{0-2}{1-0} = -\frac{2}{1} = -2$.

5.

* Since the area of the circle is 100π, the radius is 10. Once the center and radius of a circle are given, the circle is uniquely determined. Therefore the answer is One, choice (B).

6.

*** Solution using strategy 31:** When we cut and unfold the cylinder we get the following rectangle.

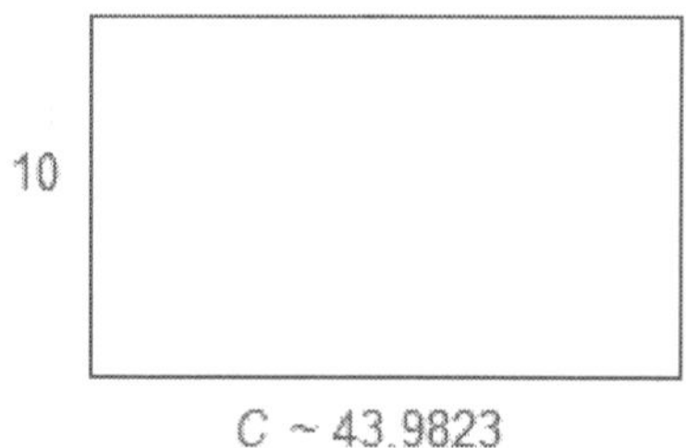

Notice that the width of the rectangle is the circumference of the base of the cylinder. Thus the width is $C = 2\pi r = 2\pi(7) = 14\pi$ inches.

The **lateral** surface area of the cylinder is the area of this rectangle.

$$L = 10(14\pi) = 140\pi \text{ inches.}$$

We also need the area of the two bases. Each of these is a circle with area $A = \pi r^2 = \pi(7)^2 = 49\pi$ inches. Therefore the total surface area is

$$S = L + 2A = 140\pi + 2(49\pi) = 238\pi \sim 747.699 \text{ inches.}$$

To the nearest integer this is **748** inches.

7.

* First note that the base radius of the first cylinder is 5 and the base radius of the second cylinder is 7. Therefore the volume of the first cylinder is $V = \pi r^2h = \pi(5^2)(6) = 150\pi$ and the volume of the second cylinder is $V = \pi r^2h = \pi(7^2)h = 49h\pi$. We set the two volumes equal to each other and solve for h.

$$49h\pi = 150\pi$$

$$h = \frac{150}{49}, \text{ choice (D).}$$

8.

* PQ will be greatest when it is a diameter of the sphere.

We are given that $(\frac{4}{3})\pi r^3 = 972\pi$. Thus $r^3 = (972)(\frac{3}{4}) = 729$, and $r = 9$. So the radius of the sphere is 9, and therefore the diameter of the sphere is $(2)(9) =$ **18**.

9.

* Since we multiply 5 by 2 to get 10, we multiply k by 2 to get 22. Therefore $k =$ **11**.

10.
* The diameter of the sphere is the long diagonal of the cube.

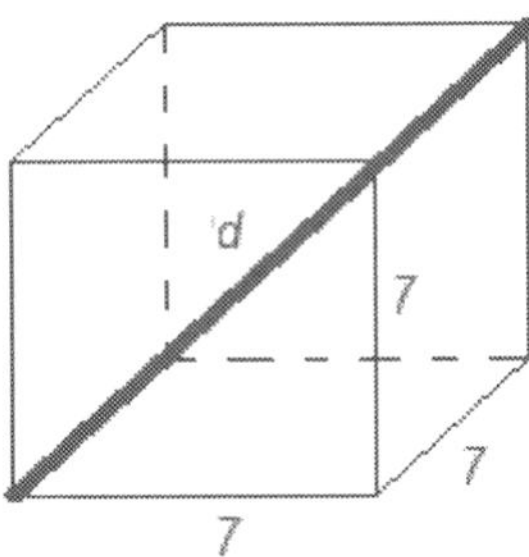

* Since the volume of the cube is 343, the length of a side of the cube is 7 (we get this by taking the cube root of 343). Thus, the diameter of the sphere is given by $d^2 = a^2 + b^2 + c^2 = 7^2 + 7^2 + 7^2 = 49 \cdot 3$.

So $d = 7\sqrt{3}$, and the radius is $r = \frac{d}{2} = \frac{7}{2}\sqrt{3}$.

Putting this in our calculator, we get that $r \sim 6.0621778$ which we truncate (or round) to **6.06**.

11.
* The following picture illustrates the solution.

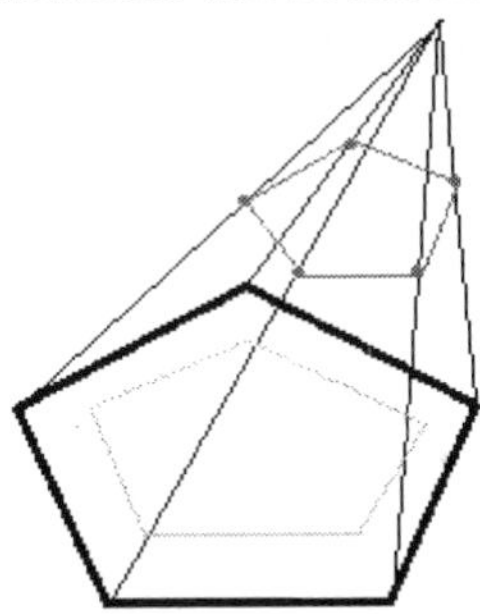

We have plotted points at the midpoint of each edge not in the plane of the base, then attached them with line segments drawn on the triangular faces. Finally, we lightly sketched the projection of the resulting pentagon onto the base. We see that the answer is choice (B).

12.
* **Solution:** We draw a right triangle inside the cylinder as follows.

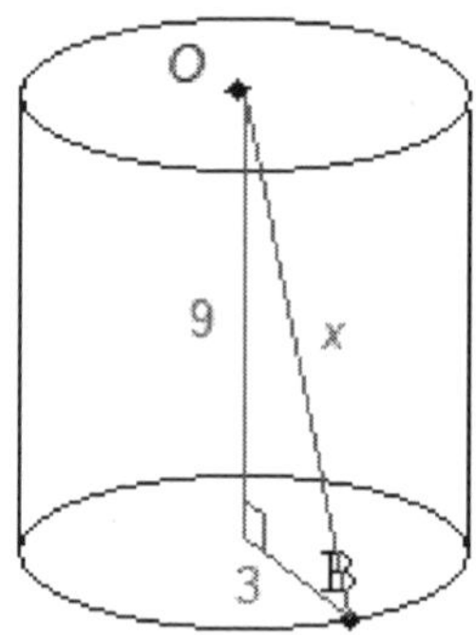

Note that the bottom leg of the triangle is equal to the radius of the circle (not the diameter) which is why it is 3 and not 6. We can now use the Pythagorean Theorem to find x.

$$x^2 = 3^2 + 9^2 = 9 + 81 = 90$$

So $x = \sqrt{90} \sim 9.4868$. So we grid in **9.48** or **9.49**.

OPTIONAL MATERIAL

CHALLENGE QUESTIONS

1. Draw a rectangular solid with sides of length a, b and c, and let the long diagonal have length d. Show geometrically that $d^2 = a^2 + b^2 + c^2$.

2. A cube is inscribed in a cone of radius 1 and height 2 so that one face of the cube is contained in the base of the cone. What is the length of a side of the cube?

Solutions

1.

Let's begin by drawing a picture.

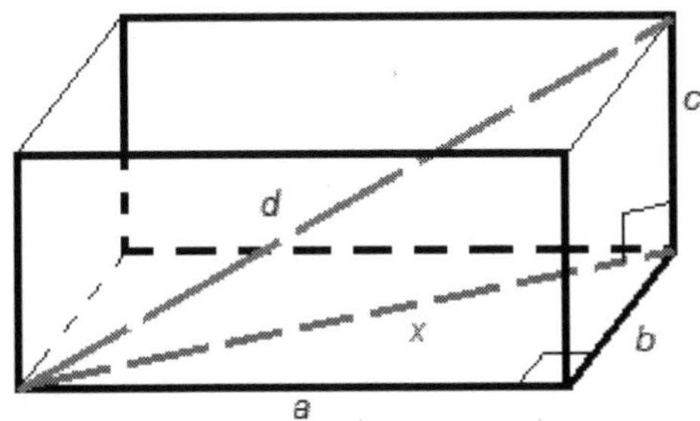

We first use the Pythagorean Theorem on the right triangle with sides of length a, b, and x to get $x^2 = a^2 + b^2$. Then we use the Pythagorean Theorem on the triangle with sides of length x, c, and d to get

$$d^2 = x^2 + c^2 = a^2 + b^2 + c^2.$$

2.

Let x be the length of a side of the cube. Slice the cone from the vertex to the base so that it cuts through the diagonal of the square base of the cube. We get the following picture.

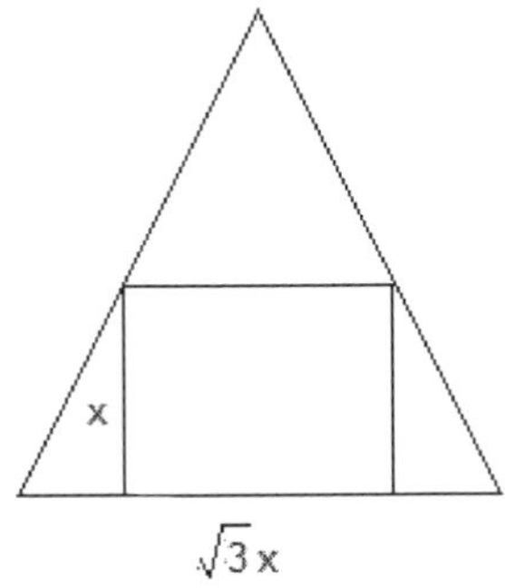

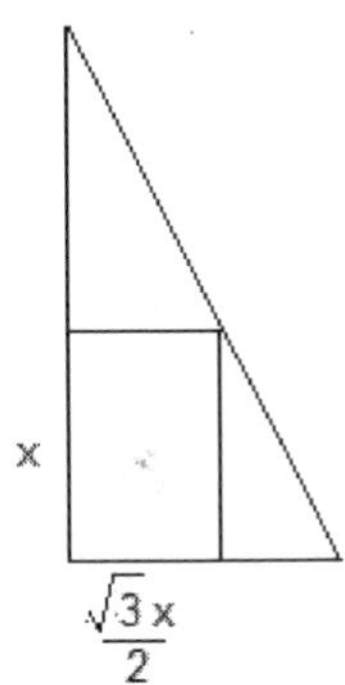

We can now set up the following ratio: $\frac{1}{2} = \frac{1 - \frac{x\sqrt{2}}{2}}{x}$. Cross multiplying gives $x = 2 - x\sqrt{2}$ or $x + x\sqrt{2} = 2$. So we have $x(1 + \sqrt{2}) = 2$, and therefore $x = \frac{2}{1+\sqrt{2}}$. By rationalizing the denominator, this can be simplified to $x = 2\sqrt{2} - 2$.

Lesson 24
Mixed Problems

Reminder: Before beginning this lesson remember to redo the problems from Lessons 4, 8, 12, 16 and 20 that you have marked off. Do not "unmark" a question unless you get it correct.

Try to solve each of the following problems. The answers to these problems, followed by full solutions are at the end of this lesson. **Do not** look at the answers until you have attempted these problems yourself. Please remember to mark off any problems you get wrong.

Level 4: Number Theory

1. If r is an integer, which of the following must be true about $6r+11$.

   (A) It is even.
   (B) It is odd.
   (C) It is greater than 11.
   (D) It is greater than r.
   (E) It is divisible by 17.

   -1, -2, -2, -3, -3, -3, -4, -4, -4, -4, -5, -5, -5, -5, -5, ...

2. Every negative integer $-n$ appears in the sequence above n times. In the sequence, each term after the first is less than or equal to each of the terms before it. If the integer -18 first appears in the sequence as the nth term, what is the value of n?

Level 4: Algebra and Functions

3. A carpenter spent a total of \$5.44 for nails and screws. Each screw cost 2 times as much as each nail, and the carpenter bought 6 times as many nails as screws. How much, in dollars, did the customer spend on screws? (Disregard the \$ sign when gridding your answer.)

4. If a is 7 less than half of b, what is b in terms of a?

   (A) $14a$
   (B) $2(a-7)$
   (C) $2(a+7)$
   (D) $\frac{a+7}{2}$
   (E) $\frac{a-7}{2}$

Level 4: Geometry

5. The points (0,4) and (5,4) are the endpoints of one of the diagonals of a square. What is a possible y-coordinate of one of the other vertices of this square?

6. In the xy-plane, line k passes through the point (0,-3) and is parallel to the line with equation $5x+3y=4$. If the equation of line k is $y=sx+t$, what is the value of st?

Level 5: Number Theory

7. If $a^8b^7c^6d^5>0$, which of the following products must be positive?

   (A) ab
   (B) ac
   (C) bc
   (D) ad
   (E) bd

8. If $n\leq -5$. which of the following has the least value?

   (A) $\frac{1}{(n+3)^2}$
   (B) $-\frac{1}{(n+3)^2}$
   (C) $\frac{1}{n+3}$
   (D) $\frac{1}{n+4}$
   (E) $\frac{1}{n-4}$

Level 5: Algebra and Functions

9. Let Δa be defined as $\Delta a = a^2 - a$ for all values of a. If $\Delta b = \Delta(b-2)$, what is the value of b?

10. If 9 times b is 5 more than the square of a, where a is an integer, what is the smallest possible value of b?

    (A) 8
    (B) $\frac{5}{9}$
    (C) 0
    (D) -9
    (E) It cannot be determined from the information given.

Level 5: Geometry

A C B
3^n $k \cdot 3^n$ 3^{n+3}

11. On the number line above, point C is the midpoint of $\overline{AB}$. If n is positive, what is the value of k?

12. The slope of line segment AB is 7. If A has coordinates $(4, a)$ and B has coordinates $(7, b)$, what is the value of $b - a$?

Answers

1. B	5. 1.5 or 6.5	9. 3/2 or 1.5
2. 154	6. 5	10. B
3. 1.36	7. E	11. 14
4. C	8. D	12. 21

Full Solutions

1.

Solution using strategy 4: If we let *r* = 0, then we have 6*r* + 11 = 11. So we can eliminate choices (A), (C), and (E). Now let's try letting *r* = -10. It follows that 6*r* + 11 = -49 < -10. So we can eliminate choice (D). Thus, the answer is choice (B).

*** Direct solution:** The product of an even integer and any other integer is even. Therefore $6r$ is even. The sum of an even integer and an odd integer is odd. Therefore $6r + 11$ is odd, choice (B).

2.
* -1 appears 1 time, -2 appears 2 times, and so on until we get to -17 which appears 17 times. Finally we stop at the first instance of -18. So we have $n = 1 + 2 + 3 + ... + 17 + 1 =$ **154**.

Remark: There are several ways of computing this sum. Here are a few.

(1) Do it directly in your calculator.
(2) Let's formally write out the sum of the numbers from 1 through 17 forwards and backwards, and then add term by term.

$$\begin{array}{c} 1 + 2 + 3 + \ldots + 17 \\ \underline{17 + 16 + 15 + \ldots + 1} \\ 18 + 18 + 18 + \ldots + 18 \end{array}$$

We are adding 18 to itself 17 times, so that $2(1 + ... + 17) = (18)(17) = 306$. So $1 + 2 + 3 + ... + 17 = \frac{306}{2} = 153$. Finally we add 1 to get **154**.

(3) Use the arithmetic series formula to get $\frac{(17)(18)}{2} + 1 =$ **154**.

(4) Use the sum feature on your calculator.

3.
*** Solution using strategies 3 and 4:** Let's assume that the carpenter bought 1 screw. It follows that the carpenter bought 6 nails. By guessing and checking we find that each nail is \$.68 and therefore the screw is 2(.68) = \$1.36 (check: 6(.68) + 1.36 = 5.44). So we grid in **1.36**.

Remark: If we let s be the cost of the screw, we can formally find the cost of the screw by solving the following equation: $s + 6(\frac{s}{2}) = 5.44$. In this case we have $4s = 5.44$, so that $s = \frac{5.44}{4} =$ **1.36**.

4.
Solution using strategy 4: Let's choose a value for b, say $b =$ **20**. Then half of b is 10, and 7 less than half of b is $10 - 7 = 3$. So $a = 3$. We now substitute $a = 3$ into each answer and eliminate any choice that does not come out to 20.

(A) 14*3 = 42
(B) 2(3 – 7) < 0
(C) 2(3 + 7) = 2*10 = 20
(D) (3 + 7)/2 = 10/2 = 5
(E) (3 – 7)/2 < 0

Since (A), (B), (D) and (E) are incorrect we can eliminate them. Therefore the answer is choice (C).

Important note: (C) is **not** the correct answer simply because it is equal to 20. It is correct because all 4 of the other choices are **not** 20. **You absolutely must check all five choices!**

Remark: Note that in choices (B) and (E) we did not need to finish the computations because each of these numbers is negative.

* **Algebraic solution:** "7 less than half of *b*" = "7 less than $\frac{b}{2}$" = $\frac{b}{2} - 7$. We now solve for *b*.

$$a = \frac{b}{2} - 7$$
$$a + 7 = \frac{b}{2}$$
$$2(a + 7) = b$$

This is choice (C).

Remark: Note that "*x* less than *y*" translates to $y - x$. Also note that $y - x$ is not the same as $x - y$. In the expression "*x* less than *y*," the numbers reverse positions when we write the algebraic equivalent.

5.

Solution using strategy 28: Let's begin by drawing a picture.

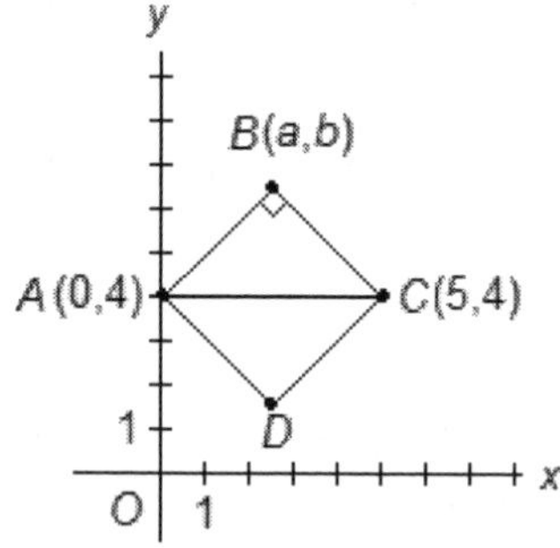

Note that *a* is midway between 0 and 5, so that *a* = 2.5. Also note that line segment $\overline{AB}$ is perpendicular to line segment $\overline{BC}$. This means that the product of the slopes of these segments is -1 (see remark below). So

$$(\frac{b-4}{2.5-0})\cdot(\frac{4-b}{5-2.5}) = -1$$
$$(\frac{b-4}{2.5})\cdot(\frac{4-b}{2.5}) = -1$$
$$(\frac{b-4}{2.5})\cdot(\frac{b-4}{2.5}) = 1$$
$$(\frac{b-4}{2.5})^2 = 1$$
$$\frac{b-4}{2.5} = \pm 1$$
$$b - 4 = \pm 2.5$$
$$b = 4 \pm 2.5$$

So $b = 4 - 2.5 =$ **1.5** or $b = 4 + 2.5 =$ **6.5**.

Remarks: (1) Perpendicular lines have slopes that are negative reciprocals of each other. This means that if $\overline{AB}$ has slope m, $\overline{BC}$ has slope k, and $\overline{AB}$ and $\overline{BC}$ are perpendicular, then $k = -\frac{1}{m}$. This is equivalent to $mk = -1$. That is **the product of the slopes of perpendicular lines is -1**.

(2) Points B and D have coordinates (2.5,6.5) and (2.5,1.5), respectively.

* **Quick solution:** Let's draw line segment $\overline{BD}$ in the figure used in the last solution.

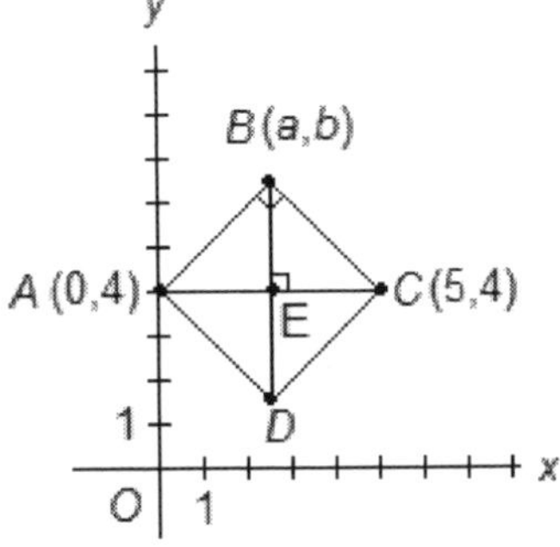

Note that 4 congruent isosceles right triangles are formed. Let's use triangle ABE (we can use any of the four). Since $\overline{AE}$ has length 2.5 and triangle ABE is isosceles, $\overline{BE}$ also has length 2.5. So $b = 4 + 2.5 =$ **6.5**.

6.

* **Solution using strategy 28:** Let's put the given line into slope-intercept form so we can easily see its slope.

$$5x + 3y = 4$$
$$3y = -5x + 4$$
$$y = -\frac{5}{3}x + \frac{4}{3}$$

So the given line has a slope of $m = -\frac{5}{3}$. Since line k is parallel to this line it has the same slope. The y-intercept of line k is given to be (0,-3). So the equation of line k in slope-intercept form is $y = -\frac{5}{3}x - 3$. It then follows that $s = -\frac{5}{3}$ and $t = -3$. Therefore $st = (-\frac{5}{3})(-3) = \mathbf{5}$.

Remarks: (1) If a line is written in the **general form $ax + by = c$**, then the slope of the line is $m = -\frac{a}{b}$. In this problem, the given line is in general form with $a = 5$ and $b = 3$. Therefore the slope of the given line is $-\frac{5}{3}$.

(2) A point on a line is the y-intercept of the line precisely when the x-coordinate of the point is 0. This means that if you are ever given that a point of the form $(0,w)$ is on a line, then in the slope-intercept equation of the line $b = w$.

* **Quick solution:** The given line is in the general form, so that the slope of the line is $m = -\frac{5}{3}$. Line k is parallel to the given line and therefore also has slope $-\frac{5}{3}$. The y-intercept of the line is given as (0,-3) so $b = -3$. Thus, the equation of line k in slope-intercept form is $y = -\frac{5}{3}x - 3$. It follows that $s = -\frac{5}{3}$ and $t = -3$. Therefore $st = (-\frac{5}{3})(-3) = \mathbf{5}$.

7.

Solution using strategy 4: Let's choose values for a, b, c, and d that make the given expression positive. Let's try $a = 1$, $b = -1$, $c = -1$, $d = -1$. Then $a^8b^7c^6d^5 = (1)(-1)(1)(-1) = 1 > 0$. So the given condition is satisfied. Now let's check the answer choices.

(A) (1)(-1) = -1

(B) (1)(-1) = -1

(C) (-1)(-1) = 1

(D) (1)(-1) = -1

(E) (-1)(-1) = 1

So we can eliminate choices (A), (B), and (D). Let's try another set of numbers, say $a = 1$, $b = 1$, $c = -1$, $d = 1$. In this case we now have $a^8b^7c^6d^5 = (1)(1)(1)(1) = 1 > 0$. Let's check the remaining answer choices.

(C) $(1)(-1) = -1$

(E) $(1)(1) = 1$

So we can eliminate choice (C), and the answer is choice (E).

* **Advanced Method:** In order for the given product to be positive, *b* and *d* must have the same sign. Therefore *bd* must be positive, choice (E).

Remark: The advanced solution depends on the fact that when you raise a negative number to an even power you get a positive number, and when you raise a negative number to an odd power you get a negative number.

8.

* **Solution using strategy 4:** Let's choose a value for *n*, say $n =$ **-5**, and substitute this into each answer choice.

(A) $1/(-5 + 3)^2 = 1/4$
(B) $-1/(-5 + 3)^2 = -1/4$
(C) $1/(-5 + 3) = -1/2$
(D) $1/(-5 + 4) = -1$
(E) $1/(-5 - 4) = -1/9$

The answer is choice (D).

9.

* $\Delta b = b^2 - b$ and

$$\Delta(b - 2) = (b - 2)^2 - (b - 2) = b^2 - 4b + 4 - b + 2 = b^2 - 5b + 6.$$

So, we have $b^2 - b = b^2 - 5b + 6$.

Cancelling b^2 from both sides gives us $-b = -5b + 6$. Adding $5b$ to both sides gives us $4b = 6$. Therefore, $b = \frac{6}{4} = \frac{3}{2}$. So we can grid in **3/2** or **1.5**.

10.

* We are given that $9b = a^2 + 5$. We will make *b* smallest by letting $a = 0$. In this case $9b = 0^2 + 5 = 5$. So $b = \frac{5}{9}$, choice (B).

11.

*** Solution using strategy 4:** Since the answer is a number we can choose any positive number for n. Let's take $n = 1$. Then the 3 numbers from left to right are 3, $3k$ and 81. So 3k should be the average of 3 and 81.

$$3k = \frac{3 + 81}{2} = \frac{84}{2} = 42.$$

Thus $k = \frac{42}{3} =$ **14**.

Solution showing the independence of *k*: $k \cdot 3^n$ should be the average of 3^n and 3^{n+3}. So we have

$$k \cdot 3^n = \frac{3^n + 3^{n+3}}{2} = \frac{3^n + 3^n 3^3}{2} = 3^n\left(\frac{1 + 27}{2}\right) = 3^n\left(\frac{28}{2}\right) = 14 \cdot 3^n.$$

Thus, we have $k =$ **14**.

12.

*** Geometric Solution:** To get from 4 to 7 we travel right 3 units. So to get from a to b we must travel $3 \cdot 7 = 21$ units. So $b - a =$ **21**.

Algebraic solution: Using the formula for slope we have

$$m = \frac{b - a}{7 - 4} = \frac{b - a}{3}.$$

Since we are given that $m = 7$, we have $\frac{b - a}{3} = \frac{7}{1}$. Cross multiplying gives us that $b - a = 7 \cdot 3 =$ **21**.

Lesson 25
Number Theory

Try to solve each of the following problems. The answers to these problems are at the end of this lesson.

Full solutions to these problems are available for free download here:

www.thesatmathprep.com/28Les800.html

Level 3: Number Theory

1. Which of the following is equal to $\frac{x+48}{12}$?

   (A) $\frac{x+24}{6}$

   (B) $x+4$

   (C) $4x$

   (D) $\frac{x}{12}+4$

   (E) $\frac{x+4}{6}$

Level 4: Number Theory

2. The sum of 12 positive even integers is 46. Some of these integers are equal to each other. What is the greatest possible value of one of these integers?

3. A mixture is made by combining a red liquid and a blue liquid so that the ratio of the red liquid to the blue liquid is 17 to 3 by weight. How many liters of the blue liquid are needed to make a 420 liter mixture?

$$110a + 17b = 4417$$

4. If a and b are positive integers in the equation above, what is one possible value of $a + b$?

5. A certain exam lasts a total of 4 hours. Each part of the exam requires the same amount of time, and 10 minute breaks are included between consecutive parts. if there are a total of 4 breaks during the 4 hours, what is the required time in minutes, for each part of the test?

2, 50, 4, 50, 6, 50, 8, ...

6. In the sequence above, all odd-numbered terms beginning with the first term are the consecutive positive even integers. The even-numbered terms are all 50. What is the difference between the 51st term and the 50th term?

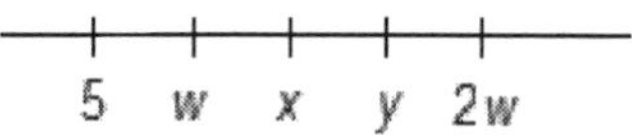

7. If the tick marks are equally spaced on the number line above, what is the value of y?

8. When the positive integer k is divided by 14 the remainder is 4. When the positive integer m is divided by 14 the remainder is 9. What is the remainder when the product km is divided by 7?

9. Each term of a certain sequence is greater than the term before it. The difference between any two consecutive terms in the sequence is always the same number. If the third and tenth terms of the sequence are 46 and 81, respectively, what is the ninth term?

LEVEL 5: NUMBER THEORY

10. If x and y are each positive integers less than 20 and $\frac{x}{y}$ is equivalent to $\frac{3}{5}$, how many values of x are possible?

11. A cheetah ran 12 miles at an average rate of 50 miles per hour and then traveled the next 12 miles at an average rate of 43 mile per hour. What was the average speed, in miles per hour, of the cheetah for the 24 miles?

SURVEY RESULTS

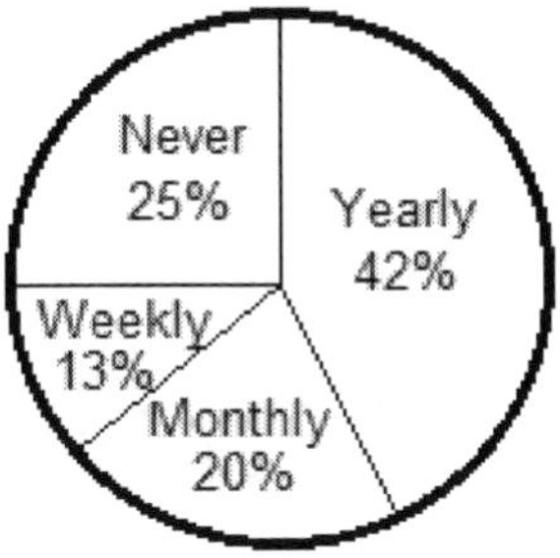

Never 25%
Yearly 42%
Weekly 13%
Monthly 20%

12. The circle graph above shows the distribution of responses to a survey in which a group of people were asked how often they donate to charity. What fraction of those surveyed reported that they donate at least yearly?

Answers

1. D	5. 40	9. 76
2. 24	6. 2	10. 3
3. 63	7. 12.5	11. 46.2
4. 41	8. 1	12. 3/4 or .75

LESSON 26
ALGEBRA AND FUNCTIONS

Try to solve each of the following problems. The answers to these problems are at the end of this lesson.

Full solutions to these problems are available for free download here:

www.thesatmathprep.com/28Les800.html

LEVEL 3: ALGEBRA AND FUNCTIONS

1. At a pet store, each frog is priced at \$1 and each salamander is priced at \$8. Jeff purchased 14 amphibians at the store for a total price of \$42. How many frogs did Jeff purchase?

2. If $18x + 42y = 66$, what is the value of $3x + 7y$?

LEVEL 4: ALGEBRA AND FUNCTIONS

3. For any real numbers r and s such that $r \neq s$, let $r \cdots s$ be defined by $r \cdots s = \frac{r-s}{r+s}$. If $r - s = 63$ and $r \cdots s = 9$, what is the value of r ?

$$\frac{5}{\sqrt{x-7}} = 6$$

4. For $x > 7$, which of the following equations is equivalent to the equation above?

   (A) $25 = 36(x - 7)$
   (B) $25 = 6(x - 7)$
   (C) $25 = 6(x - \sqrt{7})$
   (D) $5 = 36(x - 7)$
   (E) $5 = 6(x - 7)$

5. For all numbers a and b, let $a \forall b = a^2 - 3ab^2$. What is the value of $|5\forall(2\forall 1)|$?

6. Last month Joe the painter painted many rooms. He used 3 coats of paint on one third of the rooms he painted. On two fifths of the remaining rooms he used 2 coats of paint, and he only used 1 coat of paint on the remaining 24 rooms. What was the total number of coats of paint Joe painted last month?

7. If $x \neq 0$ and x is directly proportional to y, which of the following is inversely proportional to $\frac{1}{y^2}$?

   (A) x^2
   (B) x
   (C) $\frac{1}{x}$
   (D) $\frac{1}{x^2}$
   (E) $-\frac{1}{x^2}$

LEVEL 5: ALGEBRA AND FUNCTIONS

8. If $xy = 22, yz = 10, xz = 55$, and $x > 0$, then $xyz =$

9. If $x^2 + y^2 = k^2$, and $xy = 8 - 4k$, what is $(x + y)^2$ in terms of k?

   (A) $k - 4$
   (B) $(k - 4)^2$
   (C) $k^2 - 4k + 8$
   (D) $(k - 2)^2 + 4$
   (E) $(k + 4)^2$

10. Let $||x||$ be defined as the sum of the integers from 1 to x, inclusive. Which of the following equals $||21|| - ||20||$?

   (A) $||1||$
   (B) $||2||$
   (C) $||5||$
   (D) $||6||$
   (E) $||21||$

$$x = 36z$$
$$y = 36z^2 + 5$$

11. If $z > 0$ in the equations above, what is y in terms of x?

(A) $y = \frac{1}{36}x^2 + 4$

(B) $y = \frac{1}{36}x^2 + 5$

(C) $y = \frac{1}{36}x^2 + 36$

(D) $y = \frac{1}{6}x^2 + 4$

(E) $y = x^2 + 36$

12. If $|-3a + 15| = 6$ and $|-2b + 12| = 4$, what is the greatest possible value of ab?

Answers

1. 10	5. 35	9. B
2. 11	6. 116	10. D
3. 35	7. A	11. B
4. A	8. 110	12. 56

Lesson 27
Geometry

Try to solve each of the following problems. The answers to these problems are at the end of this lesson. Full solutions to these problems are available for free download at **www.thesatmathprep.com/28Les800.html**

Level 3: Geometry

1. The sum of the areas of two squares is 85. If the sides of both squares have integer lengths, what is the least possible value for the length of a side of the smaller square?

2. Which of the following is an equation of the line in the xy-plane that passes through the point (0,-7) and is perpendicular to the line $y = -6x + 2$?

   (A) $y = -6x + 7$
   (B) $y = -6x + 14$
   (C) $y = -\frac{1}{6}x + 6$
   (D) $y = \frac{1}{6}x - 7$
   (E) $y = \frac{1}{6}x + 7$

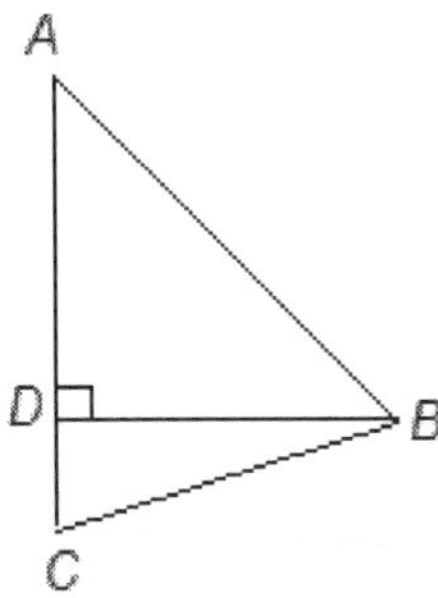

Note: Figure not drawn to scale.

3. Triangle ABC has the same area as a rectangle with sides of lengths 5 and 7. If the length of $\overline{AC}$ is 10, what is the length of $\overline{BD}$?

Level 4: Geometry

4. When each side of a given square is lengthened by 3 inches, the area is increased by 45 square inches. What is the length, in inches, of a side of the original square?

    (A) 3
    (B) 4
    (C) 5
    (D) 6
    (E) 7

5. The length of each side of an equilateral triangle will be doubled to create a second triangle. The area of the second triangle will be how many times the area of the original triangle?

6. Line k contains the point (4,0) and has slope 5. Which of the following points is on line k?

    (A) (1, 5)
    (B) (3, 5)
    (C) (5, 5)
    (D) (7, 5)
    (E) (9, 5)

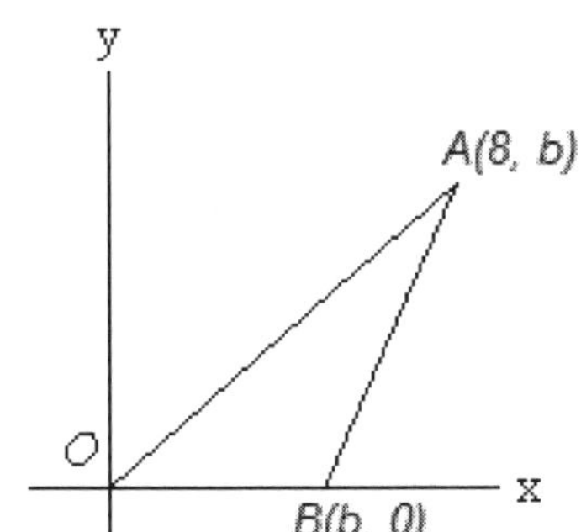

Note: Figure not drawn to scale.

7. In the xy-plane above, the area of triangle OAB is 32. What is the value of b?

8. In triangle DEF, $DE = DF = 10$ and $EF = 16$. What is the area of the triangle?

LEVEL 5: GEOMETRY

9. In the xy plane, line k has equation $y = \frac{2}{9}x + 5$, and line n has equation $y = \frac{1}{4}x + b$. If the lines intersect at the point with coordinates $(a, \frac{2}{3})$, what is the value of b ?

10. If the length of a rectangle is increased by 40%, and the width of the same rectangle is decreased by 40%, then the area of the rectangle is decreased by $x\%$. What is the value of x?

11. A sphere with volume 36π cubic inches is inscribed in a cube so that the sphere touches the cube at 6 points. What is the surface area, in square inches, of the cube?

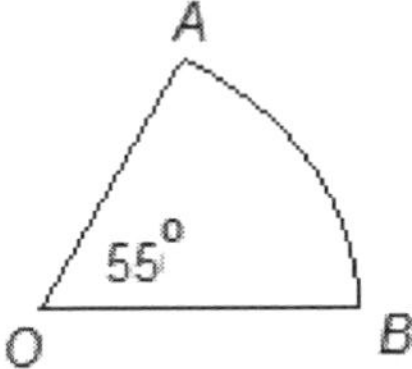

12. In the figure above, AB is the arc of a circle with center O. If the length of arc AB is 7π, what is the area of region OAB to the nearest integer?

Answers

1. 2	5. 4	9. 5.54
2. D	6. C	10. 16
3. 7	7. 8	11. 216
4. D	8. 48	12. 252

Lesson 28
Probability and Statistics

Try to solve each of the following problems. The answers to these problems are at the end of this lesson.

Full solutions to these problems are available for free download here:

www.thesatmathprep.com/28Les800.html

Level 3: Probability and Statistics

1. There are y bricks in a row. If one brick is to be selected at random, the probability that it will be cracked is $\frac{3}{11}$. In terms of y, how many of the bricks are not cracked?

    (A) $\frac{y}{11}$
    (B) $\frac{8y}{11}$
    (C) $\frac{11y}{8}$
    (D) $\frac{3y}{11}$
    (E) 11y

Level 4: Probability and Statistics

2. The integers 1 through 5 are written on each of five cards. The cards are shuffled and one card is drawn at random. That card is then replaced, the cards are shuffled again and another card is drawn at random. This procedure is repeated one more time (for a total of three times). What is the probability that the sum of the numbers on the three cards drawn was between 13 and 15, inclusive?

3. The average (arithmetic mean) of 17 numbers is j. If two of the numbers are k and m, what is the average of the remaining 15 numbers in terms of j, k and m?

   (A) $\frac{k+m}{17}$
   (B) $17j + k + m$
   (C) $\frac{16j-k-m}{17}$
   (D) $\frac{17j-k-m}{15}$
   (E) $\frac{17(k-m)-j}{15}$

4. Exactly 4 musicians try out to play 4 different instruments for a particular performance. If each musician can play each of the 4 instruments, and each musician is assigned an instrument, what is the probability that Jerry will play the tuba?

5. A farmer purchased several animals from a neighboring farmer: 6 animals costing \$50 each, 10 animals costing \$100 each, and k animals costing \$200 each, where k is a positive odd integer. If the median price for all the animals was \$100, what is the greatest possible value of k?

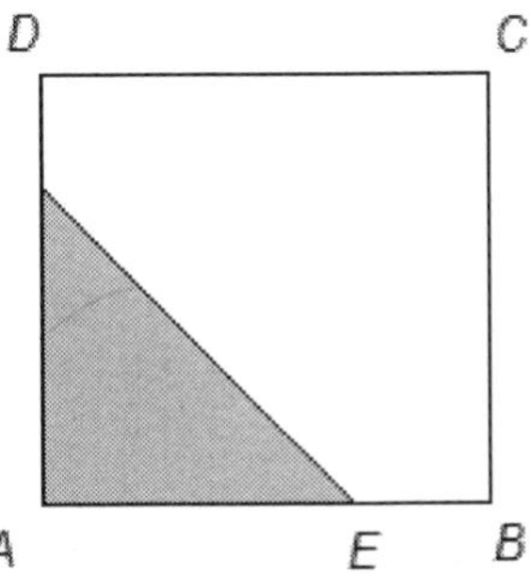

Note: Figure not drawn to scale.

6. In the figure above, $ABCD$ is a square, the triangle is isosceles, $EB = 9 - 2c$, and $AD = 9$. A point in square $ABCD$ is to be chosen at random. If the probability that the point will be in the shaded triangle is $\frac{2}{9}$, what is the value of c?

7. The average (arithmetic mean) age of the people in a certain group was 32 years before one of the members left the group and was replaced by someone who is 10 years younger than the person who left. If the average age of the group is now 30 years, how many people are in the group?

LEVEL 5: PROBABILITY AND STATISTICS

8. How many integers between 4000 and 7000 have digits that are all different and that increase from left to right?

9. A group of students take a test and the average score is 90. One more student takes the test and receives a score of 81 decreasing the average score of the group to 87. How many students were in the initial group?

10. How many positive integers less than 7,000 are multiples of 11 and are equal to 7 times an even integer?

11. Seven cards, each of a different color are shuffled and placed in a row. What is the probability that the blue card is placed at an end?

12. A five digit number is randomly generated using each of the digits 1, 2, 3, 4, and 5 exactly once. What is the probability that the digits 2 and 3 are not next to each other?

Answers

1. B	5. 15	9. 2
2. 2/25 or .08	6. 3	10. 45
3. D	7. 5	11. 2/7, .285 or .286
4. 1/4 or .25	8. 15	12. 3/5 or .6

AFTERWORD
YOUR ROAD TO SUCCESS

Congratulations! By completing the lessons in this book you have given yourself a significant advantage in SAT math. Go ahead and take a practice SAT. The math score you get should be much higher than the score you received before completing these lessons.

If you found that you were still getting many problems wrong in the last four lessons, this means that you can still show improvement by going through this book again. You can also use these last four lessons to determine exactly what you need more practice in. For example, if you got all the questions correct in Lesson 25 (Number Theory), then there is no need to review the number theory lessons in this book. But if you found, for example, that you got some questions wrong in Lesson 27 (Geometry), you may want to spend the next week or so redoing all the geometry lessons from this book.

For additional practice you may want to read *320 SAT Math Problems Arranged by Topic and Difficulty Level.*

If you decide to use different materials for practice problems please remember to try to solve each problem that you attempt in more than one way. Remember – the actual answer is not very important. What is important is to learn as many techniques as possible. This is the best way to simultaneously increase your current score, and increase your level of mathematical maturity.

I really want to thank you for putting your trust in me and my materials, and I want to assure you that you have made excellent use of your time by studying with this book. I wish you the best of luck on the SAT, on getting into your choice college, and in life.

Steve Warner, Ph.D.
steve@SATPrepGet800.com

Actions to Complete After You Have Read This Book

1. **Take another practice SAT**

   You should see a substantial improvement in your score.

2. **Continue to practice SAT math problems for 10 to 20 minutes each day**

   You may want to purchase the *SAT Prep Book of Advanced Math Problems* for more Level 3, 4, and 5 problems.

3. **Use my Forum page for additional help**

   If you feel you need extra help that you cannot get from this book, please feel free to post your questions in my new forum at www.satprepget800.com/forum.

4. **Review this book**

   If this book helped you, please post your positive feedback on the site you purchased it from; e.g. Amazon, Barnes and Noble, etc.

5. **Claim your FREE bonuses**

   If you have not done so yet, visit the following webpage and enter your email address to receive an electronic copy of the *SAT Prep Official Study Guide Math Companion*, and solutions to all the supplemental problems in this book.

www.thesatmathprep.com/28Les800.html

About the Author

Steve Warner, a New York native, earned his Ph.D. at Rutgers University in Pure Mathematics in May, 2001. While a graduate student, Dr. Warner won the TA Teaching Excellence Award.

After Rutgers, Dr. Warner joined the Penn State Mathematics Department as an Assistant Professor. In September, 2002, Dr. Warner returned to New York to accept an Assistant Professor position at Hofstra University. By September 2007, Dr. Warner had received tenure and was promoted to Associate Professor. He has taught undergraduate and graduate courses in Precalculus, Calculus, Linear Algebra, Differential Equations, Mathematical Logic, Set Theory and Abstract Algebra.

Over that time, Dr. Warner participated in a five year NSF grant, "The MSTP Project," to study and improve mathematics and science curriculum in poorly performing junior high schools. He also published several articles in scholarly journals, specifically on Mathematical Logic.

Dr. Warner has over 15 years of experience in general math tutoring and over 10 years of experience in SAT math tutoring. He has tutored students both individually and in group settings.

In February, 2010 Dr. Warner released his first SAT prep book "The 32 Most Effective SAT Math Strategies." The second edition of this book was released in January, 2011. In February, 2012 Dr. Warner released his second SAT prep book "320 SAT Math Problems arranged by Topic and Difficulty Level."

Currently Dr. Warner lives in Staten Island with his two cats, Achilles and Odin. Since the age of 4, Dr. Warner has enjoyed playing the piano—especially compositions of Chopin as well as writing his own music. He also maintains his physical fitness through weightlifting.

BOOKS BY DR. STEVE WARNER